History of Highland Hospitals Project

Case Study No 4

The Hospitals of Inverness

Their Origin and Development
1650-2000

JC Leslie and SJ Leslie

History
of Highland Hospitals

Old Manse Books

First published in the United Kingdom 2017
by
Old Manse Books
Avoch
Ross shire IV9 8RW
Telephone 01381 620412
Email   jim.leslie1@ tesco.net

ISBN
978-0-9569002-3-4

Also published by Old Manse Books in the
History of Highland Hospitals Series

The Hospitals of Skye
The Hospitals of Nairn
The Hospitals of Lochaber

Contents

Glossary of Terms
used in this book which may be unfamiliar

Area	1 acre (4840 yards^2) = about 0.4 hectares (4,000 metres^2)
Length	1 yard (just under a metre) = 3 feet. 1 foot = 12 inches (1 inch = 2.65 cm)
Money	Decimal coinage began in 1972. Until then:- £1 = 20 shillings(s); 1 shilling = 12 pennies(d). Written as (e.g.) £23 13s 10d or £23/13/10. Until the 1940s, guineas (g) were often used for donations. 1 guinea = 21 shillings.
Erysipelas	Until the 20th century, a common skin inflammation especially on the face.
Fever	A general term for an infectious disease. Before the 20th century it was often not precisely identified but was likely to have been most often typhus (see also page 4).
Itch	A 19th century general term for skin disease. The most common was scabies.
Phthisis	Archaic term for pulmonary tuberculosis or similar disease of the lungs but still used to describe a wasting condition.
Feu / feued	A remnant of the feudal system where vassals held land from a lord or superior in return for serving him e.g. in war. Vassals paid superiors to avoid military duty and this system continued until 1974. When land with a feudal superior was purchased it also had to be feued from the superior. Feudal superiors were entitled to annual feu duty.
Lunacy	A general term for mental illness. The sufferers were called lunatics. See footnote on page 197.
Pauper	A destitute individual legally maintained by the parish under the 1845 Poor Law. In the 19th century, they were often distinguished from the 'deserving' or 'respectable' poor who survived without parish support.
Probationer	A trainee nurse.
Timbury unit	Social / health care facilities for elderly with mental health issues in Scotland. Based on the Timbury Report of 1979.

Abbreviations used in this book

AR	Annual Report	EMS	Emergency Medical Service
Bal	Balance	ENT	Ear, Nose and Throat
Exp	Expenditure	LGB	Local Government Board
Inc	Income	Med Super	Medical Superintendent
In-pat	In-patient	MO	Medical Officer
OS	Ordnance Survey	MOH	Medical Officer of Health
Out-pat	Out-patient	p.a.	Per annum (yearly)
na	Not available	(R)NI	(Royal) Northern Infirmary
TB	Tuberculosis	NHS	National Health Service

Capacity of hospitals and bed numbers

The capacity of hospitals was measured in bed numbers. However, rising national standards often reduced a ward's bed capacity over time as more space per bed was stipulated. Also, early hospitals were simple affairs designed mainly to give patients just good food and rest while they recovered. As the range of treatments expanded, more hospital space was required for ancillary services such as laboratories. Hospitals, therefore, had often to physically expand merely to maintain their existing capacity.

Hospital Administration

After the NHS was formed in 1948, the Northern Region Health Board ran Highland hospitals. Until then, the RNI had been independently managed as a voluntary hospital and local authorities (see below) ran the other Inverness hospitals except Raigmore which from its opening in 1941 was run directly by the Department of Health. From 1952- 1974, there was an Inverness Hospitals Board of Management but Craig Dunain Hospital had its own board. In 1974, a complete reorganisation created the Highland Health Board and, after 1984, Raigmore had its own board. There have been several reorganisations since then.

Local Authorities

Regarding public health and welfare, parishes and burghs were the unit of administration from 1845 until 1889 when parishes were grouped into districts and counties were also given responsibilities for health. From 1929, burghs and counties ran public health, much of which – but not all – was taken over by the NHS in 1948 (See also page 6).

Preface and Acknowledgements

The authors are most grateful for the support and encouragement from many and to Dr David Alston for writing our foreword.

We particularly wish to thank Highland Archive Centre which also administers NHS Highland Archives. Its staff are unfailingly helpful with a strong client focus which is outstanding. Also Jamie Gaulkroger at Am Baile who manages a most valuable resource. We wish to acknowledge the work of Janine Donald who, as a former member of Am Baile staff, completed an index of newspaper articles which continues to be of much value to us.

We much appreciate the help of Yvonne Hillyard at the Scottish Dictionary of Architects also the staff of Highland Libraries, National Records of Scotland, National Library of Scotland, Historic Environment Scotland and Highland Historic Environment Record.

Our thanks to Dr. Helen Bryers, Mrs Elspeth MacRae, Prof. Alastair Munro, Mr Robert Polson, Mrs Pat Ross and Mr Colin Waller who have all kindly read and commented on the text. A very special thanks to Moira Leslie for her extensive editorial work.

We also thank: - Dr David Bisset, Ms Juliet Chaplin, Miss Elspeth Luke, Mr JMF Macleod, Mrs Anne Macintosh, Mers Neil and Duncan Martin, Mrs Netta MacIntyre, Mrs Elspeth MacRae, Mr Willie Morrison, the late Dr Patrick Zentler-Munro, Mr & Mrs (Dolly) Paterson, Mr Robert Polson, Dr Ken Proctor, Dianne and Linda Sturrock; Mrs Tennant, Mrs Sam Riddick, Ms Nyree Roxburgh, Mr Bob Shanks, Mrs Rena Tracy and Ms Maimie Thompson.

We thank the following for photographs, pictures and maps:-
Am Baile (page 176, 177); Archives.com (page 108); British Newspaper Archive (page 67, 223); Fort George Museum (page 151); Highland Archive Service (page 16, 24, 37, 53, 59, 102, 107, 113, 152, 169, 204); NHS Highland (page 23, 67, 75, 78, 89, 109, 114, 115, 116, 117, 118, 119,

120, 121, 122, 123, 126, 127, 128, 129, 130, 132, 133, 134, 135, 136, 137, 163, 164, 165, 179, 182, 185, 209, 211, 212, 214, 218, 229, 234, 238); Highland Historic Environment Record (page 66); Miss Elspeth Luke (page 105); Mrs Netta MacIntyre (page 59, 63); Mrs Anne Mackintosh (page 221); Mr JMF Macleod (page 170); Mrs Elspeth MacRae (page 91, 123, 126); Mitchell Library (page 64, 65); National Records of Scotland (page 39, 40, 154, 159, 180, 198); Mrs S Riddick (page 136); Scotsman (page 155); SSAFA per Judith Chapman (page 150); Mrs Tennant (page 160); St Andrews University (page 17); UHI (page 66); the late Dr PL Zentler-Munro (page 88). The quality of some maps and photographs in the book has suffered due to their age and condition.

We are also most grateful to very many members of the public who continue to share information with us. Although many may feel that the information they have seems insignificant, taken along with other parts of the historical jigsaw it can be invaluable.

To all of the above, we are most grateful but any errors and omissions remain the responsibility of the authors. Note that in some establishments, especially nursing homes, it has not been possible to ascertain with certainty the exact dates of opening and closing.

We acknowledge the work of TC Mackenzie (RNI) and William Browne (Raigmore) whose books are seminal works. Also the work of Martin Whittet and Ian Macleod who wrote a comprehensive account of Craig Dunain at its centenary. In the 1980s and 1990s, Raigmore hospital administrator George Maclean and others began an archive which captured many of the changes of that period as well as of the earlier history including interviews with retiring staff who had worked many years in the hospital and, again, this has been of great value in putting together this study.

Key Dates in the History of Inverness Hospitals

1652   Cromwell's Citadel opens and includes a hospital, pharmacy, physician and surgeon.

1746   Balnain House and Dunbar's Hospital are used as temporary hospitals following the battle of Culloden.

1804   Northern Infirmary opens as Highland's first general hospital.

1832   Forbes Dispensary opens and is active in that year's and subsequent cholera epidemics. Dunbar's Hospital also used for cholera victims.

1832-4 First major extension at Northern Infirmary.

1845   Poor Law transfers care of the poor from Kirk sessions to new parochial boards.

1846   Inverness Parochial Board opens poorhouse in Dunbar's Hospital.

1859   Englishton Asylum opens. It closes in 1866 after Inverness District Lunatic Asylum (Craig Dunain) opens.

1861   New Inverness Poorhouse opens at Muirfield.

1864   Inverness District Lunatic Asylum (Craig Dunain) opens.

1866   Major reconstruction of Northern Infirmary.

1870   Separate fever wards built at Northern Infirmary.

1877   Inverness Burgh opens Citadel Hospital for smallpox and cholera.

1881   Major extension at Craig Dunain.

1894   Northern Infirmary opens Bona Convalescent Home which closes in 1918.

1898   New operating theatre, Victoria Nurses Home and Tweedmouth Chapel open at Northern Infirmary.
Major extensions at Craig Dunain - work continues until 1904.

1907   TB Sanatorium opens at Northern Infirmary.

1913   TB Sanatorium opens at Craig Dunain.
Highland's first maternity home opens at Fort George.

1915 Hedgefield becomes a wartime convalescent hospital for military personnel. Also Leys Castle from 1917. Both close in 1919.

1917 Inverness Burgh and County open Culduthel Fever Hospital.

1919 Bowmont Centre for Child Welfare opens in Church Street. Later becomes the Ida Merry Maternity Home and moves to Craigmonie.

1923 TB Sanatorium opens at Culduthel Hospital.

1928 Foundation stone for Northern Infirmary reconstruction laid.

1930 Reconstructed Northern Infirmary opens and becomes 'Royal'.

1936 New Nurses Home and TB Sanatorium at Craig Dunain.

1940 Rosedene Maternity Hospital opens. Ida Merry Home closes.

1941 Raigmore Emergency Services Hospital opens.

1948 National Health Service takes over all hospitals.
Dunain House acquired as extension to Craig Dunain.

1949 Forbes Dispensary closes.

1955 Paediatric ward opens at Raigmore Hospital.

1969 Craig Phadrig opens for patients with learning disabilities.

1971 Phase 1 of new Raigmore Hospital opens and includes new Inverness Central School of Nursing and Post Graduate Medical Centre, rebuilt in 2007 as the Centre for Health Science.

1985 Queen opens Phase 2 of Raigmore Hospital. Remaining acute services move from RNI which becomes a community hospital. Hilton Hospital closes.

1989 Culduthel Hospital closes.

2000 Craig Dunain and Craig Phadrig hospitals close. New Craigs opens.

The History of Highland Hospitals Project

NHS Highland serves a vast area and many of its smaller rural hospitals, now long closed, are increasingly hazy memories. Aware of this, in 2008, Steve and Jim Leslie drew up a plan for the study of the history of Highland hospitals. With the help of a group of prominent individuals, they were awarded grants from NHS Highland Research & Development and UHI Centre for History for a pilot project and, in 2010, produced a report documenting the history of over 60 establishments in Highland. It remains the only overview of the history of Highland hospitals.

However, many gaps in our hospitals' stories remained and it was felt that some of the missing sources may well lie within communities. The authors, therefore, began further extensive research and the publication of low cost A5 booklets on hospitals in each part of the Highlands.

The History of Highland Hospitals Project is a non-profit making venture. Returns from sales go towards the printing of the next booklet although, being mainly of local interest, sales are limited and printing costs continue to be supported by fund raising by Steve Leslie through the NHS Endowment Fund.

The booklets are self-published and Old Manse Books was set up to manage this. Booklets are distributed through local outlets or directly from the authors. Other forms of dissemination continue - talks, a website, responding to individual enquiries and presentations on plasma screens in waiting rooms such as at Nairn and Raigmore Hospitals.

Part of this project is to identify sources which may be forgotten or not widely known and this continues to be successful. We also rely on piecing together many small items of information from local knowledge and we are most grateful to the many people who help us in this.

More details about the project and other information can be found on our website at http://www.historyofhighlandhospitals.com

Foreword

As both an historian and the chair of NHS Highland it is a particular pleasure to have been asked to write the Forward to *Hospitals of Inverness and surrounding areas* – the fourth volume of the Leslies' history of Highland hospitals.

As in earlier volumes, the authors bring to the topic an understanding of medicine and health care in the Highlands in the widest sense, aware of the links with social care and sensitive to the challenges of finance, management, recruitment, and social attitudes. They celebrate successes but are not afraid to identify failures both in health care and in Highland society, such as the growing, rather than decreasing, stigma of mental illness within communities in the later 1800s, the poor treatment of venereal disease in the early 1900s, and the stigma attached to tuberculosis in the 1930s.

Central to the book are detailed histories of Raigmore Hospital and the earlier Northern Infirmary. But the Leslies also rescue from obscurity smaller institutions such as the Forbes Dispensary in Inverness's Huntly Street. The dispensary 'provided free medicine and treatment to the poor for well over a century' although its lack of status reflected 'a very stratified society with the poor only accommodated if they were deserving'. The institution, if not the attitude, is something of which Inverness, and the Highlands, should be proud and I will see the building with different eyes now when I walk along the riverside.

I found much to savour in the detail of the book and was heartened to read that, from 1911, the Inverness Poorhouse registered births as taking place at '40 Old Edinburgh Road' in order to reduce the stigma of being 'born in the poorhouse'. And this illuminated for me another piece of Highland history, for I knew that it had been at least a small comfort in the harsh childhood of the author Jessie Kesson (Margaret Grant Macdonald) born there in 1916 to an unmarried mother and an unnamed father. Brought up in an Elgin slum, her mother simply told her that she had been born at that address in 'a big house with flower gardens'. Jessie was taken into care when her mother contracted syphilis and only discovered that 40 Old Edinburgh Road was the 'workhouse' (as she called it) when she visited after her marriage in 1937. She went on, of course, to be a leading Scottish writer.

This is a readable, thoroughly researched, and well referenced book, which not only records the history of the hospitals of Inverness and the surrounding areas but also sheds light on many aspects of Highland social history.

Dr. David Alston
Chair
NHS Highland

Hospitals of the Highlands – an Overview

We all know where our local hospital is and most of us will have visited it at some time in our lives. However, the modern hospital has evolved greatly from its relatively simple 19th century form when, for many poor people in overcrowded housing, its main benefit was often to provide space and reasonable diet to allow recovery from an illness. Before the 19th century, there is little evidence of any hospital, in the modern sense, within the Highlands. There are references to medieval hospitals, for example in Caithness, but they probably offered hospitality to travellers rather than medical care. The Dominican Friars apparently had a 15th century hospital in Inverness and 16th century charters to Inverness from Mary Queen of Scots (1567) and James VI (1591) both mention a hospital but we have no evidence of its location. In 1589, Inverness Burgh paid a lawyer to manage its hospital accounts and Inverness Kirk Session records mention a hospital in the 1660s 'which from other information must have existed in 1641'.[1] Dunbar's Hospital in Inverness dates from 1668 but it was intended as an almshouse as, most likely, were its predecessors. In Inverness, Cromwell's Fort (1652-62) appears to have contained Highland's earliest modern hospital. It had a 'row of buildings called the Line' with accommodation 'for sick soldiers' and 'an apothecary shop' (pharmacy). It also had a surgeon, Mr Miller, and a physician, Dr Andrew Monro.[2] Balnain House and Dunbar's Hospital were used as short term military hospitals after the Battle of Culloden in 1746 and there are later 18th century references to a military hospital on Castle Street and a hospital in Academy Street in Inverness but we have no details of their work.[3]

The first voluntary hospital in Scotland was established in Edinburgh in 1729. Inverness opened its Northern Infirmary in 1804 and, apart from the cities, it was the third town in Scotland to have its own hospital. In 1847, Nairn followed suit and, apart from wartime hospitals including Raigmore, all other pre-NHS hospitals were established by 1914. Voluntary hospitals were set up by local associations, often assisted by a bequest of property, land or capital. They depended on regular subscribers, annual church collections and, most importantly, one-off donations or legacies. Often, specific improvements were funded by an individual donation. Hospitals were not financially viable without this support and patient fees, where charged, seldom met the cost of the individual's treatment. This was despite local doctors giving their services free. There were salaried doctor posts in some fully endowed hospitals (see next paragraph) such as the Belford in Fort William and the Seaforth Sanatorium in Maryburgh - also in the privately run Grampian Sanatorium (now St Vincent's) in Kingussie and in institutions run by local authorities such as psychiatric hospitals, fever[i] hospitals and poorhouses. The Northern Infirmary had a salaried resident medical officer to support the work given gratis by local doctors.

Outside Inverness, most Highland communities were small and their resources were insufficient to support a hospital so that most local hospitals which were established were endowed by wealthy individuals. Some of these, such as the Gesto in Skye, existed on their original endowment until taken over by the NHS. Others, such as the Bignold in Wick, sought and achieved voluntary status when endowment funds dwindled. Some voluntary hospitals received major endowments late in their history. For example, in 1906, Nairn's new hospital was mainly financed by one donation from Ecuador. This exemplifies the amount of funding from abroad which many hospitals received either as donations from ex patriots or from those returning home after making their fortune. It is particularly apparent in the north Skye hospitals and in the initial funding of the Northern Infirmary. Owners of sporting estates and their shooting season guests also made important financial contributions. A notable example is Arthur Bignold who financed the hospital of his name in Wick. Such donations partly compensated for the lack of a prosperous middle class outwith Inverness although indigenous landowners were also prominent in health care provision such as Colonel Seaforth and Sir Kenneth Mackenzie in Ross and Cromarty.

---

[i] For brevity, we often use 'fever' rather than 'infectious or communicable disease'. Before the 20th century, the specific disease was often unclear – typhoid, typhus, and influenza were recorded as 'fever' although most cases were probably typhus.

By the 1920s, Scottish general hospitals had large waiting lists but, apart from the Northern Infirmary, Highland hospitals were often underused. Indeed, local hospital managements were often concerned by the number of potential local patients who preferred to go to Inverness or to larger centres. The North traditionally used Edinburgh and the West Highlands and Islands[i] looked towards Glasgow and attracting patients from these areas to Inverness was a challenge. In 1920, over 800 Highland patients were treated in city hospitals (table below) and it was noted then that more use could be made of Highland hospitals. At the time, the total number of beds in Highland's general hospitals was 210. On the face of it, local hospitals may have struggled to cope if all Highlanders had gone to their local hospital but, of course, many were going elsewhere for specialist treatment not available locally.[4]

In-patients from Highland in city hospitals 1920

Hospital	Patients from Highland
Glasgow Royal Infirmary	103
Western Infirmary, Glasgow	230
Edinburgh Royal Infirmary	361
Victoria Infirmary, Glasgow	40
Aberdeen Royal Infirmary	77

Voluntary associations and wealthy individuals were not alone in developing hospitals. In 1845, the Poor Law Act established parochial (parish) boards which replaced the Church of Scotland (the Kirk) in administering poor relief and care for the sick poor. Many parishes established poorhouses[ii] and Inverness used Dunbar's Hospital until it built its new poorhouse at Muirfield. The low population of other Highland parishes meant that several had to combine to build a Combination[iii] Poorhouse. The first was the Easter Ross Combination near Tain in 1850. Others followed at Latheron, Fortrose, Thurso, Portree and Bonar Bridge. Inverness Poorhouse was successful but the others were too remote from much of their large catchment area and

---

[i] The West Highlands and Islands still use Glasgow.
[ii] Called workhouses in England.
[iii] Refers to the combination of parishes and not to the functions of the poorhouse.

remained underused. Poorhouse residents were often sick and infirm and poorhouses became partly hospitals for the chronic sick.[5]

The 1929 Local Government Act swept away the poor laws putting the new health authorities - counties and burghs - in charge of former poorhouses. Many Scottish poorhouses became local authority hospitals but Highland lacked the necessary resources and its poorhouses largely remained a refuge for the destitute, chronic sick, mentally ill, vagrants and unmarried mothers all to an extent thrown together in establishments which were 'ill-equipped, inadequately staffed and often structurally unsuitable'.[6]

In the 21st century we have a single point of access to medical care and integrated health and social welfare services. Therefore, it is hard to imagine the administrative fragmentation of the past.[i] Parishes shouldered an increasing range of public health duties for which, in rural areas especially, they were woefully too small. The 1889 Local Government Act combined parishes into larger districts[ii] but also required them to employ a medical officer of health and to provide hospital accommodation for fever patients, tasks which were beyond the financial resources of many rural districts. By then, some hospitals such

---

[i] It was not until 1911 that the Scottish Board of Health was formed with an administrative focus on health matters at government level. In 1912, there were 12 separate bodies dealing with the public's health in the Highlands not counting the individual districts and burghs and the committees of voluntary and endowed hospitals. The Highland crofter who fell sick had a range of possible provision – district fever ward (public health committee) if he was infectious, the poorhouse sick ward (public assistance committee) if he became a pauper, the local voluntary hospital or sanatorium (trustees) if one existed and if he could be recommended by a subscriber, the district lunatic asylum (district lunacy commission) if he had mental health issues – but only if he was a pauper otherwise there was only the fee paying Royal Asylums such as in Montrose. None of this provision was likely to be coordinated and more often the sufferer stayed at home, discouraged by the unfamiliar uncertainty of it and the potentially long uncomfortable journey. The 1929 Local Government Act did much to co-ordinate provision but left mental health separate and each voluntary hospital continued to administer its own cases.

[ii] Mainland Inverness shire became 4 districts instead of 28 parishes.

6

as the Northern Infirmary and Dingwall's Ross Memorial had fever wards which were available to local authorities but, before 1889, there were few fever hospitals - although Wick's Harrow Hospital existed from at least 1870 (probably the earliest in Highland), and Inverness opened its Citadel Hospital in 1877. After 1899, most areas had access to fever wards but some authorities like Nairn were slow to make any provision. In addition, cottages were set aside or small 2 ward huts of corrugated iron and wood were built as emergency accommodation for highly infectious cholera and smallpox cases.[i]   After 1900, both diseases declined markedly and they mostly sat empty. By 1917, several were 'in a state of disrepair' and 'unfitted for the reception of patients'.[7]   Wester Ross had tents on hand for fever patients and tents were used in the 1922 Raasay typhus outbreak. Skye and the Black Isle had horse drawn hospital vans which could be pulled to the outbreak area and used to accommodate patients or nurses. By the mid-19th century, tuberculosis was a growing concern and the first purpose-built sanatoria were at Kingussie, Invergarry and Maryburgh.   By 1920, most parts of the Highlands had adequate sanatorium provision but, for many years, other effects of tuberculosis remained unprovided for and osteomyelitis was only effectively treated once orthopaedics became established at Raigmore after 1941.

Roads were notoriously bad in the Highlands. In 1928, surgeon AJC Hamilton arrived in the Highlands and later described the roads then as 'narrow, devious and rough' noting that a 10 mile stretch between Drumnadrochit and Invermoriston was signposted as 'dangerous'. As a result, patients coming from a distance often arrived at hospital in a 'very shocked and moribund condition' and mortality rates were high. As the roads and ambulances improved, infectious diseases facilities were centralised, a process encouraged by the 1929 Local Government Act. In 1917, Culduthel Hospital in Inverness became the main fever hospital for the Burgh and County and ultimately for the Highlands before infectious diseases diminished.[8]

---

[i] Some were temporary and not all are documented nor their location remembered. A popular manufacturer was Speirs of Glasgow (see also page 62)

Most Highland hospital provision was not centralised until the mid-20th century but, in 1864, the opening of the Northern District Lunatic Asylum centralised mental health provision from the outset. Craig Dunain, as it was later called, catered for the mental health needs of 'pauper lunatics' from the entire north of Scotland, including the Western Isles, and its wide catchment ensured an inexorable rise in patient numbers. In 1860, it had 200 residents and, by the turn of the century, this had risen to nearly 600 and its history is one of continual adaptation and expansion to meet this need. A major problem was the failure to establish mental health facilities elsewhere in the Highlands, despite several attempts to get underused poorhouses converted. The result was a constant pressure on Craig Dunain and the virtual exile of many vulnerable patients from the support of distant family and community, often a separation by language and culture as much as by distance.

Despite the success of Craig Dunain, there was a lack of provision for the mentally and physically disabled and it was not until 1970 that Craig Phadrig was opened - more than 50 years after the government had recommended such provision. By then, belief in large institutions was diminishing and a change in policy saw the development of facilities to meet the different needs and treatments of patients in a variety of establishments including specialist geriatric wards in local hospitals. Both Craig Dunain and Craig Phadrig closed in 2000 and were replaced by New Craigs.

Until the 1860s, few nurses had any training. Indeed, matrons were often called housekeepers, a term which described the perceived job. However, the success of pioneers such as Florence Nightingale led to city training schools and, by the 1870s, the Northern Infirmary had its own training scheme. By 1900, much of the Highlands had voluntary district nursing associations, most with at least one highly trained Jubilee or Queen's nurse.[i] Nursing associations were well supported by articulate, affluent women who also promoted a child and maternity care agenda but struggled against the inertia of male dominated public bodies.

---

[i] Set up at Queen Victoria's jubilee and the most highly trained district nurse.

The 20th century saw the first nursing homes some of which also maintained an agency of trained nurses for hire.

Until the 1940s, most Highland births were at home and hospital births were mainly for 'difficult cases'. Some hospitals such as the Belford in Fort William and the John Martin in Skye had designated maternity beds from the outset but most Highland hospitals had limited maternity provision. By the 1920s, there were maternity beds in nursing homes often run along with, or by, nursing associations such as Wick's Henderson Nursing Home and the Viewfield in Inverness but the first maternity home in Highland opened in 1913 for military wives at Fort George. By the 1920s, some hospitals had maternity wards such as at Grantown which opened an extension in 1926 and poorhouses continued to have small maternity wards until the late 1940s. The 1937 Maternity Act obliged local authorities to provide improved maternity facilities but an inability to agree to maternity provision at the Royal Northern Infirmary (RNI)[i] forced the opening of Rosedene Hospital in Inverness. In 1947, a temporary maternity ward opened at Raigmore Hospital followed by a 50 bed unit in 1951 when it became Highland's main centre for maternity, being the only hospital with the capacity to deal with the post-war baby boom and the increased expectation of giving birth in a hospital. Eventually, smaller maternity units such as the Pope Hospital in Sutherland, at Nairn and at Dingwall were phased out in favour of the specialist back up medical facilities which could be provided centrally.

During the First and Second World Wars, many large houses, such as Dunrobin Castle, became temporary military hospitals. Most closed at the end of the war except Forse House in Caithness and Glencoe House in Lochaber which continued as hospitals after 1945. During the First World War, a large hutted military camp at Cromarty had a field hospital and, across the Firth, the Admiralty built a naval hospital at Invergordon which, in 1921, was purchased by Ross and Cromarty as its (later named) County Hospital. During the Second World War, Wick lay at the centre

---

[i] The Northern Infirmary was renamed the Royal Northern Infirmary in 1930.

of four military airfields and the RAF took over Bignold Hospital with the civilian hospital transferred to the new Lybster High School. The major development of the Second World War was the EMS hospital at Raigmore, one of seven in Scotland, which substantially increased Highland's hospital beds.

Despite the increasing provision of hospitals and doctors, many in early 20th century Highland still had difficulty in accessing medical care. The 1912 Dewar Committee[i] found medical services 'near to collapse' and the state funded Highlands and Islands Medical Service (HIMS) was formed which set up a comprehensive GP and district nurse service - a forerunner of the National Health Service (NHS).[9] Although the number of hospital beds was thought insufficient and access to them difficult, support for hospitals was limited to essential grants to the financially challenged Mackinnon Memorial Hospital in Skye and Belford Hospital in Fort William. In 1924, HIMS funded surgeon posts at Stornoway and Lerwick but it was not until 1929, after additional state funding, that posts such as the consultant surgeon in Caithness and Sutherland and a visiting consultant physician based in Inverness were afforded. The RNI, firmly established as Highland's main hospital, was the obvious base for consultants with a regional remit. These consultants who, from 1944, included the Raigmore orthopaedic surgeon, ran clinics across the Highlands where GPs and their patients could benefit from their specialist expertise.

In 1948, the new Northern Region Health Board inherited a variety of functioning establishments. In the table on page 12, bed numbers, which varied over time, are indicative only. Some such as Meadowside at Kincraig and the Ross Memorial in Portree had been unused for years and are not listed. Some establishments were remote and in poor condition such as the Inverness-shire Sanatorium at Invergarry. Most were underfinanced, even the outstandingly successful RNI, and some were destined to close as soon as better facilities could be developed.

---

[i] Chaired by Inverness-shire MP Sir John Dewar, the committee undertook a large survey of medical provision and health care in the Highlands and Islands.

What the NHS provided was regional coordination, something which had eluded previous managements, and this allowed establishments in favourable areas to expand at the expense of the less advantaged. Some services became redundant such as the hard-working Nursing Associations and the largely forgotten Forbes Dispensary in Inverness which was one of the longest lasting in Scotland, having provided free medicine and treatment to the poor – in their thousands - for well over a century.

By the mid-1950s, the demise in fever cases, particularly tuberculosis, was matched by the rise in need for geriatric care. St Vincent's in Kingussie changed from a TB sanatorium to entirely geriatric cases in one conversion in 1956. Other fever hospitals, such as at Invergordon and Cambusavie in Sutherland, made a similar if not quite so abrupt change.

Under the NHS, a lack of capital delayed developments until the 1960s. Once finance was available, smaller peripheral hospitals, or ones where expansion was difficult, gave way to more favoured sites but it was only in the 1990s that NHS Highland could close some hospitals which, 40 years previously, had been regarded as temporary. By then, the empowerment of local communities and the perceived value of local institutions had grown and closure was not the straightforward process it had been in the early 1950s, the Gesto in Skye being a notable example.

The financial balance between centralisation of specialist facilities and maintenance of local general facilities has been a long and ongoing debate. While local communities want facilities as close to home as possible, the need for access to specialised facilities has long been recognised. As a provider of specialist facilities, Inverness, over the years, has not been the first choice for many parts of the Highlands despite the dominance of its Infirmary. However, Inverness has the continued advantage of being Highland's administrative centre. That and the wartime development of a large hospital at Raigmore - and its subsequent expansion – has allowed Inverness to maintain its centrality to Highland medical care.

Highland Hospitals in 1950

Name	Beds	Note
Craig Dunain (psychiatric)	930	Closed 2000.
Raigmore	408	
Royal Northern Infirmary	221	
Muirfield, Inverness	114	Became Hilton. Closed 1989.
Swordale, Bonar Bridge	57	Became Migdale. New hospital 2012.
Ross Memorial, Dingwall	42	
Dunbar, Thurso	36	
Belford, Fort William	32	New hospital opened in 1965.
Bignold, Wick	28	Replaced by Caithness General 1986.
Lawson Memorial, Golspie	26	
Town & County, Nairn	25	New hospital opened in 2010.
Ian Charles, Grantown	20	Part of NE Region until 1974.
Gesto, Edinbane, Skye	12	Closed 2006.
Nicolson, Strathpeffer	12	Rheumatology. Closed 1992.
Mackinnon, Broadford	8	Extended in 1965.
John Martin, Uig	7	Replaced by Portree Hospital 1964.
Maternity		
Rosedene, Inverness	18	Closed 1951.
Glencoe House	16	General from 1956. Closed 2009.
Cromarty	10	Closed 1953.
Henderson, Wick	8	Replaced by Caithness General 1978.
Pope, Helmsdale	5	Reopened 1949. Closed 1977.
Infectious Diseases		
County, Invergordon	131	Mainly pulmonary tuberculosis (TB).
Culduthel, Inverness	87	Closed 1990.
Cambusavie, Sutherland	41	Also treated TB. Closed 1989.
Town and County, Wick	28	Also treated TB.
Pulmonary Tuberculosis		
St Vincent's, Kingussie	40	Geriatric from 1956. NHS from 1986.
Inverness-shire Sanatorium	16	Closed 1951.

The Inverness Area

As will be gathered from the preceding chapter, much of the history of Inverness hospitals is closely tied into the history of Highland hospitals.

Inverness sits at a strategic location in the Eastern Highlands and, as such, was often seen in the past, certainly by the Scottish Crown, as a lowland outpost as much as a Highland capital. At times it appears to have had an uneasy relationship with parts of the lands to the west and north. However, by end of the 18th century, Inverness saw itself as the focus of all of the north, a concept which contributed much to the planning and founding of the Northern Infirmary which was very much the creation of the leading citizens of Inverness Burgh and especially of its Provost William Inglis whose enthusiasm put Inverness at the forefront of hospital development in Scotland and who promoted the project as a *Northern* rather than *Inverness* Infirmary.

Inverness appointed a municipal doctor or burgh physician in 1680,[i] possibly its first, for 'attending and visiting the sick and diseased persons of this brugh'[10] and it seems likely that, as with poor relief, medical assistance was delivered in the community. The 19th century saw the steady growth of the Northern Infirmary and the development of public welfare and health through the building of the Poorhouse at Muirfield and the establishment of the Citadel Hospital for emergency fever cases. Apart from the latter two, Inverness Burgh and nearby County areas saw their health care responsibilities as being met through the Infirmary and this sometimes led to tensions over payment for statutory services such as providing for infectious diseases and, later, for maternity. At times, there seems to have been fairly poor communications between the managers of the Infirmary and the Burgh which seems rather strange given that prominent members of the Town Council dominated the Infirmary management.

---

[i] Aberdeen appointed a burgh physician in 1503, apparently the first in Scotland.

From at least 1915, the Burgh[i] supported the health of mothers and children through assistance to local child welfare groups. Few maternity cases went to the Infirmary which apparently only dealt with 'difficult' births but had an obstetrician[ii] on the staff from at least 1914. By the 1930's, despite increasing public concern about childbirth mortality and adequate provision of maternity facilities, the Burgh seems to have had no strategy other than try to persuade the Infirmary (unsuccessfully) to receive cases and, eventually, in 1941, was forced to open Rosedene as the area's first maternity hospital.

Inverness Burgh was more active in providing for infectious diseases. In 1877, it established the Citadel Hospital for highly infectious smallpox and cholera but it continued to rely on the fever wards of the Infirmary until 1917 when, along with the County, it opened Culduthel Hospital. With subsequent investment in the 1920s and 1930s and local government changes in 1929, Culduthel assumed a regional role providing specialist treatment for a range of infectious diseases and, in the late 1940s, the hospital site was seen as a potential contender to Raigmore as Inverness' second general hospital.

During the First World War, the Infirmary treated mainly naval personnel and Hedgefield and Leys Castle served as temporary Red Cross hospitals. The Infirmary's role in the Second World War was reduced when, in 1941, Inverness was chosen for one of Scotland's seven new Emergency Medical Services (EMS) Hospitals and, by the early 1940s, there was accommodation for over 500 beds at the new Raigmore, far outstripping the RNI's peacetime complement of just over 200.

Over the years, increasing demand encouraged the expansion of the Infirmary and this was most marked around 1930 after which King George V granted the prefix 'Royal'. Expansion continued in the 1930s encouraged by its growing regional status as the base for consultants with

---

[i] For brevity we normally use the term Burgh rather than Inverness Town Council.
[ii] However, this would have been a general practitioner with a special interest rather than a specialist in the modern sense.

a Highland wide remit the appointment of whom was often grant supported by the Highlands and Islands Medical Service. By 1950, seven Highland consultant doctors were based in Inverness including surgery, orthopaedics, general medicine, obstetrics, Ear, Nose and Throat (ENT), ophthalmology and dental surgery. These consultants ran clinics across the Highlands. Raigmore Hospital contained specialist services from the start notably orthopaedics and, by the early 1950s, had provided much needed maternity facilities which were essential in coping with the post war baby boom and the growing expectation of hospital births.

From then on, the story is of expansion at Raigmore with the development of new specialties in health, replacement of the EMS barrack-style separate wards, and transfer of services and departments from the RNI and from Culduthel when it closed in 1989. The RNI meanwhile developed into the present community hospital. Raigmore Hospital continues to provide a degree of specialty which is unprecedented in an area which has the largest catchment area (larger than Belgium) with the lowest population density of any hospital in the United Kingdom.

Inverness has dominated medical provision in the Highlands and this has increased as communications in a topographically difficult area have continued to improve, allowing faster travel from a wider area. The extent of present day dominance, however, was not a foregone conclusion and it is interesting to speculate what might have been the present position had Tom Johnston, Secretary of State in the late 1930s, not made the decision to site a wartime hospital at Raigmore.

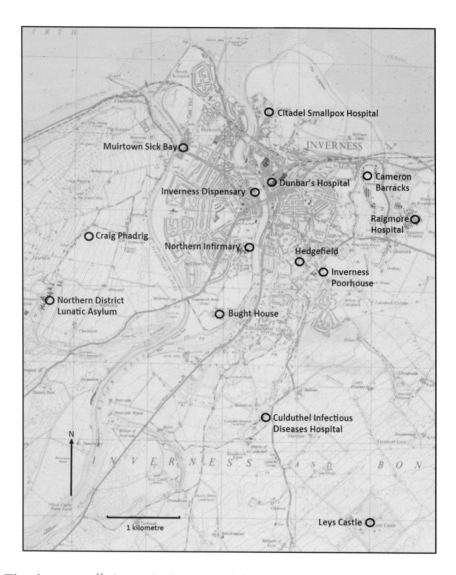

The above map[11] shows the location of the hospitals of Inverness in their original names. Most were peripheral to the town when they opened. The Asylum was deliberately located at a distance from the urban area and the location of Culduthel, at about 3 kilometres distant prompted a plea from the public for a bench to be set half way so that relatives could rest on their way to visit patients.

Dunbar's Hospital
Academy Street
1668

Dunbar's Hospital has often been noted as the first recorded 'hospital' in Inverness[i] but the term is used in its medieval sense of an almshouse to accommodate the old and infirm (bedesmen) rather than the sick[ii] per se. The photograph on page 22 shows a bedesman carved above one of the dormer windows. The other 6 dormers can be seen in the photograph above (from c1900). Alexander Dunbar, Provost of Inverness built his 'hospital' in 1668, probably using stone from the demolished Cromwell's Fort. In 1683, he handed it over to the Kirk Session specifying that the ground floor be used as a grammar school and

---

[i] See also page 3.
[ii] However, in 1721, the Kirk Session minutes note that an upper loft was let to the Magistrates as a 'Hospital for the Regiment of Fusiliers' but we have no details.

Burgh weigh house. The upper floors were for the use of the Burgh's poor but there appear to be no records of the Kirk Session ever using it for this purpose. Instead it was used as a school, library and a variety of other[i] rent yielding uses.[12] On John Wood's map of 1821, it is named the Old Latin School and it was known locally as the Old Academy.

Dunbar's was used during the cholera outbreaks[ii] of 1832 and 1834[13] where a handbill announced that 'the Medical Gentlemen have made an arrangement by which one of their number will be in constant attendance day and night at the hospital (Old Academy, foot of Church St.)'. The building was obviously known as the Old Academy and not as a hospital which suggests it did not have any pre-existing medical function. Moreover, the building was not the obvious choice for cholera victims and the local Board of Health considered the Town Hall, Northern Meeting Rooms and a new build on Castlehill before settling on Dunbar's.[14] The Northern Infirmary also supplied beds to the Inspector of the Poor in the outbreak of 1849 and it seems likely that the Inspector would have used part of Dunbar's given that he already administered it, although definite evidence of this has not been found.

By 1840, the Committee of the Legal Administrators of the Poor which administered Inverness' poor fund was exploring the possibility of opening a poorhouse and approached the Kirk Session which apparently had considerable funds designated for the poor.[iii] However, the Session refused funding, being prepared to go to court over it, and would not allow the use of Dunbar's as a poorhouse. Over the winter of 1844/45, the Committee opened a small 'poor's house' on the Green of Muirtown but, at Whitsunday (15 May) 1845, apparently under pressure and with the impending Poor Law, the Kirk allowed the 'poor's house' to be

---

[i] In 1792, a proposal to lease it to the Burgh as a poorhouse came to nothing.

[ii] In 1832, the Infirmary supplied beds to Inspector of the Poor for cholera victims.

[iii] Before 1845 it was the Kirk's duty to support the poor. It collected funds for the purpose including fees for hire of a mort cloth which draped the coffin at burials. The evidence suggests that Inverness Kirk Session could be less than assiduous in supporting the poor either through spending its funds or in its use of Dunbar's. However, by the 1830s, it was apparently over-whelmed by the number of destitute.

moved to Dunbar's 'by way of an experiment'. This new Inverness Poorhouse incorporated the redundant weigh house which had contained the town's lamp and fire engines. In late 1846, the Parochial Board carried out renovations when the old spire[i] was removed and a house was built in the yard for the Inspector of the Poor. A large expansion of Dunbar's was planned and generally agreed with the Session but did not go ahead due to the unsuitability of the site.[15]

The 1845 Poor Law had transferred responsibility for looking after the poor from the Kirk Session to the new Parochial Board and disputes over resources continued. The Session believed it owned Dunbar's and all the poor relief money which it had collected before 1845, and Dunbar's use as a poorhouse was 'only during its pleasure'. The Parochial Board considered that it was entitled to Dunbar's but did not take its case to court.[ii] Accordingly, there was an impasse which probably impeded any appropriate development of the facility.[16]

The new 'poor's house' was initially intended as a refuge for the infirm, aged and friendless to pass their last days in peace and quietness and 'not so out of humanities reach' and this continued to be an important function. At first, the Poorhouse held only 4-6 elderly women and there was great reluctance to use it, some stating that they would rather die than enter it. In 1846, it never contained more than 10-12 residents who were 'bed ridden and friendless paupers' and a few deserted children.[17] Figures for May 1847 show 2 male, 7 females and 3 children.

Initially, paupers were merely boarded and a Keeper of the House, Mr Fraser, was paid a levy for each resident but, by 1848, it was thought more cost effective to increase the number of residents (see page 21) and that year Miss Jessie Walker, a Gaelic speaker from Glasgow, was appointed sole matron at £20 p.a. Residents now were expected to work. Orphaned[iii] or abandoned children were kept there until they could be

---

[i] The spire is shown on Slezor's 'Prospect of Inverness' of 1693.
[ii] The outcomes of court cases elsewhere suggest it would have lost.
[iii] The frequent epidemics significantly increased the number of orphans.

boarded out and this increased – the 1861 census shows that 25 of the 66 residents were children, including 5 infants who were looked after by the matron and trained for a job in service - which most gained on leaving. Also kept there under Sheriff's warrant were 'fatuous' people[i] as a less costly, but also more humane, alternative to sending them to an institution elsewhere and, in 1858, there were 6 resident.

Capacity and occupancy

	Capacity	Residents
1850	59	36
1852	60	40
1854	58	43
1856	55	41
1858	63	65
1860	65	57

The capacity of Dunbar's was set at around 60 (table on the left) but this was unrealistic and, as the number of residents steadily grew, it became increasingly overcrowded and difficult to manage and was seen as inadequate by the Board of Supervision.[ii] In 1857, a report on Dunbar's accommodation indicated the difficulties of working and living there. The building had 3 storeys. On the ground floor was a female dormitory with its floor below the level of the yard so that the walls were always damp. The toilets were in a boarded off part of the room. Matron had a sitting room and bedroom but her toilet was not partitioned off so 'for her comfort' she slept in her sitting room. The ground floor also held the kitchen with a servant's bedroom opening off it. The first floor had a male and a female dormitory each with a boarded off convenience adjacent to each other. There was a bath accessible to either ward but the area was too confined to be of use and the only portable bath was too cumbersome. The male and female dormitories on the second floor had only one communal toilet and one washing place. Off the passage was a mortuary which also contained the bedding and clothing store.

There was no probationary ward for receiving and cleansing new admissions and no fumigation facility so that lice spread easily from the clothes of new admissions. There was no dining room and meals were

---

[i] A Scottish legal term for those with learning difficulties.
[ii] The Board of Supervision in Edinburgh oversaw the operation of the Poor Law.

taken in the dormitories. Unlike many poorhouses, there was no refractory ward (isolation room) for unruly residents but a room in a thatched cottage in the yard accommodated 'two undesirable women'. The cottage also contained a lumber store and carpenter's shop. There were no separate sick wards and no separate accommodation for the children. There was no proper laundry and, on wet days, washing had to be hung up to dry in the kitchen or dormitories. The yard extended from Church Street to Academy Street and was surrounded by a 7 foot wall and contained the customary piggery. It was also the airing court for the residents but there was no segregation and all residents mixed together.[18]

Inverness registered paupers 16th August 1857[19]

Permanent Roll	468
Occasional	177
Orphans	26
Resident in Poorhouse	49
Lunatics in asylum[i]	26

It was no wonder that, the following year, the Inspector of the Poor again reported that Dunbar's was overcrowded and noted 'the impossibility from its old construction of a proper classification of residents' and stated that 'the necessity for a new building presses itself more and more on your committee and officials'. In 1856, the Kirk Session planned to erect a school house and teacher's residence in the Poorhouse yard[ii] which would further constrict space. Also, Dunbar's accommodated only a small percentage of the parish paupers who were, as in many parishes, mainly supported at home (table above). In contrast to a decade earlier, accommodating paupers in a poorhouse rather than support at home was now generally seen as more efficient. Poorhouses were also increasingly used as a 'test of pauperism'. Applicants for poor relief were offered a place in the Poorhouse and when they refused, as the vast majority did, they lost benefits. All this further encouraged the construction of a larger poorhouse.

---

[i] They had to be sent elsewhere for example to Morningside in Edinburgh.
[ii] Which appeared not to happen.

21

The Poor Law had instituted formal state support for paupers and any treated in the Infirmary were charged to the Parochial Board. However, as elsewhere, the parish employed its own medical officers,[i] and used Dunbar's to house bed ridden and chronically ill cases. Dr MacDonald, Inverness MOH, speaking in 1919, had been 'unable to obtain any records of medical work' in Dunbar's although 'there were undoubtedly sick housed there'. Indeed, no records of the treatment of the sick within Dunbar's have been subsequently discovered but this is not unusual for Highland poorhouses.[20]

Staffing seems to have been minimal. Miss Walker, as matron, seems to have had an onerous role although, by 1851, she had a nurse and servant

 to help care for the 45 residents. In 1855, she was head hunted by the Infirmary and, although she was not appointed there, her salary was raised to match that of the Infirmary matron (£30). In late 1860, she left to get married and was replaced by widow Mrs Martha Fraser for the short period until the Poorhouse moved to Muirfield. In late 1861, residents were transferred to the new Inverness Poorhouse and, by October 1862, Dunbar's Hospital was advertised to let for residential and commercial use.[21]

Dunbar's Hospital
Dormer window with carved
bedesman

---

[i] Dr Manford was MO in 1946 and Dr Mackintosh was MO when he died in 1850. Dr Manford and Dr Mackay shared the work from 1850 until at least 1859.

Inverness Poorhouse
(Muirfield Institution / Hilton Hospital)
Old Edinburgh Road
1861

By the mid-1850s, Dunbar's Hospital was becoming increasingly unsatisfactory as a poorhouse and, in late 1858, the Inverness Parochial Board feued[i] an 8-acre site at Muirfield on the southern outskirts of the town. A new Inverness Poorhouse was designed by James Matthews and William Lawrie[ii] who were chosen over local architects Alexander Ross and George Rhind. In 1859, the tradesmen, who were mostly local, were selected as shown on the left.[22] The date on the building (photograph above) is 1860 which presumably marks its physical completion since it was not occupied until the following year.

Trade	Firm	Cost
Mason	Cumming	£2,470
Carpenter	Duff	£2,097
Plasterer	Hogg (Montrose)	£333
Ironwork	Smith & Mackay	£103
Slater	Russell	£337
Plumber	Black	£333
Glazier	Macleod	£93
	Total	**£5,766**

---

[i] See page ii for more details of the feudal system.

[ii] An Aberdeen firm. Lawrie ran the Inverness office - the main one after 1877.

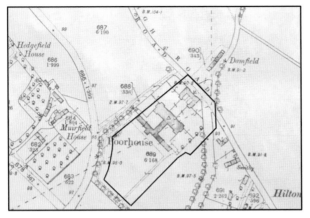

The 6 inch Ordnance Survey map (left) from 1870[23] shows the Poorhouse site[i] with its grounds (outlined) lying to the south. The design was typical of the time and strongly influenced by the Board of Supervision in Edinburgh. At the entrance was the separate gatehouse which contained porter's lodge and probationary wards with hot and cold baths which all new admissions had to endure. Here, new entrants' clothes were fumigated and stored and they were re-clad in Poorhouse clothes. The separate gatehouse can be seen clearly on the map above but it is now mostly demolished (photograph on page 23). Flanking the main entrance were the governor's quarters and committee room. The more infirm residents occupied the rest of the ground floor (males on the right and females on the left). The first floor housed the more robust residents including large day/work rooms and also a school room and dormitories for children. The attics were used as large wards. The main dining room was central at the rear of the main building and was also used as a chapel. Further back and parallel with the main block was a single storey block containing kitchens, stores, mortuary and confinement cell. Most of the building survives.

In 1861, a further £2,000 was spent on completing the building and out-houses and the whole cost was financed by a bank loan to be repaid over 30 years. The new Poorhouse opened on 21st November 1861 with 61

---

[i] See map on page 16 for its location.

residents[i] who transferred from Dunbar's Hospital.[24] Dunbar's matron did not transfer to the new Poorhouse and Mr and Mrs D MacFie[ii] were appointed governor and matron at a combined salary of £120 p. a. There was also a nurse and servant. The Poorhouse was administered by a committee to whom the governor reported every three months. Poorhouses have been described as being run like prisons and the governor had substantial authority over the residents whose lives were strictly controlled. Residents were allowed out of the Poorhouse only one day per month for a maximum of six hours but males and females could not go out on the same day. Mothers of illegitimate children and all women under 35 years old were not allowed out at all. Only after 1905 could husband and wife occupy the same apartment but this was subject to the discretion of the governor. Discipline was strictly enforced and the Poorhouse had male and female punishment cells which seem to have been regularly used. In 1903, the annual Board of Supervision inspection noted that the cells were dark, unventilated, had no seat or bed and would not be licensed for a criminal. The inspector doubted if the committee realised the severity of placing residents there – for up to 12 hours in winter in unheated conditions. The committee's response was to install a seat and assure the inspector that a bed was available if required.

Restrictions also applied to the staff. The governor and his wife each had 3 weeks annual leave but they could not go off together because one of them had to be in charge.[25] As elsewhere, nurses' lives were strictly controlled. In 1860, there was little differentiation between the role of nurse and servant but, by the 1880s, there was a national drive to establish trained nurses in poorhouses. At first, the Poorhouse committee resisted but it had appointed one by 1889. Initially, a high turnover was blamed on the job being too hard and, in 1900, a domestic servant was employed to assist and hot water was brought closer to the sick wards. However, turnover was still quite high and it was difficult to fill posts. Nurses

---

[i] By December 1861, there were 12 men 30 women and 17 children. Initially, female residents dominated (around 60% at the 1871 and 1881 censes) but this predominance later reduced. In 1903, 55% of the accommodation was female.
[ii] Married on 24/11/1861, 3 days after the Poorhouse opened.

earned £30 per year with board and lodging and 21 days annual leave and, by January 1905, there were *Rules for Trained Nurses* which set a strict daily timetable[i] (below). In 1903, there was still only one nurse and none at night and the annual inspection noted that, although there were only officially nine sick residents, there were actually 35 when infirm patients were included. The inspector could see no real distinction between the two groups in nursing terms and recommended that the state nursing grant be stopped until there was more adequate nursing including appointing a night nurse. The latter happened in 1911 but there was still just one nurse on duty apart from matron until 1926 and, by then, there were around 40 sick beds. The numbers of sick in the table opposite, therefore, underestimate the number of ill people in the Poorhouse. The spikes in numbers e.g. 1886 possibly represent fever outbreaks

Nurse's daily timetable 1905

Cup of tea	7.00am
On duty	7.00am - 8.45am
Breakfast	8.45am - 9.30am
On duty	9.30am - 12.45pm
Dinner	12.45pm - 1.30pm
On duty	1.30pm - 4.45pm
Tea	4.45pm - 5.15pm
On duty in ward	5.15pm - 8.30pm

The Parochial Board employed two medical officers[ii] one of whom visited daily. They examined all new residents on arrival and attested to their fitness for work. New arrivals had their immediate medical needs met such as eradicating head lice and ensuring that they did not suffer from any infectious disease but it was not until 1904 that the smallpox vaccination of all new entrants was mandatory.[iii]

---

[i] Infirmary nurses worked a similar pattern (see page 59).

[ii] In December 1864, one of the medical officers, 'in the interest of science,' removed the head of a 4-year-old 'idiot child' who had died after living in the Poorhouse for about a year. The head was sent to his house apparently in collusion with a Depute Commissioner in Lunacy. Although the 1832 Anatomy Act allowed unclaimed bodies of the poor to be used for dissection, such action underlined the fear many had of the poor being used for medical experimentation and this kept medical students out of poorhouses for many years (Hamilton The Healers).

[iii] Vaccination had been generally available from the 1860s.

Unlike other Highland poorhouses, Inverness had a high occupancy. Accommodation was initially planned for 200 residents but it became clear that this was too high and subsequent figures are lower. By 1905, it had been reduced to 150 and, in 1906, attic conversion increased capacity by only 10 beds including 27 sick beds. Correspondence at the time indicates the restraints put on the local authority by the Local Government Board[i] in Edinburgh as, through increasing regulation, it tried to ensure adequate living space for residents.[26] Fortunately, actual occupancy was well short of official capacity as shown in the table below.

There was much emphasis on austerity and economy. Craft and trade skills of residents were utilised, for example, boots and clothes were made in-house, unless the only resident tailor died, as happened at one point. In 1864, 'strong scotch tweed' was substituted for moleskin[ii] and residents evidently were identified by their 'uniform'. If a resident absconded wearing house clothes, it was treated as theft and the police informed. Diet was basic[iii] consisting of porridge twice a day with buttermilk or treacle, soup with potatoes or bap (roll) and 1.5 ounces of meat three times a week[27] although there was extra food on New Year's Day and a Christmas dinner of mutton donated by a town solicitor. Residents were allowed to 'attend divine service on Sundays' and a chaplain was also appointed, initially at £15 p.a. but later raised to £30 p.a. and, by 1863, the sick and bed ridden received additional spiritual instruction on Wednesday afternoons.

Residents & sick 1870-1910 at mid-November

Year	Total residents	Sick
1870	77	9
1874	88	23
1878	83	12
1882	87	10
1886	86	26
1890	65	6
1894	101	8
1898	86	7
1902	86	10
1906	77	22
1910	83	24

---

[i] In 1894, this succeeded, with extra powers, the Board of Supervision (page 20).
[ii] It is said that men originally wore white moleskin suits with large pearl buttons but this does not seem likely.
[iii] Compare this with that in the Asylum (page 213).

The Poorhouse gradually became less austere. In 1900, the Committee agreed to 'charitable entertainments' and residents had regular visits, gifts and entertainment from local organisations and individuals. In December 1927, the governor noted that 'treats' included special Christmas and New Year[i] meals and a concert and choir performance. By 1914, there was the beginning of a library and copies of local papers were donated. From 1919, tea as well as porridge was served for breakfast. In 1911, Inverness Poorhouse was the first in Scotland to have 40[ii] Old Edinburgh Road rather than Inverness Poorhouse recorded on birth certificates 'thus eliminating any taint of pauperism which in later life might be a hindrance to the person concerned'. Although in this aim it was singularly unsuccessful.[28]

Poorhouses aimed to be as self-sufficient as possible. The grounds had a 6 acre garden and, in 1862, a gardening sub committee was formed, the land ploughed and the foreman of Howden Nurseries asked to select suitable trees and plants. A gardener was employed and a piggery built. It is likely that a cow was kept for milk as happened elsewhere. The land continued to be worked into the 1950s.[iii] Apart from work in the grounds, the main tasks were chopping firewood, the sale of which brought income, and household tasks although, by the 1870s, there were often insufficient able bodied residents and domestic servants had to be employed. Interestingly, it was seldom possible to persuade outside paupers to take up such employment even when they lost their allowance as a result of their refusal to work.

There was always a number of children and their welfare was an ongoing issue. In 1910, there were 110 children accommodated over the year. Most were eventually removed by their parents but 11 were boarded out,

---

[i] There was a tradition of celebrating the old New Year (12 January) at Muirfield. In 1934, 61 prominent (male) Inverness citizens were invited. A former nurse remembers it included lots of doctors (Inverness Our Story Bk1). It seems unlikely that the residents were involved.

[ii] Street numbers changed and it became 80 Old Edinburgh Road in 1934.

[iii] It was important in the 1940s to the extent that a new tractor was purchased.

three adopted, three sent to an Industrial School[i] and five, who had been convicted of theft and placed in the Poorhouse by the police, were sent to a reformatory. Eight were still resident at the end of the year. Numbers continued at a high level. In 1915, 58 children were admitted and this rose to 73 in 1917.[29]

Initial plans for a resident to teach the children foundered when he left and the children went to Raining's School[ii] run by the Society for the Promotion of Christian Knowledge. However, the Society later refused to have them and, by 1871, the children were attending Culcabock School to the east. The Poorhouse committee regularly examined the children in reading, spelling and arithmetic and, by 1869, the precentor of the High Church was teaching them singing. From 1863, children were boarded out locally over the summer and autumn, essentially as domestic labour, for £1 payment to the Parochial Board and there was later much concern about their welfare and treatment while boarded out. In 1869, the Board of Supervision ruled that children could not be separated from their mothers and sent out of the Poorhouse.[30]

Staff had to cope with ongoing change and uncertainty. In 1915, Oldmill Poorhouse[iii] in Aberdeen was converted to a wartime hospital and 60 of its residents were sent to Inverness until after the war. In 1916, two wards were temporarily set aside for phthisis (pulmonary tuberculosis) cases because the Citadel Hospital was required for an outbreak of cerebrospinal meningitis. In the mid-1920s, the economic depression and the prospect of work on the Inverness-Glasgow road brought many itinerant workers to the area. Many of them arrived exhausted and homeless and required temporary accommodation in the Poorhouse and

---

[i] Run by the Royal Society for the Prevention of Cruelty to Children. Like ragged schools they took destitute children and gave them education and a trade. The first was in Aberdeen in 1846. Initially voluntary, they were later legalised by act of parliament. They differed from reformatories in that their pupils had not committed a serious crime (See footnote page 74).
[ii] Now demolished, it was situated at the top of Raining's Stair in Inverness.
[iii] Later part of Woodend Hospital (Glenburn Wing).

this continued into the 1930s.[i] In 1932, there were 524 admissions and 476 discharges both of which reduced considerably the following year when the road work had finished. Vagrants who often came and went daily were accommodated in the separate porter's lodge. The three maternity beds were often occupied by mothers who were in some distress so that their arrival was usually a sudden rather than planned event. All this work of checking in and out fell upon the matron and nurses who were already struggling with oversubscribed sick wards. Administrative staff were then unheard of.

As the table on page 27 shows, numbers of sick varied but began to increase steadily in the 20th century and accommodation for them became insufficient. By 1910, the 24 sick beds were full and there were often sick in the ordinary wards. It was impossible to segregate infectious cases such as phthisis although 'itch and offensive cases' were isolated in the probationer wards in the gatehouse. In 1911, attic space was converted to dormitories which allowed expansion to 43 sick beds which the governor considered ample although, by 1917, sick beds had again increased to 26 male, 19 female and 5 children.[31] By then, all the sick wards, a maternity ward, nursery and staff accommodation were contained on the first floor and, apparently, a male and female ward were reserved for 'the respectable sick poor'.[32] Medical officers continued to visit the sick daily and the other residents monthly but, despite rising numbers of sick, nursing staff did not increase until the 1920s.[33]

Facilities were slow to improve and there was no hot water system until 1901.[34] In 1908, central heating was installed, it being noted that it was impossible to maintain temperatures in the sick wards in winter. However, there was still a shortage of water so that the recommended one bath per week for residents was instead one per fortnight. There was no heating in the attic rooms until 1919 when gas radiators were installed and, in 1921, electric light was introduced. In 1926, a new governor's house was opened and the redundant governor's family quarters in the main building provided space for accommodation for two

---

[i] Local authorities had to accommodate homeless which they did at the Poorhouse.

nurses and a medical inspection room. The 1920s saw a steady rise in the numbers of sick (table below) as well as the infirm but little change in staffing despite the increasing workload.

Muirfield selected statistics 1920 - 1926[35]

Numbers at the end of	1920	1922	1924	1926
Total residents	67	72	98	121
Sick	26	23	34	36
Resident children[i]	7	4	5	5
Matron	1	1	1	1
Day nurse	1	1	1	1
Night nurse	0	0	0	1

In the 1920s, there were administrative changes to the Poorhouse but little evidence of a change in conditions. In 1921, it was renamed Muirfield Institution[ii] but greater changes were to come. The 1929 Local Government Act swept away much of the old Poor Law and poorhouse sick wards, like all other public health, became the responsibility of counties and burghs. From 1930, the new Inverness Joint Hospital Board administered the sick wards (as well as Culduthel and Citadel hospitals) and Mr Bewglass, Muirfield's governor, also became Clerk to the Board. The official capacity was 40 sick beds but there was continual overcrowding, a fact highlighted strongly in annual reports from the governor and medical officer. They also stressed that little had changed under the new administration. There was no hot water at night, heating was mainly by open fire and the laundry machine which had been installed in 1907 was worn out. Basic aspects were lacking such as bedside lockers but, more importantly, sanitary facilities were outdated and inadequate for hospital cases. In 1934, the governor noted that the delay in rectifying the situation could no longer be attributed to local government reorganisation but the problem seems to have been that there was no obvious in-house solution.

---

[i] Resident children were those who could not be boarded out due to sickness or special needs. They had their own ward and were looked after by a nurse.
[ii] This is earlier than most in Highland. All did eventually change names but the latest - Nairn Poorhouse - did not become Balblair Home until 1934.

In the early 1930s, the Department for Health agreed that it was not cost effective to upgrade the outdated building and a new build at Culduthel would also remove patients from the stigma of the poorhouse which still pervaded Muirfield. However, plans for this were only finalised in 1939, delayed by the Second World War (page 184) and then overtaken by the new hospital at Raigmore. Meanwhile, the uncertain future of the institution prevented any strategic planning of facilities or staffing and, indeed, no substantial refurbishment was done until the 1950s.

In 1935, the Burgh MOH reported that Muirfield was 'totally unsatisfactory for the patients for which it has to cater' and the following year was more expansive calling it 'unsuitable in every way', 'wards badly ventilated' and 'laundry and kitchen arrangement entirely unsatisfactory'. There were only four baths in the whole building – two male and two female. In 1938, the governor noted that there had been no structural alteration to the wards since it opened in 1860 when no thought had been given to medical care.

In 1938, a government survey described Muirfield as a building with narrow central corridors and poorly lit but well ventilated wards although the latter point is at variance with the earlier views of the medical officer. Its accommodation included 54 beds for the chronic sick, a nursery ward for six children and places for certified mental patients.[i] The recommendation was for chronic sick to continue until the planned (but never built) provision at Culduthel was ready and thereafter Muirfield would have 'chronic sick mental cases'.[36]

---

[i] Despite provision being available at the Northern District Asylum.

Muirfield selected statistics 1933 - 1937[37]

	1933	1934	1935	1936	1937
Cases treated	243	231	254	244	290
Ordinary at 31 st Dec	27	30	23	23	21
% Ordinary	22%	23%	23%	24%	18%
Infirm at 31 st Dec	22	24	22	22	20
Chronic Sick at 31st Dec	65	65	50	48	67
Children at 31st Dec	8	13	6	3	10
Total resident at 31 st Dec	114	119	101	98	113
Births pa	14	15	15	14	14

Ordinary residents were fit but were unable to support themselves.
The Infirm could not work and needed care but not intensive nursing.
The Chronic Sick were bed ridden.

As the table above shows, the initial capacity of 40 sick beds now had to accommodate well over 60 at times and, in addition, the children and infirm also required care. This amounted to around 80% of the total residents. The throughput of cases also increased being 112 p.a. in 1921, 196 p.a. in 1930 and, as the table above shows, approaching 300 p.a. by the late 1930s. In July 1932, Inverness Burgh boarded out able-bodied residents to the underused Ness House in Fortrose to increase accommodation for infirm, sick and maternity but this appears to have ceased by 1935.[38]

The table on page 34 shows the classification of ailments recorded by the medical officer. It seems that many residents at Muirfield suffered from unspecified conditions associated with old age and debility which may have defied closer diagnosis or perhaps a closer diagnosis was not sought. Certainly the generality of the description of cases contrasts with contemporary RNI reports and makes year on year comparisons difficult. Note the regular number of maternity cases (births) which later went to Rosedene.[39]

As well as pressure on facilities, financial pressure on Muirfield also increased because, with better social welfare, there were fewer fit residents and few former tradesmen so that the hospital had to pay for maintenance jobs which previously would have been carried out by its own residents. This was particularly the case in 1937 when the Government's Unemployment Assistance Board took over support for able bodied cases. Also, as the economy recovered in the 1930s, there were more jobs so that the more active residents found work.

Muirfield classification of sick cases[40]

	1934	1935	1937	1938
Diseases of the nervous system	40	45	29	42
Diseases of the circulatory system	29	34	52	51
Diseases of the respiratory system	20	23	24	26
Diseases of the digestive system	16	8	7	12
Diseases of the genito-urinary system	13	6	10	12
Accidents	13	11	22	26
Senility	8	10	20	22
Ante and post-natal	24	36	28	21
General condition e.g. rheumatism	64	43	48	69

In 1938, nursing staff consisted of three fully trained and five trainees (probationers). The shortage of nurses was regularly reported but apparently could not be increased due to insufficient nurses' accommodation. A nurse remembers that, in 1939, patients were mainly those who could not live on their own and that the small maternity unit dealt with many births by unmarried mothers. She remembers the hard work and being on night shift on her own.[41]

During the Second World War, three downstairs rooms were set aside as an ARP[i] station and First Aid post. Muirfield also had to accommodate the families of some armed forces personnel, posted to the area, whose wives and children had followed them and turned up homeless on the doorstep. The porter still stayed in one half of the gatehouse and still locked the gates each night. The other half of the gatehouse stored patients' clothes and housed two old men. The number of children was concerning and particularly high at over 20 in 1943 thus increasing the pressure for a children's home.[42]

---

[i] Air Raid Precautions – later Civil Defence.

The contrast between Muirfield's sick wards and those in Culduthel Hospital (page 175) is interesting. Both were run by the same local authority board but their staffing and accommodation levels were quite different. There were approximately 3 patients per nurse at Culduthel and this level of staffing was maintained - if numbers of in-patients increased, staff numbers seemed to rise accordingly. By contrast, there were at least twice as many patients per nurse at Muirfield and staffing levels were fixed so that they just had to cope when numbers increased.

In 1948,[i] Muirfield transferred to the new Health Board and, in 1951, the official capacity of 114 was split equally between the Board and the local authorities. At the 1951 census, it had 87 patients and 12 resident staff. By mid-1953, the Burgh had moved out its infirm to its recently acquired 'old people's homes' at Ach an Eas and Rossal. The County took much longer to act and although it had acquired Aigas House, it thought Muirfield patients were 'unsuitable' for it. Eventually, in 1958, after some considerable pressure from the Health Board which was trying to cope with the rising demand for chronic sick beds, County patients were moved out to Burgh housing while their new Home at Burn Road (Burnside) was constructed. Until 1956, when separate lodging houses were provided, both Burgh and County retained the gatehouse for male vagrants - women and child vagrants were still accommodated in the main building. Numbers of patients in Muirfield continued at around 90.

In 1955, there were substantial alterations and the top floor was converted into nurses' accommodation. In 1960, the hospital was extensively modernised.[43] This included new central heating, demolition of the gatehouse and porter's lodge, a day room for patients, new ward kitchens and additional bathrooms and toilets/sluices. On 8th November 1961, it was officially re-opened as Hilton Hospital[ii] with 80 beds. During the refurbishment, 40 female patients were accommodated at Culduthel

---

[i] After 1948, former poorhouses with a majority of bed-ridden residents transferred to the new health boards otherwise they remained with the local authority. In Highland, only Muirfield and Swordale (Migdale) transferred to the health board.
[ii] This name had been suggested in 1950 by the Council of Social Services, Inverness.

and 20 male at Invergordon. In 1963, the former governor's house was converted to nurses' accommodation.[44] However, the hospital's facilities were still outdated and, after being considered as a possible Health Board headquarters, it closed in August 1987 and patients were transferred to the new long-stay geriatric wards at the RNI.[45] The building has now been converted to residential use.

Governors and Matrons

1861- 1904	Mr & Mrs D MacFie	Mrs MacFie assistant matron until Mr MacFie's death in Aug 1910.
1904-44	Mr & Mrs Bewglass	Appointed from 17 applicants. Mrs Bewglass retired in 1935.[46]
1944	Thomas Allison	
1935-51	Miss Joan Mackenzie	Initially acting matron then matron from 1939. Died suddenly.[47]
1951-57	Miss A Chisholm	
1957-65	Miss CG Bain	Retired.
1965 -	I O Mackay[48]	

The proceeds of colonial expansion

The next section deals with the Northern Infirmary and a large part of its funding in the early half of the nineteenth century came from aboard. Many local people had close contacts with military regiments in Bengal and with planation managers in the Caribbean – some local families owned plantations. Much use was made of those contacts so that both areas sent back many donations – perhaps as much as one third of the initial funding. At the time, slave labour was the main workforce in Caribbean plantations. Therefore, it can be said that our main Highland hospital was partly funded by the proceeds of slavery and imperial conquest. Funding from abroad and from the profits of British colonies continued to play an important part in the funding of other Highland hospitals such as at Nairn and in Skye although, by then, slavery had been abolished in the British Empire for some time.[49]

The Royal Northern Infirmary[50]
1804

This stately dome on Ness's banks upreared
Commands respect and long will stand revered... [i]

By the late 18th century, aspiring towns such as Inverness increasingly viewed a general hospital as an essential acquisition. In 1797, a committee was formed under Provost Inglis[ii] (left) and, at a meeting of 'noblemen and gentlemen' on 25 October 1798, a 'general view' was agreed. This was followed by an appeal in the Edinburgh Courant which contained a list of around 100 subscribers promising around £1,900. It noted the need for a hospital accessible to the sick poor of the Highlands and stated that Inverness was the 'most centrical' location.[51]

The hospital plan was supplied by Alexander Laing, architect in Edinburgh,[52] for which he was paid £17.[iii] It was approved on 11 September 1798 and, in March 1799, an Infirmary committee of two Provosts and six Bailies held its first meeting which agreed a mason's contract of £1,680 with James and Alex Nicol of Kintessack near Forres and Hugh Suter of Inverness. Some days later, John Smith[iv] from Banff was selected as architect to complete the carpentry, 'plaister work', plumbing and slating for £1,300. The Infirmary owned land south of

---

[i] From a poem by the *Clachnacuddin Bard* when the Northern Infirmary opened.

[ii] William Inglis of Kingsmills was Inverness Burgh Treasurer (1775) and Provost (1797-1801). In 1787, he entertained Robert Burns, on his Highland tour.

[iii] He also designed the town steeple and court house in 1789-91.

[iv] John Smith, often quoted as the Infirmary's architect, just coordinated the trades. Actually, his architect brother James, an Inverness magistrate, did much of it. James designed many local buildings e.g. Tain Royal Academy and is listed in Colvin's Biographical Dictionary of British Architects. John is not and details on him are sparse. The Aberdeen city architect of the same name was not born until 1781.

Old Edinburgh Road next to Aultnaskiach and it was investigated as a possible site but a trial well produced no water. Instead, in early 1799, a 4 acre site beside the River Ness was feued from Fraser of Torbrek. The well-known picture below[53] from 1823 shows the Infirmary on the far left and illustrates the relative separation of the hospital from the rest of the town. On 6th May 1799, following a large procession, the foundation stone was laid by the 'Right Worshipful the masters of the (three) different (freemason) lodges' amid some ceremony. The rest of the day was then spent with 'genuine harmony and conviviality'.[54]

Provost Inglis, the hospital's prime mover, pursued potential subscribers vigorously. He established agents in London, Bristol, Edinburgh and Glasgow and a considerable number of donations came from the south of Britain and from ex patriots, especially those involved in colonial plantations (of which there were many) in the East and West Indies and Demerary (Guyana) (see page 36).[55] Much also came from the military overseas such as Canada and India.[i] By August 1800, the total collected was £7,381. Colonel Mackenzie sent over £1,000 in rupees, £677 of which was raised from his 78th Highlanders then based in Bengal and included £336 from 'non-commissioned officers, drummers and privates'.[56]

---

[i] In a review of 1927, the Infirmary managers acknowledged that a 'great, if not the greater, part of the fund of the institution was contributed by our countrymen at a distance, and particularly in the East and West Indies' (Inv. Courier 10 January).

The completion date was set at August 1801 but building work was slow and the death of Provost Inglis in February 1801 reduced momentum. The delays were partly due to rapidly rising costs[i] in materials and labour although the architect blamed the masons and later sought compensation which indeed was given to both.[57] There was a government embargo on shipping and more materials had to be moved by expensive land cartage. By May 1803, subscriptions stood at nearly £8,000 and the total cost of erecting the building and making up the grounds was £4,236. Furniture cost £152 but this also included £13 for the Infirmary's first milk cow.[ii]

The original Northern Infirmary[58]

While the building design (above) was impressive it was not ornate. In a letter of 1799 to John Fraser of Achnagairn, Provost Inglis was clear on his philosophy. In rejecting a hospital plan received from architect Colin Farquhar of London as too gaudy he stated, 'Our object is to erect a decent building which will do credit to the liberality of the Subscribers, but by no means to forget that it is to be inhabited by the sick poor for whom to provide anything beyond comfortable accommodation would be absurd.' The building was 'of three storeys with a central three-bay block, capped by a pediment supported by giant order Corinthian pilasters raised over the ground floor. This block was linked by single-storey quadrants to two-storey pavilions' each of which had four vaulted lunatic cells on the ground floor (see also page 197 onwards).[59]

---

[i] The managers managed to recoup £5 by letting out the site for summer grazing.
[ii] The Infirmary may have kept more than one. It was selling two in 1844.

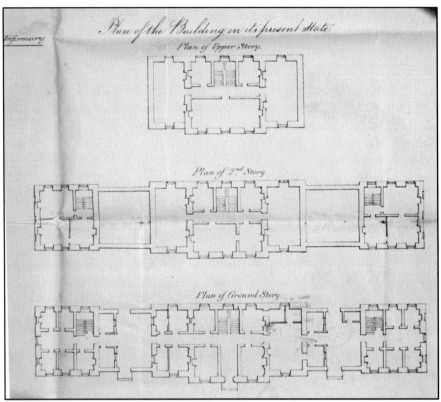

Plan of the original Northern Infirmary[60]

In the plan above, the main door opened onto a lobby and main staircase. To the right was a parlour and matron's room with a bed closet. The kitchen was a larger room with a bed closet to accommodate the cook. To the left of the entrance was the clerk's room, medicine store and two bathrooms. The lunatic cells can be clearly seen at each end of the ground floor. Upstairs was the large 'directors' room'[i] and the resident house surgeon's accommodation. The upper storeys held four main wards and several smaller rooms with the 'operations room' on the 2nd floor. The managers stated that the hospital could accommodate 60 patients and 20 lunatics but this seem exaggerated. Even after the 1835

---

[i] Infirmary records refer to directors and managers. We just use the term manager.

extensions (page 48), there were under 60 beds and the 8 lunatic cells were each only 8 feet square - far too small for 20 patients.[61]

The hospital opened on 25th May 1804. A procession of 'all the respectable inhabitants of the town' walked from the Town Hall and, after prayers from senior minister Rev. Alexander Fraser and a speech from Provost Alex. Mackintosh, 'the doors were thrown open'. As with laying the foundation stone, the opening ceremony prompted a day of festivities by the gentlemen of the area with 'many loyal and patriotic toasts' drunk. The plaque on the hospital (above) is rather misleading. For many years, it was believed erroneously that the hospital opened in 1803 and not 1804. Also, Provost Inglis was the main promoter but he did not open the hospital and had died in 1801.

The new Infirmary was ready to receive patients on the 1st June but the first patient, Elspet Munro from Urquhart parish, Ross-shire, was not admitted until 3rd July. The delay was possibly due to the suspicion of this new institution within the local populace, a sentiment not unusual in Scotland at this time when standard medical practice was still to purge and bleed sufferers. The first fever patient (typhus), was Alex. Mackenzie, a soldier with the 78th Highlanders, who was admitted in November. A second fever sufferer was admitted the same month and the nurse also became infected. By February 1805, Elspet Munro had recovered and agreed to stay on to assist matron until a nurse could be found. In these early days, many patients were cured by rest and good diet which took a long time and it was the only cure at the time for Elspet who had a tubercular swelling on her knee.[62]

Patients had to be at their beds at meal times and visiting time which was 10 am -12 noon each morning (10-11 am and 3-6 pm from 1837). They went to bed at 9.00 pm and rose at 7.00 am in summer and 8.00 am in winter months. The sexes were strictly separated except, it appears, in the lunatic cells (page 197). If able, patients were expected to assist around the hospital. In 1806, medical attendant Dr Forbes prescribed that a convalescent patient help out in the hospital garden as part of his recovery and, in 1818, two shovels were purchased for convalescing patients to extend the gravel walk in the grounds.

Initially, staff consisted of matron, nurse, cook, two maid servants and a porter who seems to have had considerable status. Porter William Fraser was the first member of staff appointed in February 1804 and, at £15 p.a., was paid considerably more than the matron (£12 p.a.), house surgeon (£12 p.a.), nurse (£6 p.a.) and domestic staff (£4 p.a.). He was in charge of the grounds including the vegetable/fruit gardens and a milk cow[i] which supplied the hospital. He was 'keeper of the insane' and apparently responsible for much of their wellbeing (page 197).

The matron was housekeeper and often known as such. She was responsible for the furnishings, domestic equipment and supplies for which she accounted weekly to the managers. She directed the nursing and domestic staff and, like them, lived in. The duties of the nurse were essentially to feed the patients and ensure they took any medicines. She fetched the food from the kitchen and monitored the diet which seems to have been strictly controlled since visitors were not allowed to bring in food or drink. She kept the wards clean and tidy. Nurses were required to have both English and Gaelic and were instantly dismissed if they accepted any gift from a patient.

As in most voluntary hospitals, local doctors[ii] were honorary (unpaid) 'medical attendants'. They attended the hospital in rotational blocks and visited patients daily at noon, normally two being on duty at any one time. They had to consult each other in difficult cases and where an operation was required. From the outset, there was a resident 'House Surgeon,

---

[i] The house surgeon bought and sold the cow and annual calf.
[ii] Apart from laudable philanthropy, being an honorary doctor to the local hospital could advance a doctor's private medical practice on which most depended.

Clerk and Apothecary' who was 'master of the house'. The post was normally given to a newly qualified doctor who was in charge of the hospital staff and accountable to the medical attendants for medical treatment. He made up the medicines and looked after the medical instruments. The ability to speak Gaelic was of prime importance, many patients having Gaelic as their first language and, in the 1840s, there was a large outcry when a non-Gaelic speaker was appointed. The house surgeon was not allowed to have his own patients. Later, the Clerk's post was separate and part time until 1884. In 1891, the Clerk and Collector post included being general administrator as well as keeping and presenting the accounts and statistical information. He worked at the Infirmary from 10am - 4.00 pm each day. By 1923, the post incorporated that of treasurer. Lists of matrons, medical attendants and resident house surgeons are shown from page 93 on.

The management committee, normally chaired by the Provost of Inverness, consisted of the Inverness magistrates and ministers, the county sheriff and annually elected subscribers. The managers appointed an honorary secretary and treasurer. A committee of five managers plus medical attendants met in the hospital each Friday,[i] toured the hospital and visited the wards to receive feedback from patients and staff. This continued for many years, certainly until the end of the century.[ii] The committee collected donations from the charity box at the gate which is still there (right) and dispensed discipline to patients, for example, where there was accusation of theft. It also disciplined staff - around 1845, a nurse was sacked for using foul and abusive language. The meeting approved all matron's supplies, received a report on patients from the medical attendants and assessed any admissions and discharges. The managers

---

[i] Some years later they met in the Town House. Met fortnightly in the early 1930s.

[ii] From 1887, ward visits were enhanced by a Ladies Visiting Committee.

interviewed patients due to be discharged and this continued at least until the 1860s. The managers also questioned the 'keeper of the insane' on his work but there is no evidence of them visiting the cells and neither the medical attendants nor the keeper were apparently required to report on the 'lunatic' patients. By 1806, patients came from all over the Highlands and Moray and, by 1809, a large number of parishes contributed to the funds (table below). Of the money collected, Inverness contributed 32%. The two Urquhart parishes (see table), Abernethy, Nairn, Petty and Bolleskine together contributed a further 24%. Patients also came from parishes which did not contribute and this was deplored by the managers for many years.

Parishes contributing to the Northern Infirmary in 1809

Inverness area	Inverness, Kirkhill, Ardersier, Fort George, Kiltarlity, Dores, Petty.
Easter Ross	Killearnan, Knockbain, Tain, Edderton, Tarbat, Resolis, Nigg, Urray, Contin, Logie Easter, Cromarty, Fearn, Roskeen, Urquhart.
Wester Ross	Lochcarron, Gairloch, Applecross.
Strathspey	Abernethy.
Moray	Dyke, Rafford, Kinloss.
Nairn	Ardclach, Nairn, Calder (Cawdor).
Great Glen	Boleskine, Urquhart.

Although emergency cases were admitted immediately, gaining admission to the Infirmary was not straightforward. Patients had to be recommended by a subscriber and required a certificate from their parish minister confirming that 'his circumstances entitled him to the benefits of the Institution' as well as a certificate from a doctor confirming his suitability for admission.[63] It was many years before outlying doctors' recommendations alone were acceptable - not until 1889 for doctors in the parishes contiguous with Inverness and 1899 for doctors[i] from the northern counties.[64] From the start, military cases were regularly admitted through the recommendation of their commanding officer (and

---

[i] By 1898, doctors sent over 80% of admissions. Church ministers only 4%. (AR)

44

guarantee of maintenance payment) there being 26 between 1806 and 1811. Employers were expected to pay for their sick servants if admitted. As elsewhere, companies formed agreements with the Infirmary to receive patients from their workforce such as the Caledonian Canal Company in the early 19th century, railway companies from the 1860s and, in the 1890s, British Aluminium at Foyers. Those recommending patients had to ensure their funeral expenses if they died during their stay.

Patients were not admitted if they could be treated as out-patients. 'Incurables' were not admitted nor those requiring regular nursing unless it was also paid for. 'Insane patients' were not admitted if they had suffered their condition for more than a 12 month period or had been released as incurable by any other institution. They had to have a certificate of insanity and have their maintenance paid weekly in advance. 'Idiots' (i.e. those with learning difficulties) were not eligible for admission. It has been noted that the cells were designed for mentally ill patients who were also sick but no evidence of this can be found and the impression is that they were largely admitted as a control measure.

In-patients per annum 1804 – 16

Year	Admissions
1805*	68
1806	56
1807	34
1808	47
1809	70
1810	82
1811	97
1812	110
1813	74
1814	99
1815	126
1816	127

*incorporates
July – December 1804

The hospital was for the poor but society distinguished between the 'deserving poor' and the 'dissolute' as they were called and only the former would have been likely to receive a recommendation. Better off families treated their sick at home, having sufficiently large accommodation to do so.

As shown in the table (left), early numbers in the Infirmary were fairly low but steadily increased. There were normally between 10 and 20 in-patients at any one time although this varied and there were none in July 1807. Patients often stayed for many weeks thus reducing potential annual capacity. In the 1820s, numbers increased further - there were 218 admissions in 1825 and 216 in 1828

45

although a quarter of the latter were fever patients from an outbreak in the Burgh. Out-patients were treated from the start although no record of them was kept until 1817. By 1820, they numbered about 300 p.a. and increased to around 400p.a. in the mid-1920s[i].[65]

Northern Infirmary cases May 1804 – August 1809[66]

Ailment	No.	Ailment	No.	Ailment	No.
Ulcers	54	Fever	27	Dyspepsia	17
Phthisis	16	Diseased Joints	14	Rheumatism	13
Paralysis	10	Syphilis	10	Scirrhous Mammae*	9
Scorbutus*	8	Carious Bone*	7	Cancerous Lip	6
Diseased Eyes	6	Tumours	6	Scrofula*	5
Abscess	5	Ascites	4	Fractures	4
Amenorrhoa	4	Anasarca*	4	Luxations*	4
Hypochondria	3	Burns	2	Erysipelas	2
Ischuria	2	Measles	2	Vermes*	2
Jaundice	1	Diabetes	1	Concussion	1
Dyspnoea	1	Dysentery	1	Hydrothorax	1
Haemoptoe*	1	Haematuria	1	Sore throat	1

*Archaic terms (modern terms in brackets) - anasacra (peripheral oedema); carious bone (osteomyelitis); haemoptoe (haemotysis); luxation (dislocation); scirrhous mammae (breast cancer); scorbutus (scurvy); scrofula (tuberculous lymphadenitis - TB swelling of lymph nodes usually in neck); vermes (worms).

In the first five years the Infirmary treated a large range of ailments (table above) and there were 32 operations. Fever cases were frequent and variable in number and included smallpox in the epidemics of 1812 and 1815 although the initial rules had excluded such cases. The first death occurred in July 1806 and, by 1809, there had been 6 deaths (2% of patients). Hospitals did not admit patients who were clearly dying in an effort to break the public perception that hospitals were 'the last shift'. However, it was not until 1830 that the managers noted that 'the prejudices (of local people) against hospitals are fast disappearing'.[67]

---

[i] 1,545 in total from 1817 – 1821 and 3,245 from 1817 - 1825.

The problem of lack of funding was ever present. Initially, it was due to the building overspend[i] and, soon after opening, a public appeal for funds was made and again in late 1805. Government assistance was sought – 'the same aid which has been granted to the Infirmary at Aberdeen' – and, from 1805, after meeting the 'Secretary at War' in Inverness,[ii] a grant of £91 p.a. was received (15-20% of total income) but was withdrawn after 1821 'for reasons of economy'. In 1808, Lachlan Mackintosh of Raigmore, lately of Calcutta, forwarded many donations from Bengal, which prompted a Gaelic poem to commemorate his benevolence. In 1809, the managers made a further appeal for funds stating that 'expenditure very considerably exceeded the receipts'.[iii] In both 1806 and 1809 the appeals resulted in considerably enhanced donations.[68]

Annual income varied greatly mainly due to variations in donations, subscriptions and church collections (table below) which together made up 70% of income and the nervousness about funding is understandable. However, over the first 20 years, income exceeded expenditure by just over £2,000 (about 15% of income) although this includes one-off legacies and donations. In this period, 67% of expenditure was on 'House Expense' and salaries with 7% spent on medicines.[69]

Finances 1810 – 1825 (£)
(selected years)

Year	Income	Balance
1810	597	+137
1813	526	+197
1816	908	+176
1819	745	+49
1822	591	+12
1825	486	+89

As elsewhere and for much of the Infirmary's history, patient fees went only a small way towards costs. Substantial donations were required to meet running expenses and extensions and improvements normally required a specific appeal or substantial donation. By 1805, there were annual church collections[iv] usually on the first Sunday

[i] In 1804, the Infirmary had about £3,000 which it invested at 5% - half of it with the Burgh. Capital rose to over £4,000 within a decade but was still considered a very small endowment to ensure sufficient income from its investment.
[ii] It was anticipated that the hospital would treat members of the armed forces.
[iii] But only in 1808 (deficit of £148). 1805-7 showed a total surplus of £366.
[iv] The mechanism by which parishes donated.

in the New Year and potential contributors were reminded by a notice in the local press the previous week. From at least the 1830s, ministers were sent a copy of the annual report so that they were fully aware of the benefits to patients.

The management expected parishes, which sent patients, to donate to the hospital and, over the years, made recurring pleas and exhortations bordering on threats. In 1811, the management felt 'reluctant to receive patients from other parts of the country unless they contribute towards this institution'. In 1834, despite impassioned appeals, only 27 parishes were contributing - fewer than before (table page 44) - and, in 1841, the managers 'resolved not to admit anyone from parishes who do not contribute enough to the funds'.[70] There is no evidence of them ever doing so but the issue rumbled on. Few parishes from the far north or from the far west contributed probably because, at this time, the west looked towards Glasgow and Caithness[i] towards Edinburgh for hospital services. By the mid-19th century, the proportion of income from parish collections had fallen considerably and the hospital relied much more on its growing investments (table page 52).

1830s – 1860s
Patient numbers had gradually increased as did the ambitions of the managers and, in the late 1820s, this prompted the first review of the hospital building. Until then, the only change was a gardener's house, built in 1817, and a separate garden entrance the following year which allowed much of the gardens to be let out for the rest of the century.[71] In 1830, a written appeal for major improvements as well as to increase revenue, with plans attached, was sent to 600 prominent citizens. It noted rising patient numbers and advances in medical treatment which required new accommodation. This yielded a poor response and a further letter was issued. By 1831, over £1,000 had been raised but the initial estimate of £1,200 had increased to £2,000. Work started in 1832 and was complete by 1835 but improvements to the kitchen and laundry, estimated at £600, could not be afforded. It was not until 1839, that the

---

[i] In 1741, the first patient in Edinburgh's second Infirmary was from Caithness.

managers judged it prudent to once again make a public appeal but less than half the required sum was realised and there was a reminder four months later. The work was finally completed in 1840.[72]

The architect was William Burn, Edinburgh[i] with the work overseen by local architect Robert Caldwell. An improved water supply was installed and accommodation extended by 30 beds,[ii] two private[iii] wards, water closets (wc's) and baths[iv] with hot and cold water the lack of which had been an issue with the medical attendants for some years. All this allowed 'a better classification of patients', especially the segregation of fever cases. The frontage of the hospital was unchanged but a wing was added to the rear with a laundry and kitchen and operating theatre above. The first floor was mainly fever wards and the second floor had the main wards plus 2 day rooms. There were now 10 lunatic cells on the ground floor and 4 on the first floor. The rest of the ground floor contained accommodation for the 'lunatic keepers', house surgeon and matron.[73]

These improvements largely sustained the hospital for the next 30 years. Around 1844, gas lighting was introduced and, in 1848, wc's were installed in the fever wards. In 1857, the porter's lodge beside the gate (photo on right) was built at a cost of £337,

[i] He promoted the Scottish baronial style and designed Inverness Castle in 1836.
[ii] The house surgeon noted that this nearly doubled the bed numbers.
[iii] Their precise purpose is not clear but may indicate a growing local confidence in the hospital by the middle classes. They were certainly used by affluent visitors to the area and may have been partly designed for such use.
[iv] Two baths were installed for the 'exclusive accommodation of the public' and, in 1934,'Ladies and Gentlemen' were 'respectfully invited to patronise them'!

designed by architect Thomas Mackenzie[i] of Elgin who gave his services free. The clock on the lodge portico from 1903 commemorates the coronation of Edward VII.[74]

Selected in-patient numbers 1832 – 49

Year	Total in-patients	In-patients at 1st Jan	Total out-patients	Operations
1832	179	22	110	7
1833	162	6	161	21
1835	237	26	154	17
1838	381	35	145	18
1842	385	32	194	10
1844	352	28	68	12
1847	464	25	83	10
1849	279	25	61	14

In the early 1830s, patient numbers were unusually low, the house surgeon ascribing this to the hospital renovations and to the cholera epidemics.[ii] Thereafter, in-patient numbers rose fairly sharply (table above) and, by the 1850s, were 300-400 p.a. Variations in numbers from year to year were mainly due to fever outbreaks which were sporadic and unpredictable. From 1832, out-patient consultations for vaccinations, eye, ear, throat and dentistry were largely provided to the poor by the Forbes Dispensary (page 189) and this substantially reduced out-patient expansion with numbers still well under 100 p.a. in the 1860s. As can be seen in the table above, the number of operations at this time was fairly low and continued at that level for many years.[iii]

---

[i] Who designed Nairn Town and County Hospital which opened in 1847.
[ii] Cholera was treated elsewhere (pages 18 and 167) but the epidemics subdued normal social interaction. Potential Infirmary patients would have avoided close contact with others and be more likely to stay at home. There was also a cholera outbreak in 1849 and it is tempting to ascribe that year's low patient numbers to it.
[iii] Until the use of chloroform from around 1850, operations were traumatic and very risky. Also, the mortality rate from hospital operations was much higher than for those carried out at home usually due to infection and it was not until after the 1860s that antiseptics and asepsis made hospital operation relatively safe and allowed Infirmary operations to increase.

This was a time of significant advances in medical practice. The principles of science were increasingly applied to medicine and there was much debate on the training of doctors culminating in the Act of 1858 which regulated doctors' qualifications. Inverness doctors seem to have responded to national and international initiatives. 1828 saw the first specialty when Dr Forbes[i] became visiting physician and Dr Macdonald visiting surgeon. In 1838, the Infirmary received the gift of a hydrostatic bed, then a recent invention.[ii] In 1847, Dr Manford used ether in an operation.[iii] Later that year, two operations were performed by Dr Nicol using chloroform, within a month of its demonstration by James Simpson in Edinburgh.[75] The first microscope was acquired in July 1851.

Finances 1834 – 1862 (selected years) (£)

Year	Inc.*	Exp.	Bal.	Note
1834	609	557	+52	1829-33 total deficit is £686.
1844	778	1,083	-305	
1848	909	1,062	-153	Deficit for past 5 years is £922.
1850	587	713	-126	£2,000 legacy (John Cheape, Ayrshire).
1853	672	855	-183	
1858	737	791	-54	
1862	1,079	1,214	-135	Much improved donations.

*Figures exclude one-off large donations and legacies.

The financial business of the Infirmary at this time (table above) is one of fighting against constant deficits and watching legacies and donations absorbed into running costs instead of being used for structural improvements. Both income and expenditure rose over the period but also varied considerably from year to year. Expenditure was linked to the numbers of patients. Fever epidemics were costly and exacerbated by the cost of alcoholic drinks which were thought to be a cure, a belief which survived until the 1920s when they were still prescribed in Culduthel Hospital. Alcohol was thought to cure other diseases in the 19th century and hospital diet often included its consumption. Medical

---

[i] Not the same as the one linked to the Dispensary.
[ii] Invented in London c1830 by Scottish doctor Neil Arnott to relieve bedsores.
[iii] First demonstrated publicly as an anaesthetic in Boston, USA the previous year.

treatment has largely stopped using alcohol as a treatment although the general public seems to have retained a stubborn belief in its efficacy!

Income had initially depended heavily on donations from subscribers and others and on church collections both of which had to compete with other charitable demands. Over the period, income relied increasingly on interest from investments (table below) which tended to be more predictable. In 1856, following a succession of large deficits, a local appeal turned the tide through many one-off donations although the situation had again become difficult by the 1860s. As Victorian affluence and philanthropy increased, one-off donations, as well as legacies, increased in both number and size. There were also increasing numbers of charity events. In 1833, a charity ball for Infirmary funds was held in the Northern Meeting Rooms and, in 1843, an 'Infirmary Ball' raised £140 and, thereafter, this became an annual event although they more often yielded £40-50.[76]

Sources of income (excluding legacies)

Year	1834	1866
Interest on capital	23%	31%
Donations	8%	26%
Church Collections	26%	17%

In the first half of the 19th century, parishes recommended patients for treatment, often through a church minister. It was sometimes unclear who was responsible for any due payment of fees and, by the 1840s, some parishes owed the hospital a considerable amount, or so the hospital claimed. In 1936, following several attempts to contact a parish minister about non-payment for a mentally ill patient now recovered, the Keeper was sent to the minister's house to deliver the patient home to him personally. After the 1845 Poor Law, there were also disputes with parochial boards over payment for paupers. By June 1846, the Infirmary managers were legally pursuing Inverness County, Inverness Burgh and Dingwall Burgh and a dispute with Ross-shire parishes lasted into the 1860s.

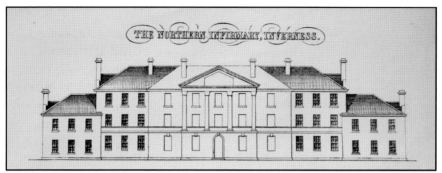

The Northern Infirmary Improvements 1864-66: Front Elevation

The number of patients steadily increased and the accommodation was quite stretched in the fever and smallpox outbreak of summer 1864. There were 163 fever cases of which 25 died, including a nurse, and several patients in the surgical wards were cross infected emphasising the need for building improvements. Essentially, the fever and smallpox wards needed to be better separated from each other and from the general wards and the medical attendants thought that convalescent wards would allow recovering fever and smallpox patients to improve faster. Therefore, a major refurbishment was planned and the funding appeal in the press noted the above reasons for the initiative but also the growing population, the advances in medical science and the desire not to be left behind by the rapidly developing hospitals of the cities.

In 1865-66, the hospital was extended by building over the pavilions and quadrants[i] which increased accommodation by 24 beds, including 4 convalescent wards, to over 80 beds in total. Final costs were just under £2,500 and the work was completed in June 1866 with architects Matthews and Lawrie.[77] Despite this large improvement, completely separate fever wards (the North Block) were opened within six years (page 60) which illustrates the effect of the continual rise in standards on

---

[i] Compare the above elevation with the drawing on Page 39.

hospital construction and expenditure.[i] It may also reflect the continual pressure of fever cases which continued to dominate the range of ailments treated (tables below). Note that there were only 19 different types of operations which, by modern standards, seems far too few to ensure that doctors built up any expertise but they would of course have performed many other operations outside the hospital.

Northern Infirmary cases 1866-67

Ailment	No.	Ailment	No.
Fever	50	Rheumatism	9
Respiratory system	47	Fractures	9
Nervous system	29	Heart & Blood Vessels	7
Urinary & Generative organs	28	Joints	7
Digestive organs	28	Organs of sense	7
Ulcers	18	Bone diseases	6
Abscesses	17	Cancer	6
Burns	16	General Debility	5
Skin Diseases	15	Scorbutus (scurvy)	4
Venereal	9	**Total**	**317**

Northern Infirmary operations 1866-67

Amputations	7	Cancer	3
Fistulae	2	Tumours	2
Diseases of sense organs	2	Hernia	1
Diseases of urinary organs	1	Hydrocele	1

Physical improvements to the hospital continued. In 1876, the 4 acre site was extended by about 3 acres. In 1884, a telephone was installed[ii] and, in 1886, Surgeon General Fasson, Medical Superintendent of the Royal Infirmary, Edinburgh was invited to inspect the hospital. He recommended substantial changes to both management and facilities and his report formed the basis of large improvements over the next three years including a new boiler, hot water system and window ventilation.[iii]

---

[i] Brought total capacity to 90 beds in the main building (Scotsman 11 Feb 1873).
[ii] This is early – the Inverness telephone exchange opened the year after.
[iii] Dr Fasson did a similar exercise at Aberdeen City Hospital the following year.

In addition, hot water central heating was installed but each ward retained a fireplace. Two new large wards were formed by amalgamating smaller ones, funded by Mr Howden (£150) and the Northern Meeting[i] (£200) which was commemorating its centenary. The Howden and Northern Meeting wards were opened by Lady Francis Baillie of Dochfour on 28th December 1889 amid a 'large fashionable attendance'. During the refurbishment, the fever wards were used as general wards. Architects were Matthews and Lawrie and Dr Fasson declined any fee for his report although he was sent 10 guineas for expenses.[78]

Finance continued to be the prime ongoing issue and the hospital's revenue budget was regularly in deficit. A basic problem was that, even where it could be afforded, it was nigh impossible to charge patients the full cost of their treatment. Even public bodies were apparently undercharged. For example, in 1886, parochial boards paid one shilling per day for each pauper in-patient but the management reckoned[ii] that the average cost was up to 3p higher.[79] Costs varied from year to year, apparently still closely related to the number of fever cases (page 51). For example, in the fever and smallpox epidemics of 1864, the Infirmary overspent by £250. The financial deficit was lower than average when there were no fever outbreaks or where no fever patients were admitted in times of refurbishment, such as in 1888 when the annual accounts showed a surplus of £421 compared with an average annual deficit in the 1880s of nearer £500. Rising patient numbers and the costs of treatment continued to push up the deficit which, in 1902, was 60% of income.

Donations varied from year to year, for example they were much reduced during the Boer War (1899-1902), and not all were cash. It was common in Highland hospitals for many in-kind donations such as food, flowers and newspapers and, although this is less apparent in Infirmary records, there are some interesting examples. In 1846, Mackintosh of Mackintosh donated 2 tons of coal. In 1870, Mr Cameron of Muckovie sent his 'usual

---

[i] Lord Tweedmouth supplemented this by £50. He and Mr Howden (Inverness seed and plant merchant) were stewards of the Northern Meeting.
[ii] However, the management does not seem to have been averse to exaggeration.

55

liberal annual donation of chaff' (for stuffing mattresses) and, in 1887, Mr Grant of Dunean sent 12 such bags. Similar donations continued.[80]

The 1880s saw a renewed campaign to increase revenue. In 1882, the deficit was 50% of income and, the following year, a special committee recommended employing a salaried officer to raise funds and forming fund raising committees across the north. The following year, a full time clerk was appointed and collections were held at many local firms, at ships in the harbour, at local railway stations and at shops and these continued for many years. In 1885, a 2-day bazaar[i] in the Town Hall, opened by Lord Lovat, grossed over £2,000.[81] The table below shows financial details for 1886. The hospital's growing capital ensured that returns on investments were now the main source of income. Patient fees, at only £44 were apparently unusually high that year because a large number of foreign seamen were treated who, unlike local patients, would have been charged.[82] That year £4,400 was received in legacies of which £4,000 was invested. Note that, in 1886, expenditure was £2,374 giving a deficit of £480.

Sources of revenue in 1886 (£)

	1885-86	% of total
Interest on investments	814	43
Private contributions	549	29
Church collections	444	23
Patient Fees	44	2
Income tax repayment	43	2
Total income	1,894	100

By the second half of the 19th century, it was often difficult to attract house surgeons, possibly because Inverness was small and had no nearby medical school. Incumbents often did not stay long unless they were from local families and planned to practise locally (some returned as medical attendants to the Infirmary). A two year contract was introduced

---

[i] This was a common way to raise money for public enterprises. They were often run or patronised by the wealthy hence the large sums often raised.

to try to retain post holders but it seems to have been ineffective. The salary level was an issue.[i] In 1866, Dr Campbell resigned having secured a higher paid post elsewhere. His salary had been £30[ii] which was the same as the matron and less than the porter. Dr Wilson, medical attendant, attributed the high turnover of house surgeons to the low salary and the post was advertised at £40.[83] By 1873, this had been increased to £50 with little apparent effect on the high turn-over. In 1891, a proposal to upgrade the post to a residential medical officer with full control of the hospital was defeated and the problem continued.[84] At the turn of the century, the South African (Boer) War was blamed and the salary was increased by 40% but with little success. Finding a house surgeon during the First World War was nigh impossible and, in May 1915, the managers, possibly in desperation, publicised their willingness to consider a 'lady house surgeon' and advertised for a 'lady or gentleman'.[85] In 1917, the only house surgeon available was final year student Dr Brennan who required leave to sit his finals. Immediately after, he was called up for war duty and he suggested his successor Dr McIver who became the Infirmary's first female house surgeon.

Meanwhile, local doctors continued to act as unpaid medical attendants and by 1889, two were on duty at any one time. In 1953, Dr Theo Chalmers[iii] recalled that in 1904 *'the general practitioners in attendance were each allotted 12 beds, but they had to do a three months stretch of continuous attendance at the Fever Hospital. They all operated I think with one exception and no operation was carried out without the consultation of the whole staff. They tackled quite big things, and I remember Dr Mackay removing an upper maxilla (upper jaw) for malignant disease'.*[86]

---

[i] In 1836, Dr Nicol had thought that a house surgeon could be easily obtained without paying a salary, the surgeon being willing to work for his board and experience.
[ii] The house surgeon's salary had been reduced from £50 to £30 in 1828.
[iii] Born in Inverness in 1884, he graduated from Aberdeen in 1906 and became a medical missionary in India. In 1914, he joined the R.A.M.C. and served as a surgeon in France, returning to India in 1919. In 1928 he took up general practice in Inverness and became ophthalmic/general surgeon to the Infirmary.

Not being a teaching hospital and having no nearby university restricted the availability of specialist doctors. One might have thought that this would also preclude any medical students but the first record of them occurs in 1847 and, by then, there were several suggesting that they had been attending for some time.[87] Two were resident at the 1871 census and, in 1885, the managers agreed that up to five medical students be allowed to visit the wards. In 1891, rules for their visits were drawn up.

By 1860, the matron's role had increased in authority and responsibility and the post required an increasing amount of specialist training. By the 1870s, matron had joint control with the house surgeon over staff and was involved in training nurses. However, it was difficult to recruit a matron and it was clear that the post was perhaps less than desirable, prompting much discussion about the post and the staffing structures.[i] The supply of matrons had improved by the 1880s and, by 1891, Matron could hire, fire and suspend nurses and female domestic staff.

In terms of formal training, there seem to have been little to distinguish nurses from general servants until at least the mid-19th century. In the early 1820s, advertisements for nurses specified only that they be 'stout active women not under 30 years of age' with both English and Gaelic. From 1872, Nightingale[ii] nurses were trained at the Royal Infirmary, Edinburgh and, thereafter, the number and quality of nurses generally increased. The Infirmary had formal training for nurses from at least the 1870s and, in 1887, 'rules' were drawn up based on those existing in Edinburgh, Glasgow and also in Aberdeen which had recently conducted its own review of training. The training consisted of a series of lectures by the matron on nursing, by the surgeons on anatomy and bandaging and by the medical staff on physiology and medical nursing. Practical training was given by the ward sisters and probationer nurses had a 2 year training programme (3 years by the 1890s). A furniture inventory of 1890 lists a 24 seat class room and equipment, including anatomy charts,

---

[i] The 1860s saw the realisation, generally, of the benefits of trained nurses and demand may have outstripped supply in the 1870s.

[ii] In 1860, Florence Nightingale set up a nurses' school at St Thomas', London.

presumably for nurses' training. A nurse's certificate from 1886 is shown on the right. In March 1901, entrance examinations along the lines of the Royal Infirmary, Glasgow were instituted and, from 1925, Inverness was a centre for the Quarterly State Examination of Nurses. Previously, the nearest centre

had been Aberdeen. In 1932, a sister tutor post was created and, by then, there were up to 60 probationer nurses. In 1933, nurses' badges were introduced. The badge below was awarded to Mrs Netta MacIntyre in the 1940s.

A nurse's job was hard but possibly reflects life elsewhere at the time. They lived in and their lives were fairly strictly controlled. Their daily

routine was similar to that shown on page 26, starting early in the morning and not finishing until mid-evening. The night nurse then came on duty until 9.30am but probationer nurses who did much of the night work started an hour earlier. In 1901, nurses got two hours off duty three times a week, one half day holiday every fortnight and, after a year's service, two weeks annual leave.[i]

Staffing levels also changed. By the 1820s, a second nurse was required and, in 1835, there were 2 nurses, 1 cook, 1 laundry maid and 2 female servants along with a male 'keeper of maniacs' and his female assistant. In 1844, an advertisement for 2 day nurses suggests there was also a night nurse by then. By the 1880s, there was a varying number of probationer nurses and, by 1894, there were still only 3 nurses but 5 probationers.

---

[i] In the 1930s, conditions were not much better for probationer nurses. In 1936, they received £20 p.a. salary and were only allowed out 1 night per week.

Thereafter, the increase in demand for staffing was met mainly by probationer nurses with 11 by 1903, 16 in 1912 and over 20 by the mid-1920s when there were still only 6 fully trained nurses employed.[88]

Fever

From the 1870s, the treatment of fever cases, expensive as it was, became an issue and there was a growing opinion that local authorities should bear more responsibility for this public need – a view reflected in developing national legislation (see also page 174). This section looks at the evolution of fever facilities in the Infirmary and its changing relationship with the local authorities over their provision.

Infectious diseases cases had always been admitted to the Infirmary and gradually the facilities for their treatment became more isolated from the rest of the hospital in line with increasingly detailed national advice and expectation. Throughout the 19th century, the Infirmary dealt with most of the fever cases in the Inverness area. Improved facilities for fever patients had been one of the drivers of the 1866 renovations but those seem to have been almost immediately considered insufficient and separate accommodation for infectious diseases was sought. In 1866, the need was highlighted during a smallpox outbreak when patients in the surgical wards were cross infected.

In 1868, Mackintosh of Raigmore agreed to raise £500 for a fever ward and there was further fund raising. In May 1873, two fever wards[i] (40 beds), two convalescent rooms and a wash house and laundry were opened - all in a separate rectangular block (the North Block – photo page 78). However, the 1867 Public Health Act had put further public health duties, including dealing with fever outbreaks, in the hands of local authorities and there began a long running debate, often verging on dispute, between the Infirmary and the Burgh[ii] and for 'some years to

---

[i] By 1899, the fever block was split into six wards.
[ii] Although the hospital also provided fever facilities for the first two Districts of the County (mainland Inverness-shire except Lochaber, Badenoch and Strathspey), the Burgh normally led negotiations. From at least 1896, the 1st District's fever ambulance was housed at the Infirmary (MOH Annual Report).

come a tournament was ... carried on with the fever wards as a shuttlecock...' Periodically, the hospital announced the ceasing of fever admissions followed by protracted negotiations with the local authorities on the payment of fees. Often, discussions coincided with new national regulations especially the 1889 Public Health Act which gave local authorities clear responsibility for providing fever hospital accommodation. In 1893, the fever wards required upgrading to their kitchen facilities and nurses' sleeping accommodation and a 10 year agreement was made whereby the Infirmary managers would equip the wards in return for an annual payment and a fee per patient from the local authorities. By 1895, the altered fever wards were in use.[89]

However, from 1900, the fever wards were subject to ongoing criticism by Local Government Board (LGB) inspectors as well as the Burgh MOH who, in 1902, considered that the facilities were below standard and probably insufficient for the size of the population. He also thought that the fever wards were too close to the general wards, (see photograph page 78) the grounds were too confined, that the location represented a risk to the population of Inverness and that it could not be 'considered an up-to-date hospital'.[90]   In 1904, the LGB served notice on the three Inverness local authorities to provide adequate accommodation and specified a requirement of 34 fever beds instead of the existing 26 beds.[i] Four years later, its inspector found it 'out of date and unsatisfactory'. In 1910, the LGB's report was extremely critical, repeating the criticisms of the previous decade. It also noted that the wards were insufficiently isolated so that it was unsafe to treat more than two diseases at any one time and there was insufficient airing space for long term patients. Furthermore, the nurses' accommodation had just 3 beds to serve the 6 on duty so that sheets had to be changed before each use and there were irregularities in the administration. While details of the report were keenly disputed by the MOH, the continuing inadequacy of the premises were not. The following year, the LGB again found 'accommodation and arrangements not sufficient' during a diphtheria outbreak.

---

[i] The original 40 bed capacity had been reduced as increasingly stringent government regulations specified more space per patient.

The proximity of the fever wards to, and their management by, the Infirmary was, nevertheless, a considerable advantage in dealing with the inevitable irregular supply of fever patients. In autumn 1902, there were 47 fever patients at one time in the hospital but this was dwarfed in spring 1903 when there were 97. In 1904, during an outbreak of scarlet fever the facilities had to cope with 93 fever patients and many children. As part of a larger hospital, these extremes in patient numbers could just about be accommodated and, by 1904, the Citadel Hospital was available as overspill although rarely used (page 169).

Meanwhile, in 1906, the Government classified pulmonary tuberculosis (phthisis) as a notifiable infectious disease and, in 1908, after an anonymous donor[i] promised £1,600, work went ahead on a new separate, so called, phthisis block which, on 3rd October 1909, was opened by Mrs Gossip, the Provost's wife. It had a veranda to facilitate open air treatment. The architect was Alexander Ross, Inverness.

Between 1900 and 1910, although the local authorities and the Infirmary had expended considerable energy in discussing the fever wards, it was more often about costs rather than in agreeing a way forward for improved facilities. The Infirmary managers continued to believe that a considerable part of their annual financial deficit was due to the underpayment for fever patients by the local authorities. Inverness Burgh had sent 286 fever patients from 1899-1901.

From the turn of the century, the Burgh MOH had been calling for the construction of a joint[ii] fever hospital. In 1906, he made comparative costings of different types of building being much attracted by the lower costs of a Speirs[iii] wood and iron building over a stone built one. The possibility of it being sited in the grounds of the Infirmary was suggested but this did not happen and, by 1912, Inverness Burgh and adjacent

---

[i] Later identified as Mr Robert Lawrence, Inverness.
[ii] To serve the Burgh and the adjacent 2 Districts of the County.
[iii] This Glasgow firm's prefabricated buildings were used across the country as hospitals, halls etc. (page 7). One can be seen at the Highland Folk Museum.

County Districts[i] were planning their own sanatorium and fever hospital. The drawing[91] on the left may date from around this time. Several sites were considered for a new build as were several large houses including the redundant military barracks in Telford Street as well as Hedgefield and Heatherley on Culduthel Road. Eventually, in 1914, the Burgh purchased Culduthel House (page 175) and the Infirmary resolved not to deal with any fever patients after May 1914. From then, the Burgh leased (for £75 p.a.) the Infirmary fever wards[ii] which it ran with its own matron and staff[iii] until the Culduthel site was ready. Patients were transferred there from December 1917.

1890s - 1919

At the end of the 1880s, the Infirmary still retained its essential design. The plans overleaf from the 1880s[92] show the first two storeys which can be compared with the plan on page 40. Due to rising numbers and rising standards, there was now a much more generous allocation of staff space compared with 1804 when the cook had just a bed closet in the kitchen. The resident doctor and matron (still called housekeeper) occupied the space formerly making up the lunatic cells. In addition, the greater number of servants and nurses necessitated dormitories, dining rooms and sitting rooms. As well as staff accommodation, the ground floor now had private wards of which there were five single and one double in total and kitchen facilities were now much more extensive.[93]

---

[i] In 1912, the County took over the running of the sanatorium at Invergarry.
[ii] In mid-1916, the MOH said there were 45 beds which even under wartime conditions seems rather crowded.
[iii] Dr LMV Mitchell was Medical Superintendent which also included Culduthel and Citadel Hospitals. The matron post may also have been a joint one.

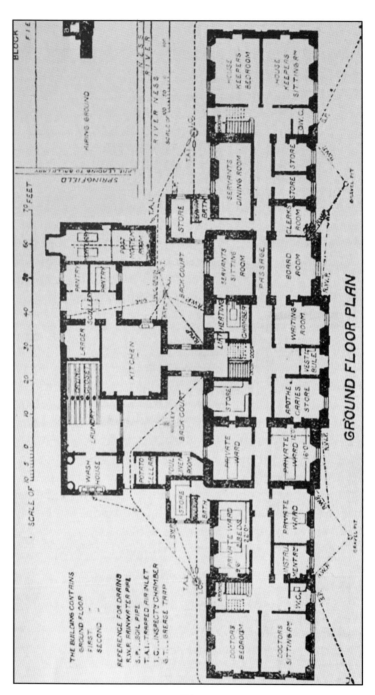

GROUND FLOOR PLAN

SCALE OF 10 5 0 10 20 30 40 50 60 70 FEET

THE BUILDING CONTAINS
GROUND FLOOR
FIRST "
SECOND "

REFERENCE FOR DRAINS
R.W.P. RAINWATER PIPE
S.P. SOIL PIPE
T.A.I. TRAPPED AIR INLET
I.C. INSPECT'N CHAMBER
G.T. GREASE TRAP

BLOCK · FIE

RIVER NESS

SPRINGFIELD

AIRING GROUND

DOCTORS BEDROOM

DOCTORS SITTING RM

HOUSE KEEPER'S BEDROOM

HOUSE KEEPER'S SITTING R'm

SERVANTS DINING ROOM

SERVANTS SITTING ROOM

PASSAGE

BOARD ROOM

CLERKS STORE ROOM

STORE

WRITING ROOM

VESTI BULE

APOTHE CARIES STORE

PRIVATE WARD

PRIVATE WARD

INSTRU
MENTS

W.C.

STORE

BATH

LAUNDRY

WASH HOUSE

KITCHEN

LARDER

PANTRY

BACK COURT

BACK COURT

POTATO CELLAR

PRIVATE WARD

STORE

64

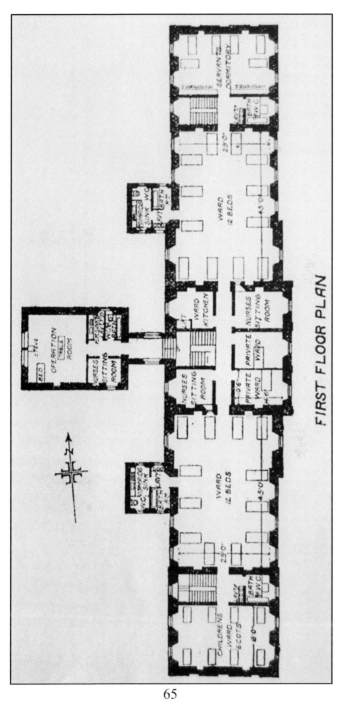

FIRST FLOOR PLAN

The 1890s saw a fresh wave of enterprise in the run up to Queen Victoria's Jubilee. In 1896-8, a two storey porte-cochere, costing around £950, was erected over the entrance to the building. Architects were Ross and MacBeth, Inverness.

The above photograph from the 1960s shows the porte-cochere on the right and, in the left foreground, the 1930 hospital entrance which was modified in 1954[i] and has since been removed.

The porte-cochere contained consulting room, clerk's office, medical library[ii] and a new operating theatre which was in use by 1897. The operating theatre (below) was described in 1927 as a large square tiled room with windows on three sides. It had no anaesthetic room. Its lit window at night, suggesting an operation taking place, became something

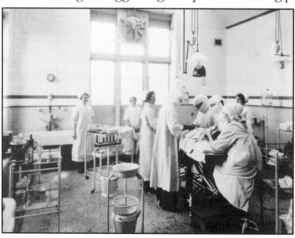

of a beacon for local people who appreciated the work of the Infirmary. The old operating theatre at the rear became maids' quarters and their former 'servants' dormitory' (plan on page 65) became a six bed ward.[94]

---

[i] It is much larger in the photograph on page 78.
[ii] It began in 1852 when Dr Forbes of London sent a collection of journals (Knox).

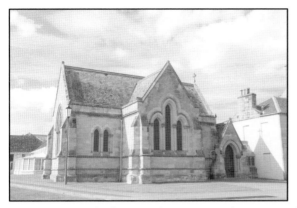

In 1896, Lady Tweedmouth[i] gave £3,000 for a chapel (left) in memory of her husband. The foundation stone was laid in 1897 and architects were Ross and Macbeth, Inverness. In 1898, the chapel was dedicated by Roman Catholic, Presbyterian and Episcopal clergy each performing a dedication from the three specially designed separate altars. This ecumenical feature of the building seems to be fairly unusual in Highland.[95] Lady Tweedmouth was not the only benefactor in 1896. £4,500 came from the estate of the Earl of Moray and £2,000 from the estate of Mr Guesdon of Nova Scotia, a native of the Highlands.[96]

In 1897, an appeal was launched for 'Victoria Jubilee Wards' for longer term sick and also for better accommodation for nurses. The appeal was very successful and, although there is no evidence of the Jubilee wards being constructed, the 13 bedroom Victoria Nurses' Home was designed by Alexander Ross[ii] and opened in

---

[i] Lord and Lady Tweedmouth owned Guisachan estate near Inverness where they pioneered the Golden Retriever dog breed and rebuilt Guisachan House and Tomich village. He died on 4 March 1894. Lady Tweedmouth was influential in Victorian society and well respected locally. She died on 20 March 1908.

[ii] Previously in partnership with MacBeth.

1898. It had a day room and was intended to be more homely than living in the Infirmary. The drawing (page 67) appeared in the press and the Home, costing £1,472, was officially opened in October 1899 by the Earl and Countess of Moray. The existing nurses' quarters were converted into wards. In 1919, an eight bedroom annex further increased nurses' accommodation.[97]

In 1903, an Infirmary centenary appeal was launched and although the response was initially disappointing, by 1904, medical staff and management were debating how to spend the proceeds. The doctors wanted an electrical (electrotherapy) department[i] but the managers decided to fund an eye ward instead. However, a suitable location could not be identified and, in 1906, the idea was dropped, the suggestion being that the hospital was too small to specialise,[ii] and, instead, electric light was installed. Nevertheless, in 1907, an electric treatment room was opened by Mackintosh of Mackintosh following donations from his family.

Northern Infirmary in-patients 1898 – 1906

	1898	1900	1902	1904	1906
Medical cases	306	342	257	245	207
Surgical cases	276	279	220	290	265
Fever cases	47	144	44	241	31
Eye cases	-	-	55	62	12
Skin cases	-	-	13	16	13
Total cases	629	765	589	854	528
From Inverness Burgh	61%	67%	57%	71%	64%
From Inverness County	23%	21%	21%	20%	24%
From Ross & Cromarty	8%	5%	8%	6%	10%
Average daily in-patients	60	82	64	86	57
Number of deaths	41	67	52	42	46
Children under 16	11%	30%	15%	32%	17%
Aged 60 and over	15%	10%	13%	10%	11%

---

[i] Infirmary doctors had been using electrical treatment since at least 1809.
[ii] Although, by then the Infirmary annual report listed eye and skin cases separately.

Patient numbers had increased and, by the 1890s, annual patient numbers were approaching 600. By then, there were normally 70 - 80 in-patients whose average stay of just over a month was little changed from 40 years earlier. The annual number of operations varied but steadily rose being 30 in 1885 and 79 in 1897. In 1903, the treasurer noted that patient numbers had risen over the previous 15 years because the general populace was now much less nervous about entering the Infirmary. However, in the table opposite, when the variable fever numbers are discounted the annual patient numbers are fairly steady at just over 600. The high numbers of children in 1900 and 1904 were also due to fever cases. Note that medical cases exceeded surgical until 1902 and, from then on, the latter increasingly dominated. Inverness Burgh and County still provided around 80% of the patients in this period.

Finance remained problematic with annual deficits of around 25% of income. In 1902, the treasurer revived the idea of systematic collections and, in 1908, the Ladies Auxiliary Association began to establish a large network of annual house to house collections. It was organised by district for example a Kilmorack, Kirkhill and Kiltarlity branch was formed in 1911. In the Inverness area, these district collections replaced the traditional annual church collections but the latter continued elsewhere. In 1920, Inverness burgh and parish collections raised £468 and the Alexandra Day[i] collection almost £200. In 1924, an Infirmary Week was started and raised £2,000 that year.[98]

The treasurer also revived another old chestnut, that of the apparent under contribution of rural parishes. The table on page 68 shows that the bulk of the patients came from the Burgh or County. Ross and Cromarty supplied less than 10% and other counties were barely represented. However, from the early years of the Infirmary, treasurers had noted the low contribution from some rural parishes and, in the early 1900s, there were detailed analyses which went on for years comparing the origin of patients with their parish contribution. In 1931, this found

---

[i] First held in London in 1912 to mark the 50th anniversary of Queen Alexandra's arrival in Britain to marry Edward VII.

that, on average, only about 30% of the cost of treating patients was received in parish donations and many rural parishes were contributing less than 10% of the cost of treating patients from their parish.[i] The analysis was given front page publicity in the local press which had the effect, as had previous such efforts, of substantially increasing income albeit for a limited time. Throughout this time, there was a continuing reliance on legacies and one-off donations to support the ongoing deficit in running costs. Some notable examples are shown in the table below.

Northern Infirmary selected legacies

Year	Amount	Benefactor
1903	£1,000	Mrs McGillivray.
1904	£1,122	Total of several legacies.
1907	£1,000	Robert Anderson's estate.
1909	£1,000	Dick Bequest.
1911	£5,000	Mrs Merry of Belladrum[ii].
1912	£2,000	David Jamie.
1916	£20,000	Miss AM Grant.
1921	£5,000	Estate of Daniel Fraser a US banker.
1922	£4,800	Estate of John Kinnaird, Birnam.

In 1916, the LGB reminded local authorities of their responsibility for setting up venereal disease clinics. Inverness Burgh made several approaches to the Infirmary, each one rejected by the managers giving the reason that there was no room. Being further pressed, the managers said they were not empowered to lease any part of the building to the local authority for such clinics. The Burgh sought the opinion of legal counsel which stated that there was no barrier to leasing the building but the Infirmary still refused amidst protracted negotiations. To be fair to the Infirmary, it does look as if the Burgh was trying to side step its legal obligations. In 1931, the Infirmary managers agreed to the building of a clinic at the hospital but the local authority, despite its statutory duty, baulked at the cost (£3,500) and put it on hold. Eventually the MOH,

---

[i] However, at the 1940 AGM, Provost Mackenzie said 'the Burgh can and should do better to support the Infirmary'.
[ii] Mother-in-law of Mrs Ida Merry (page 153).

who thought the situation 'deplorable', started clinics at the County Public Health office in Ardross Street but the only hospital treatment was in Aberdeen and this continued into the 1940s. In 1949, the new NHS combined venereal disease with dermatology and appointed a local specialist.[i]

1919 – 1939
(See page 105 for the Infirmary during the World Wars)

In 1919, with the First World War over and with infectious diseases removed to Culduthel, the Infirmary could take stock and reorganise. The former fever wards, now called the North Block, were refurbished and converted to medical wards.[ii] It also contained the electrical department and, from 1925, X-ray and UV light treatment. Surgical wards remained in the main block. The former phthisis wards (page 62), now renamed the West Wards, were used for surgical

Patient statistics (selected years)

	Average in hospital	Admissions
1919	63	744
1921	86	824
1923	91	1,011
1925	85	1,076
1927	87	1,000
1929	93	1,445

tuberculosis. All this extended patient capacity and patient numbers responded. As shown in the table above, numbers soon returned to the pre-war (1913) level of 78 patients on average in the hospital and an annual total of 832. By 1929, admissions had increased by about 60% although this seems to be due more to patients spending less time in hospital rather than to the number of occupied beds.[iii]

---

[i] Treating venereal disease was not unknown. Glasgow had a Lock Hospital from 1805 which, by 1890, had 81 beds and 3 staff and treated around 300 p.a. Lock Hospitals were originally for lepers and, like them, VD sufferers were often shunned and the disease was linked to moral attitudes which made its open treatment difficult.
[ii] At this period the hospital is listed with 108 beds in total with apparently 40 in the former fever wards which was its original capacity.
[iii] Average patient stay in the 1920s was about 28 days but this had dropped to around 20 days in the 1930s and 1940s.

The above reorganisation, along with the nurses' home extension (page 68), cost around £2,400 which along with a large deficit in running costs was quite worrying. By the early 1920s, the numbers of remaining wartime armed forces personnel had reduced considerably with a corresponding reduction in income from the government and the post war value of invested stock was low reducing income from investments. The managers were forced to borrow over £1,300 from the bank.

Unlike elsewhere in Scotland, waiting lists were relatively small but the need for major improvements became increasingly apparent. In 1926, Dr J Mackenzie, consultant surgeon to the Infirmary, gave a useful summary of the issues in his evidence to the Mackenzie Committee.[99] He noted that the hospital was outdated, an additional 60 beds were required, especially surgical, and there was no provision for maternity or venereal disease. There was insufficient staff accommodation, no provision for private patients and no convalescent home. He could also have added that new advances in medicine needed to be accommodated, the X-ray facilities were outdated[i] and the operating theatre was too small. Surgeon AJC Hamilton later noted that the corridors were dark and narrow and the sanitary arrangements in the wards were 'rudimentary'. *'What sanitary equipment there was belonged to an earlier era e.g. in one ward there was a large iron bath on wheels with a long handle for pulling it. When last seen it was being used for holding cement for the new hospital!'* In 1924, Dr DJ Mackintosh of Glasgow Infirmary (see also page 80) prepared a report on the hospital which dealt with the above issues and noted that the lack of nurses' accommodation was urgent. The report recommended Sir JJ Burnet as architect[ii] and, anticipating expansion, the managers acquired another 2.5 acres of adjacent land.[100]

---

[i] In 1901, Mrs Mackintosh of Mackintosh donated an X-ray (only 5 years after the world's first X-ray department in Glasgow Royal Infirmary). Previously, Ogston the local pharmacist had X-rayed fractures, etc. The X-ray was upgraded in 1918.

[ii] A Glasgow firm with much experience in public buildings including hospitals.

Meanwhile, a development fund had been set up which, by September 1925, had reached £40,000 and, at a public meeting in December, a £100,000 appeal was launched for the 'extension, reconstruction, and endowment' of the Infirmary. In January 1926, the decision of the managers to expand the hospital was vindicated by the publication of the Mackenzie Report (see opposite page) which identified the need for greater regional coordination of health services with Inverness[i] central to a Northern Region, one of five regions[ii] centred on the Scottish cities.

On 19th November 1927, the first sod of the new building site was cut by Mrs. Mackintosh of Mackintosh and, in May 1928, Dr Walter Elliot, Under Secretary of State for Scotland, laid the foundation stone. A range of fund raising activities began across the area. There were some very large donations. Mr Alexander Edward of Forres donated Kintail sporting estate with an annual rental of over £3,000 and value of about £45,000. Over £2,500 came from the estate of Mrs Stewart of Garth in India. Over £2,000 was donated by the Cameron Highlanders to endow two beds[iii] and the same amount came from Miss Elizabeth Hood, Darnaway Road. There were very many smaller donations and legacies and much fund raising through a variety of community activities. Local football teams and sports organisations raised £1,165 to endow a 'Sports Bed' and this included an exhibition football match between Celtic and Dundee in Clach Park.[iv] There were fancy dress parades, tennis tournaments, fetes, balls, concerts, drama productions and extensive door to door and street collections. By April 1929, £85,000 was raised and, by the end of 1930, the total had reached £124,000.[101]

---

[i] It also recommended that the Infirmary come within HIMS (see page 81).
[ii]The other Regions were centred on teaching hospitals linked to universities. Inverness had neither and therefore had reduced access to specialist services.
[iii] This was a popular way of contributing, the idea being that the returns from £1,000 invested would maintain a (named) bed in the hospital (see list page 98).
[iv] Held on 11th May 1927 before a crowd of 5000. Celtic, the Scottish Cup holders, beat Dundee 3-1.

The Children's Ward

The first development and flagship of the new Infirmary was the children's ward and this section draws together the treatment of children in the Infirmary. The Highlands, in general, seem to have been rather slow in prioritising the medical care of children. However, there is no doubt that Inverness was well aware of and influenced by events in the south and the opening of the Edinburgh Royal Hospital for Sick Children in 1860 is certain to have inspired local discussion. From 1859, the Infirmary admitted children from the Ragged School[i] gratis and the 1866 Annual Report noted that the medical attendants wanted to designate a children's ward, pointing out that one third of all Inverness children died before the age of 10 and that improved medical care was a way of combating this. At the Infirmary annual meeting Dr Wilson said that many young children in Inverness had disease and he and his colleagues thought the matter urgent. He noted that the only extra cost would be an additional nurse and that many people were willing to subscribe towards a children's ward. The meeting agreed with him.

A children's ward fund was started and, by the end of 1868, it had £1,600 and fund raising events such as concerts were being held.[102] Mackintosh of Raigmore had also promised up to £500. The initial idea was to convert one of the existing wards but there were concerns that this would reduce the hospital's flexibility in dealing with smallpox[ii] patients and it was resolved to first build a separate fever block (page 60). In 1871, Mrs Clarke of Achareidh, Nairn, funded bedding for 10 - 12 beds and, in 1873, £3,500 was received from the legacy of Miss Ettles with £1,000 earmarked for the children's ward which opened that year, although it was said that children were initially reluctant to enter it. The children's ward is shown on the plan on page 65.

---

[i] Ragged Schools provided free education for destitute children. It started in Aberdeen in 1841 then spread throughout Britain. The Inverness one in Tanner's Lane opened in 1853. By 1861, it held up to 30 boys and girls in equal numbers under the management of a married couple. Most pupils were voluntary but some were looked-after vagrants and juvenile offenders.

[ii] It seems strange that this highly contagious disease was still being managed within the general hospital.

In 1881, it was decided to use part of the children's ward for convalescing fever patients. It is not clear how much was set aside but there appears to have been no children's ward by 1897 when the Burgh suggested establishing one as part of the Queen's Jubilee celebrations.[i] This proposal was rejected by the Infirmary managers who said that treating children in a separate ward had not been a success and had been given up and they wished instead to pursue a hospice and endowment for the Inverness Branch of the Jubilee Nurses Institute. However, there must have been some local pressure. Miss Julia Mackintosh of Raigmore had left a bequest of £1,000 to start a home for sick children and, by converting an existing female surgical ward, the 'Julia Mackintosh Ward' was opened by Bishop Kelly in 1903. In summer 1922, Queen Mary, who was staying at Moy Hall visited the children's ward. By then, it had been moved[ii] to the North Block as part of the 1919 reorganisation after fever cases went to Culduthel. From the discussion that preceded this, it seems that a children's ward did not exist during the war years.[103]

York Ward Royal Visit 1948

[i] The other suggestion was to build a home for 'incurables' which did not happen.
[ii] Child surgical cases continued to be accommodated in the main surgical wards.

75

In May 1929, a new 26 bed children's ward, the Princess Elizabeth of York[i] Ward, was opened by the Duke and Duchess of York[ii] with an estimated 30,000 spectators. The photograph on page 75 is from their return visit in 1948 with Princess Margaret.[104] Numbers of child in-patients gradually increased reaching around 150 p.a. by the 1940s.

There were, however, problems. The Scottish Hospitals Survey of 1938 found the ward unsatisfactory with no protection against cross infection.[iii] In 1938, Dr Leys, medical attendant, submitted a report on the children's ward to the Department of Health rather than to the Infirmary managers which caused them some anxiety especially when the Department sent Sir John Fraser[iv] to assess the situation. He stayed for several days and returned a year later, in 1940, and found nothing had changed. His report was highly critical. Essentially, there was nothing satisfactory - staff were untrained[v] and absences were not covered, equipment was inadequate,[vi] there was no proper segregation of cases which risked cross infection, the diet was monotonous and lacked in-season green vegetables, the administration was poor and unhelpful and records[vii] were 'badly kept'. He also noted that local doctors were not referring children because of the conditions – a problem amplified by the fact that this was the only specialist children's acute facility in the region. He included a list of malpractices he had observed 'lest it be thought that the advice is towards the ideal'.

The RNI managers had some disagreement with the content of the report and there is no evidence that they took any immediate action or

---

[i] Later Queen Elizabeth but then just 3 years old.
[ii] Also the Earl and Duchess of Inverness. Later George VII and Queen Elizabeth.
[iii] Children were in 3 wards (boys, girls and infants) but there was no cubicle ward.
[iv] Professor of Surgery and Principal, Edinburgh University. He belonged to Tain.
[v] He wrote that staff displayed 'not only ignorance but the diffidence and lack of efficiency which is the result of a long period of tolerated insufficiency'.
[vi] For example, there was no proper milk storage.
[vii] A children's operating room did minor operations but the Infirmary could not provide details of the operations to the Department (nor could it give details of A & E cases or operations). By the 1950s the theatre was just used for dressings.

discussed it constructively. When, in 1942, the RNI called in paediatric specialist Professor McNeil of Glasgow his report apparently found a 'high standard' of treatment although it was only after his visit that a milk kitchen with steam steriliser was installed. Dr Leys disagreed with Professor McNeil's report and sent his own to the Department of Health. More than a year later, the RNI managers had apparently still not discussed Professor McNeil's report or sent a copy to the Department of Health and there is no evidence of any further action being taken. Gradually, the need for local specialist paediatric advice became apparent although this was not available in Highland until the early 1950s after the NHS was formed (page 130).

The Children's Ward was the first completed part of the new Infirmary but other developments were moving quickly. In March 1930, the hospital opened four wards of 28 beds each, four single and eight double private[i] wards and two operating theatres. One theatre was for ophthalmology and ENT and one theatre had a cystoscopy room with specialist urology table and X-ray – the first of its kind in Scotland.[105] One omission was a maternity ward which had appeared in earlier plans but which was not built (page 142). By March 1931, all new Infirmary buildings had been erected and all the wards were occupied, providing 150 beds.[106] At the end of the renovations, the hospital, now virtually rebuilt, was renamed the Royal Northern Infirmary[ii] and it was considered one of the most modern hospitals in Scotland. Indeed few, if any, hospitals elsewhere in Scotland[iii] achieved such modernisation in this period of financial austerity and, given the size and economic base of the local community, it was an outstanding achievement. Pages 78 and 79 give an overview of the development.

---

[i] Single wards cost 4 guineas per week and the double wards 3 guineas plus any fees the attending doctor may charge. They were intended for patients who could not afford similar treatment in a nursing home or who required special apparatus.

[ii] By permission from George V.

[iii] A recent comprehensive history of Scottish medicine states that in the 1950s all Scottish voluntary hospitals were contained in Victorian or Georgian buildings. The writers have obviously overlooked Inverness but it underlines the point.

In the photograph below the original hospital can be seen at the front. This now held administration, matron and nurses' quarters, recreation and dining rooms. The Tweedmouth Chapel is on its left and the 1898 nurses' home is in the right foreground. The large building above the 1898 nurses' home is the new nurses' home reopened as a two storey building in 1938 (page 84) - formerly the fever wards and North Block. The original building is now dwarfed by subsequent developments with the children's (York) ward behind the Chapel and behind that again are the surgical and medical wards. There was a new kitchen and store, new laundry and new boiler house. These and further details can be identified by the plan opposite although the sewing room and dispensary does not appear on the 1938 OS map. Note that the main entrance was moved to the left of the original block and this new entrance was renewed in 1954 to commemorate the 150th anniversary of the opening (photograph page 66).[107] The long white building on the right background is a new looking Inverness High School which opened as Inverness Technical School in 1937.

The New Royal Northern Infirmary c1938

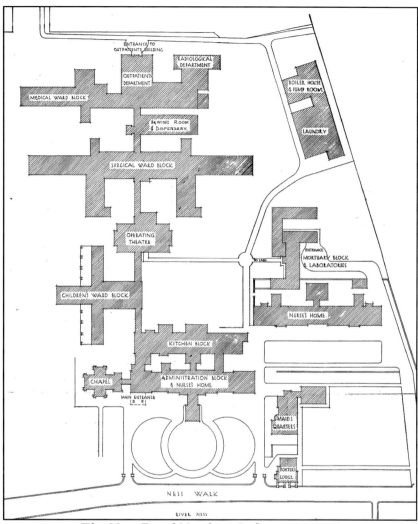

The New Royal Northern Infirmary 1930[108]

In 1803, the Infirmary had contained wards, offices, staff accommodation and a kitchen but little else. A feature of hospital development in the 19th century was the increasing space required for better segregation of cases. In the 20th century, developments in medical science and technology such as X-ray and electrotherapy required treatment rooms. Similarly, laboratory analysis steadily expanded within its own increasingly specialised facilities. In 1913, the Infirmary had set up a pathology lab initially to examine TB sputum. In 1916, Miss Jessie Grant of Annfield, Inverness left £20,000 to the hospital which she wished to be used to make improvements.[i] Dr DJ Mackintosh (see also page 72) suggested forming a bacteriologist post and, in 1920, Dr LMV Mitchell was appointed and a bacteriological laboratory set up which was equipped in 1922. This allowed specimens to be analysed locally rather than sent to Aberdeen.[ii] In 1928, Dr Mitchell was succeeded by Dr RG Bannerman who also became pathologist.[109]

In 1931, a new pathology and mortuary block was opened as well as bacteriology laboratories and facilities for radiology and X-ray/electrical (with deep X-ray therapy). The radiology and out-patient block was named the Grant Pavilion after Sir Alex and Lady Grant of Logie and Dunphail whose donation of over £20,000 had funded it. By 1931, the laboratories were handling all patients' specimens from the Burgh and from parts of the Highlands and Moray. By the mid-1930s, there was a regional service to hospitals, local authorities and general practitioners in pathology, haematology, bacteriology and biochemistry. These had developed into separate departments by 1950.[110]

In 1930, the new out-patient department[iii] (until then there had been none) had specialist ENT facilities and a small operating room for minor cases. It ran surgical, medical, ENT, dental and eye clinics. In 1936, an

---

[i] In recognition, the female surgical ward was renamed after Miss Grant's brother Surgeon Major Alexander Grant who had been Queen's surgeon (see also page 103). A plaque to his memory was unveiled in 1918 (Scotsman 20 Dec 1918).

[ii] The arrangement with Marischal College had been set up by Inverness Town Council in 1906 after several years of requests from the Inverness Burgh MOH.

[iii] X-ray and Out Patients were opened by the Prince of Wales in June 1931.

out-patients sister post was created and, by 1944, clinics also included orthopaedic, dental, skin, 'nerve' (psychiatric) and gynaecological. There were now over 12,000 attendances annually compared with under 300 in 1913.

The modern concept of continual service development was now embedded. In 1935, Pathology set up a blood transfusion service. In 1938, there were 38 transfusions in the hospital which rose to around 100 p.a. by the early 1940s and grew rapidly to over 800 by the mid-1940s. By then, a regional blood transfusion service had been formed in anticipation of war.[i] In 1935, the first electrocardiograph[ii] was installed and established as a department in 1938.[111]

Although Inverness had not been seen as the most central place[iii] by large parts of the North and West Highlands and Islands, its centrality gradually increased as much due to political and administrative factors as to improved roads. When the Highlands and Islands Medical Service (HIMS) was introduced in 1914, it was thought that visiting specialists would be of much benefit to Highland cottage hospitals. An obvious base hospital for visiting specialists was the Northern Infirmary but Inverness' relative prosperity excluded it and its hospital from the HIMS scheme.[iv] In 1919, HIMS became part of a reorganised Department of Health. This may have precipitated a review of hospital services in the north because, that year, Infirmary managers met with Dr Shearer of HIMS to discuss joint working. It was clear that Inverness was of prime importance to health care in much of the area and, as noted earlier, in 1926, the Mackenzie Committee recommended that the Infirmary be the central hospital for a Northern Region. Meanwhile, there were other

---

[i] A new blood transfusion unit opened in 1954.
[ii] Donated by the MacRae-Gilstraps and the people of Attadale, it allowed examination of the performance of patients' hearts.
[iii] In the early 1940s, specialist surgeons in the north and west referred cases to city specialists rather than Inverness.
[iv] HIMS provided medical services in areas where the population was too poor or too scattered to sustain a private medical or nursing service. The 1909 Inverness Directory lists 15 doctors, 26 private nurses and 2 community (Queens) nurses.

initiatives across Scotland to try to encourage some co-ordination between hospitals. In 1921, a Local Voluntary Hospital Committee was set up for the Highlands and Islands. In 1923 and 1924, the Marchioness of Tullibardine[i] promoted conferences in Inverness Town Hall which were seen as the start of joint working in the area.[112]

In 1922, the first grant of £1,290 was received from HIMS but financial constraint restricted the establishment of regional visiting specialists. HIMS support for hospital services did not seriously begin until after 1929 when the government doubled its funds which, in 1930, allowed the Department of Health[ii] to award the Infirmary £5,000 p.a. for the next 10 years to help it provide specialist services (consultants) for the region. It also awarded a grant that year of £1,000 for X-ray facilities.[113]

The Infirmary's expanding hospital services attracted patients from a wider area which is most marked in the increase in proportion of patients from Ross and Cromarty (table below) compared with the early 1900s when this figure was usually less than 10% (page 68).

Source of patients 1931 (% of total)

	1931	% of total
Inverness	770	35
Inverness County	700	32
Ross and Cromarty	588	26
Caithness and Sutherland	39	2
Moray and Nairn	108	5
Others	11	-
Total	2,216	100

---

[i] Also the Duchess of Atholl, she was a Highland MP and prominent in political affairs holding strong and sometimes, at the time, controversial views and known by some as the 'Red Duchess'. She was on the Dewar Committee (page 10).
[ii] In 1919, HIMS was subsumed within the Scottish Board of Health which became the Department of Health in 1929. HIMS retained its separate funding stream, but, for simplicity we refer just to the Department of Health after 1929.

Patient numbers increased rapidly in the 1930s, attracted by the new hospital facilities and the increasing centrality of the RNI as Highland's main hospital.[i] The average number of in-patients more than doubled in the period and, in 1939, averaged 197. Annual admissions increased from just over 1,000 in 1927 to over 2,600 in 1933 and had reached almost 3,500 by the end of the decade - an increase of three fold - made possible by a greater throughput of patients rather than more beds. Patients now stayed around 20 days compared with over 30 at the start of the century.

Patients at 31st December 1939
(Official bed allocation in brackets)

	Male	Female	Children	Total
Medical	31 (24)	30 (24)	10 (9)	71 (57)
Surgical[ii]	86 (62)	85 (62)	14 (9)	187 (133)
Isolation	1 (1)	1 (1)	1 (0)	3 (2)
Maternity	-	2 (2)	-	2 (2)

Accelerating demand from patients, a concept with which we are now very familiar, soon pressurised the new RNI's expanded facilities. In 1934, an extensive review by the Department of Health found that the RNI's surgical services were 'barely adequate' and that medical services were 'quite inadequate' to meet demand. In 1938, it granted £1,000 p.a. for 10 years towards the funding of a new medical block. £43,000 was required and, in 1936, treasurer Lt. Col. Mitford delivered a 'wireless' (radio) appeal which raised over £350.[114] In 1938, the medical block, built beside the radiology unit[iii], opened with 50 beds including 8 private beds[iv] and 2 isolation rooms. It brought bed numbers in the RNI to 205 and freed up more beds for surgery which was increasingly in demand.

However, demand increased even further and, despite the additional wards, there was considerable pressure on the new facilities. Compared

---

[i] AJC Hamilton noted that it was now much easier to persuade patients from the West to come to the hospital.
[ii] ENT had 22 beds and the surgical figures include 10 ENT children cases.
[iii] The radiology department was reconstructed.
[iv] The Infirmary now had 21 private beds (reduced to 10 in 1948).

with the previous year, 1939 saw 795 more in-patients, 1600 more X-rays, 1700 more laboratory cases and 22 additional staff. The table on page 83 shows that surgical cases continued to dominate the hospital's 205 beds. The table also shows a total of 273 in-patients or 33% over capacity at 31st December. This over-capacity is most marked for surgery (40%). The ensuing deficit was £6444 and the beleaguered treasurer questioned the acceptance of government grants which apparently committed the hospital to spend three times as much as it received.

Staffing continued to expand. In 1931, there had been 16 surgical and medical staff and, that year, nursing staff had increased to 52 (from 36 in 1929). The growing in-patient numbers now required a corresponding increase in staff – to around 60 nurses by the mid-1930s – and staff accommodation was again under pressure. Therefore, in 1937, work started to reconstruct the North Block and add a second storey. It opened the following year as a 60 bed nurses' home (see photograph on page 78). Domestic staff then occupied the former nurses' accommodation in the original Infirmary block.

For the rest of its history as a voluntary hospital, RNI finances continued to be a delicate balancing act but they continued to benefit from one-off donations and legacies (table below).

Selected legacies 1931 - 35

Year	Amount	Note
1931	5,000	Left by Miss JJ Anderson, daughter of local solicitor.
1932	1,050	Col & Mrs MacRae-Gilstrap (Eilean Donan. Castle) - bed for Macraes who fell in First World War
	1,000	From estate of Mrs Inglis of Newmore.
1933	21,000	From the estate of John Mackay, Quebec, Canada.
	1,100	To endow 2nd Glenurquhart bed.
	5,000	From the estate of Lady Seaforth.
	1,050	From the estate of Provost Donald MacDonald.
1934	1,000	From the estate of Miss Helen MacBean, Carrbridge.
1935	1,050	Gifted by Lord Nuffield for the Nuffield bed.
1938	1,000	From the estate of Duncan Cameron, Muir of Ord.

The increasing complexity of the RNI required increased management and administrative work (the demand for which continues). In 1937, Major W Forsyth was appointed first medical superintendent and was accommodated in the refurbished Ness House[i] which, in 1935, had been purchased for the pathologist. The private house Alton on Ballifeary Road was purchased for the dispossessed pathologist at a cost of over £2,000.

The 1930s can be seen as a turning point in medical staffing with the emergence of specialist posts as medicine continued to develop in complexity. From a fairly early date, medical attendants had specialised into surgery or medicine (although they remained general practitioners) but further specialist posts had been slower to develop. Very rarely, a specialist would be called in.[ii] In 1900, Dr Macdonald was appointed ENT surgeon, the first specialist appointment, although, like all the other medical attendants, he still dealt with a range of other cases. In 1904, plans for an eye ward were dropped and the hospital was felt to be too small to specialise but the trend had been set. In 1908, surgeon Mr James Luke was appointed and, in 1910, accepted reappointment on condition he dealt only with surgical cases, becoming the Infirmary's – and Highland's - first specialist surgeon.[iii] In 1919, Mr David Dickie was appointed second specialist in surgery. In 1927, Mr Luke died and was succeeded by AJC Hamilton who like Mr Luke made specialist visits to other parts of the Highlands notably to the Belford Hospital in Fort William. Apart from two residential medical officers, the rest of the staff were general practitioners with their own medical practice and essentially with a special interest rather than a specialty in the modern sense. GPs continued on the staff until after the NHS was established.[115]

---

[i] Formerly a nursing home (page 145) and now the Highland Hospice.
[ii] In 1889, Scottish gynaecology pioneer Lawson Tait from Birmingham operated.
[iii] He came to Inverness from Glasgow and lived at Woodville (now the Rocpool Hotel) from 1906. He was not in general practice and performed surgery throughout the Highlands. His unexpected death was much lamented. See also page 105.

The redevelopment and expansion of the Infirmary allowed a further increase in specialist posts in the 1930s. Pathology and bacteriology have been discussed above (page 80). In 1930, Dr Tainish was appointed the first radiologist.[116] He was unsalaried but received two thirds of the fees received for radiology and electrical treatment, the other third going to the hospital. He was also free to continue his private practice.

Specialist posts were increasingly supported by the Department of Health and by local authorities as the RNI increased its role as base hospital for visiting specialists to the rest of the Highlands. In 1929, the Department of Health awarded a two year grant to support an ENT specialist (EG Collins) who, by 1933, was holding clinics across the Highlands.   Other visiting specialists based at RNI included ophthalmologists Dr RD Campbell and Dr T Chalmers. From 1933, Dr Greig Anderson from Aberdeen was appointed first consultant physician and, in 1938, replaced by Dr Leys the first consultant physician appointed under a Department of Health/HIMS scheme which meant that his £1,200 p.a. salary was split equally between the Northern Counties and the Department of Health. He was in charge of 48 beds in the RNI, ran weekly out-patient clinics and visited Fort William, Wick and Thurso monthly, Golspie every two months and Stornoway every three months. This was a part time post – he also had private practice - but his regional workload increased rapidly which underlined the unmet need in the Highlands for specialist medical services.[117]

A popular impression of early general hospitals is that they were fairly severe places with a strict staff hierarchy and iron discipline, flavoured with a patient selection system which depended on subscriber recommendation or patronage. It is hard to dispel this image before the 1930s but, from then, there were changes which suggest a softening of the approach. Until 1936, probationer nurses and domestic servants were excluded from the annual staff dance – the only staff social event - and could not hold their own one. Probationer nurses were still under a very strict regime. They worked long shifts and were only allowed out one evening per week - all for an annual salary of £20. (Note Dr Leys' salary opposite.) The Second World War caused considerable changes in attitudes and, during it, social events began in the staff dining room. In 1944, a staff club was formed which raised money for a separate recreation hall[i] which they purchased second hand. It was a wooden Canadian recreation hall from Carrbridge[ii] which was in place by 1947 and, as a boost to the staff club funds, was mostly funded by the Department of Health which was trying to encourage hospitals to improve social facilities for their staff. By the late 1940s, there were regular dances, dramas, Christmas and Halloween parties and activities such as badminton, table tennis and community singing.

Patient 'comforts' also improved. In 1934, Matron had organised sales of work and had collected enough funds to install a wireless. The same year, the managers agreed to have Sunday papers on sale to patients which raised the anticipated objection from the Lord's Day Observance Association but the managers stood firm (see also page 131). In 1952, headsets were purchased for 53 beds allowing patients to listen to radio[iii] and, in 1952, a welfare fund was formed which initially derived its income from the return deposits on empty soft drinks bottles left by patients. The fund was for both patients and staff benefits and supplied many smaller items of furnishing and equipment to the hospital.[118]

---

[i] There was apparently already a brick hall built in 1931 (Farrell 2002).
[ii] Coincidentally the recreation hall at Raigmore was built in 1944 of wood by Canadian foresters based at Carrbridge (page 122).
[iii] In 1970, the Inverness Hospital Radio Service began from an Infirmary studio.

Inset Dr HJ Kirkpatrick, Dr AB Hay, Dr J Fraser, Dr EA McIntosh, DR IM Seex
Back Row Dr I Doherty, Dr Bisset, Dr Harrison, Dr Dawson, Dr Douglas
Middle Row Mr Murray, Dr JA Chalmers, Mr Gossip, Dr Michie, Mr Anderson,
Dr Edmunds, Mr Macdonald, Dr Bolster, Dr Gotlieb, Dr Scott
Front Row Mrs Kirkpatrick, Dr Chalmers, Mr Miller, Mr Hamilton, Miss Dean,
Maj Gen Paton, Dr Mitchell, Dr Bryant, Dr Wilson, Dr Bethune

The photograph above shows the medical staff of the RNI in 1948, the year in which it was amalgamated into the NHS. The voluntary organisation which founded and ran the hospital had lasted for almost 150 years and the hospital had seen its medical staff increase from three local doctors giving their services free to the group shown. In 1804, Matron had one nurse and two servants to assist her. By 1948 (photograph opposite) there were over 150 nurses and domestic staff.

At the hand over to the NHS, the RNI had 221 beds and around £55,000 in cash and investments. It had property valued at £24,000 which included a porter's lodge, two lodges on Bishops Road, Ness House, Alton, Eden Court and the adjacent property of Dunedin purchased in May 1948 as a site for expansion. It was the feudal superior on land at Hilton, Waterloo Place, Leys Town, Barnhill and Ballifeary as well as Kintail Estate which gave it an income of £345 p.a. in feu duties from around 150 properties.[119]

The table below shows the allocation of beds in the late 1940s. There were also 26 paediatric beds, two isolation beds and 20 private beds. The beds were split equally between each specialist except for medicine where the bed allocation is shown in brackets.

Specialty	Beds	Specialist
ENT	18	IM Seex and HM Urquhart
Ophthalmology	12	T Chalmers and RL Richards
Gynaecology	20	JA Chalmers and AB Hay
Surgical	76	H Miller and AJC Hamilton
Medical	48	J Ronald (18) T Scott (18), DC Wilson (12)

RNI specialist staffing 1949[120]

Area	Specialist
Surgical	2 consultants shared (Raigmore and RNI), 1 assistant at Raigmore, 1 registrar at RNI.
Medical	2 consultants shared (Raigmore and RNI), 1 assistant at Raigmore, 1 registrar at RNI. 2 assistants and registrars to be appointed
ENT	1 consultant shared (Raigmore and RNI). 2nd required.
Dermatology	1 physician.
Ophthalmology	1 consultant at RNI. 2nd to be appointed.
Gynaecology	2 consultants in Inverness.
Anaesthesia	1 consultant and 2 anaesthetists to be appointed.
Laboratories	Pathology, Biochemistry (to Raigmore), Bacteriology.

In 1949, the new health board surveyed the specialist staff and assessed the need for additional ones. Their summary as it pertained to the RNI is shown in the table above. By then, there was already some joint working with Raigmore Hospital including sharing facilities as well as specialist staff (page 139).

In early 1945, following the Heatherington Report[121] and anticipating expansion, the RNI had purchased nearby Eden Court for £7500. In 1946, the Department of Health suggested using it as a Preliminary Nursing School (combined with Raigmore) and approved its £9250 conversion which occurred in 1948. In 1950, it opened with 12 student nurses each from Raigmore and the RNI. Later there were also student nurses from Culduthel.[i] Nurses were accommodated in the former Bishop's Palace and the chapel was converted to a classroom.[122] The School was opened by Miss O Robinson OBE from the Department of Health, formerly Principal Matron of the Emergency Services Hospitals, (photo opposite). Main training still continued separately at the RNI and Raigmore but students spent time in Inverness hospitals other than their own to ensure experience of all specialties including placements at Craig Dunain and at Hilton.[ii]

---

[i] Before this, they had to go to Aberdeen for preliminary training.
[ii] A former Hilton nurse remembers feeling overstaffed by the number of students.

90

Student nurses undertook a 3-year course to become state registered nurses. In the 1950s, pupil nurses undertook a 2-year course to become state enrolled nurses and were trained at Alton in Ballifeary Road (the former house of the RNI pathologist).

By 1965, training was organised under a Central School of Nursing but facilities were located at Raigmore, Eden Court, Alton House and RNI until the new building opened at Raigmore in 1970 with 162 student and 48 pupil nurses (page 128). These included students from Ross shire and Lewis hospitals. Applications for training were now to the Central School. Previously, matrons of individual hospitals had recruited.

In the 1950s, RNI in-patient numbers continued at around 200 daily. The distribution of beds is shown in the table overleaf. Essentially the pattern was similar to that of the 1930s with surgery the main category but there were also significant numbers of ENT, ophthalmology, paediatrics and gynaecology. In 1962, in response to long patient waiting lists for ophthalmology, gynaecology was transferred to Raigmore and two wards were converted to ophthalmology which increased its beds from 16 to 28. However, a shortage of skilled nurses, later relieved by agency nurses, delayed the opening until the end of the year. In late 1971, 20 beds were established for geriatric assessment and rehabilitation which reduced the medical capacity by 22 beds.[123]

RNI bed allocation 1959-71[124]

	1959	1963	1971
Ophthalmology	16	28	28
Medicine	60	60	38
General Surgery	88	96	96
Ear Nose and Throat	30	30	30
Gynaecology	20	-	-
Paediatric	10	10	10
Geriatric assessment			20
Total	224	224	222

In 1984, a new Audiology Unit opened but there then began major changes as the planned centralisation of acute hospital facilities at Raigmore progressed and the RNI moved towards a GP led community hospital. Acute services moved to Raigmore and, by May 1986, the hospital was empty. After extensive refurbishment, 96 elderly patients were transferred from Hilton and Culduthel hospitals. After further work, in 1991, the York Ward[i] opened as Highland's first day hospital with a capacity of 20 per day. From 1999, there was major reorganisation into a new community hospital and, by April 2000, there were 30 GP beds. Further changes saw conversion of some of the former wards into residential property and, in 2004, the original hospital block became the headquarters of the University of the Highlands and Islands. The building's frontage retains much of its character, a reminder of the achievement of the people of the Highlands and Inverness across two centuries.[125]

---

[i] The 1929 children's ward.

Infirmary Staff

The following section gives details of Infirmary staff over the years. Although every effort has been made to produce a continuous record there are small gaps where details have not been found. A question mark indicates that the information or inference is uncertain or unknown.

Matrons 1803 – 1970

Until the mid-19th century, matron and most staff were rarely named in records or in press reports which makes identification challenging.

Date	Matron	Notes[126]
1804-15	Mrs Murray	Dismissed for being old and infirm.
1815-28	Mrs Elizabeth Adam	Matron appointed March '28 ?Mrs Willox.
1828-31	Mrs Willox	Resigned and set up as a midwife.
1831 - ?	?	
? -1841-?	Isabella Davidson	Recorded at census.
1844	Matron wanted. Mrs Sampson Edinburgh selected on paper but committee want to see her. ?appointed.	
1846-?	?	Matron resigned/wanted, May 1846.
1849-51	Mrs Christian Mackenzie Clark, Inverness.[127]	
1851-55	Miss Mackenzie	Dismissed as 'too old and unfit'.
1855-68	Mrs Beaton	
1868-73	Mrs Flora Wood	£30 p.a. Dismissed when matron with modern qualifications was required.
1873	Miss Greenhill	Died before starting.
1873-74	Miss Topping	Joint control, with house surgeon, of nursing staff (now includes night nurse).
1875	Miss Sarah Maguire	Includes training of nurses. Resigned. Next appointee resigned before starting.
1875-77	Mrs Helen M Robinson	Resigned apparently over staffing issues.
1878-81	Mrs Perry	Large number of applicants.
1881-91	Miss Isabella Falconer	Died in post July 1891.
'91-1905	Miss McConnachie	Became matron County Hosp. Dufftown.
1905-21	Miss Elsie CR Philp	Resigned for health reasons.
1921-28	Miss Anne Sutherland	Resigned (married AJC Hamilton).
1928-47	Miss Drysdale	Resigned after period of illness.
1947-50	Miss Dean	Resigned (married Maj. Gen. Paton).
1950-51	Miss Mary Mackay	
1951-70	Miss Eliza Low[128]	Retired.
1970	Miss ECS Morrison	

House surgeons 1804 – 1930

To save space 'Dr' is omitted unless the first name or initial is unknown.

Date	House Surgeon	Notes
1804-9	John Taylor	
1809-12	William Macdonald[129]	
1813	Hugh Fraser	?Medical attendant from 1824.
1813-4	M Bethune	?Medical attendant from 1821.[130]
1814-28	John Mackenzie	Salary £50 p.a. Medical attendant from 1833.[131]
1828	C Martin	Had shop in Bridge Street. Resigns 1828 after dispute with medical attendants.[132]
1829-30	John Grant	From Forres.[133]
1830-4	Rob. A Manford	£30 p.a.[134] Medical attendant from 1837.
1834 -6	Eric Mackay[135]	Appointed from 22 applicants.
1836-9	Roderick Fraser[136]	
1839-41	James J Ross	Medical attendant from 1856.
1842-3	Dr Kennedy[137]	
1843-5	John Wilson[138]	From Nairn. Medical attendant from 1848.
1845-6	John Mackintosh	From Auldearn. No Gaelic - local protest.[139]
1846-7	Isaac Wallace	From Nairn.[140]
1847	Dr Crearar	
1847-8	D McEwan	
1848	John Campbell[141]	
1849-51	Robert Wilson	
1851-3	Archibald Whyte	Set up practice in Nairn.[142]
1853	David Dallas	From Nairn.[143]
1854-5	Walter Scott[144]	
1855-7	John Mackenzie	From Invercannich.[145]
1857	John McGilp[146]	
1857	R Fraser[147]	
1858-9	John Cook	Pioneer in developing calf's lymph vaccination.[148]
1860	Robert Taylor	
1860-2	Robert Craig[149]	
1862	P Hume Gentle	£30 p.a. salary – same as the 'cell keeper'.[150]
1863-4	Alex Cameron	
1864-5	Donald Campbell	From Edinburgh. Resigned due to salary. Drowned with family in New Zealand in 1881.[151]
1866-8	William Macdonald from Daviot.[152]	
1868	Charles Adam	From Aberdeen.
1868-70	David Tulloch	Salary now £40p.a.
1870	Adam S Reid[153]	
1870-1	Charles Smith[154]	

1871-2	Robert Smith	
1873	F Fraser	
1873	Anthony Butler[155]	
1873-?	DF Fraser	From Dornoch.
1878-?	D MacDonald[156]	
?-1880	Dr Marshman	
1880-2	WH Brodie	From Aberdeen.[157]
1882-3	John MacPherson	From Dores at £50 p.a. Later HM Commissioner for Lunacy and Prof. Psychiatry Uni. of Sydney.
1884-5	GD Logan[158]	
1886	John Wilson Black[159]	Medical attendant from 1890.
1887-8	John Macdonald	Invernesian. Future MOH for Inverness-shire.[160]
1888	Alexander Rose Macleay	
1888-9	James Strother	
1889-91	David MacRitchie	Son of Inverness chemist.[161]
1891-2	D O McGregor	
1892	Henry R Chalmers[162]	
1892-3	Hugh E Fraser	Son of Provost. Medical attendant from 1895.[163]
1893-4	George A Williamson[164]	
1895-6	Arthur Mackintosh	Son of treasurer.[165]
1896-8	Ian G Sibbald[166]	Son of Chief Commissioner for Lunacy.
1898	C Percy B Wall[167]	Previously at Craig Dunain? (page 236) Left for post in South Africa,
1899	AN Haig	
1900-1	George G Hay	
1901-2	WE Taylor	Salary increased (£70-£100) to attract applicants.
1902	WH Eden Brand	
1902-3	JC Galloway	Died suddenly in 1903.
1903	Robert C Affleck	
1904-5	DJ Gair Johnstone	
1905-6	WE Reid	
1906-7	James M Macdonald[168]	
1907-8	Thom. E Roberts	From Inverness. Medical attendant in 1909.[169]
1909	William T Munro[170]	
1909-11	Farquhar Macrae[171]	
1911-12	L Lowrie Fyfe	
1913-4	John G Elder[172]	
1914	Charles Joubert	From South Africa.[173]
1915-6	Donald MacLeod	Final year student.
1917	Dr Brennan	Leave of absence to sit finals then called up.
1917	ME MacIver	First woman house surgeon.[174]

1918	Dr Macbean or Macvean[175]	
1918-20	Herbert Humphry	
1921	PR Riggell[176]	
1921	JW MacRae	
1922	J MacLeod[177]	
1923-5	CD Macrae Alex. M Fraser	Now two house officers - senior surgical (Dr Macrae) and junior medical.
1924-5	Alex Fraser (Later Inverness MOH),[178] R Urquhart Gillan (junior),[179] Roderick Mackay,[180] Alistair Cameron. (2)	
1925	Harvie Duncan, Alex Logan (2)	
1926	Harvie Duncan[181] E A Johnston	E A Johnston is later Medical Superintendent of Culduthel and of Raigmore Hospital.
1926-7	RC Scott,[182] JTM Symington	
1927	JA Fraser Dr Caird	JA Fraser probably still in post in 1928. Son of Professor Caird.[183]
1928	Brian Meyer[184] RS Ritson Dr Gray[185]	Ronald Maunshill also signs list of medical staff at laying of foundation stone.
1929-30	Dr Ferguson[186]	
1931	Now 3 house officer posts (renamed residential medical officer).	

Honorary Medical Attendants 1804 – 1948

Doctors are listed from the date of their election to the Infirmary unless otherwise stated. Date in brackets shows when they stopped (where known).

Date	Staff details
1804	William Kennedy (-1822), James Robertson[i] (-1815), George Forbes (-1832). Alex MacDonald later that year (died 1835).
1814	John Inglis Nicol (died of cholera 1849).[187]
1820	Managers' meeting includes Dr Innes Robertson.
1821	Dr Bethune (- before 1834).[188]
1824	Hugh Fraser (-1849), Dr D Campbell (- before 1834), Dr CJ Macdonald (died 1834). There are now 5 medical attendants.
1832	John Robertson (-1833).
1833	John Mackenzie (died 1850).
1834	Archibald Macrae (-1836), William Munro (-1841).
1836	Dr Jamieson (-1837).
1837	RA Manford (-1866).
1838	Dr S Chisholm (died 1848).

---

[i] Several times Provost. Lived at Aultnaskiach.

1844	Dr Walker (resigned 1848).
1848	John Wilson (-1880). In partnership with Dr Nicol.
1850	Roderick Fraser (-1859).
1851	Duncan Mackay (-1854 resigns in protest at dispute between managers and doctors), JG Mackenzie[189] (- before 1862), Thomas Ross (-1856 at least).
1856	James Jones Ross (-1880).
1866	Dr McNee (died 1900).[190]
1867	D Campbell (moved away 1868). ?House surgeon 1864-5.
1868	W Macdonald (-1883).
1871	Hugh Clark (died 1876).
1878	John Simpson (-1888).
1880	James Murray pupil of Lister and introduced antiseptic treatment to Infirmary operations (died 1943),[191] FM Mackenzie (-1887).
1883	Ogilvie Grant (-1889 when he became MOH Inverness-shire), DS Macdonald (-1886), WR Gibson (-1884).[192]
1884	D MacFadyen senior (-1922, died 1924), J Milne Chapman (died 1893).
1891	J Wilson Black (-1929 died 1930) specialises in ophthalmology.[193]
1893	J Munro Moir (died 1926), J Asher Forsyth (died 1911),[194] Leslie Fraser dental surgeon (died 1909),[195] AW Mackay (-1939).
1895	Hugh Ernest Fraser (-1897 when appointed Med Super Dundee RI).[196]
1897	John Macdonald (-1908) becomes first ENT consultant in 1900.[197]
1898	Gordon Lang (died 1924) began X-rays and was radiologist.[198]
1905	John W Mackenzie becomes ENT surgeon (died 1928).[199]
1908	James Luke first consulting surgeon from 1910 (died 1926),[200] Kyle Mackintosh (-1932) succeeds Leslie Fraser as dental surgeon.
1909	JE Kerr (-1910), TE Roberts (-1910), D MacFadyen Junior succeeds Gordon Lang as radiologist (- 1928).
1910	Kenneth Gillies (-1927 died 1928), DJ Kelly (-1913).
1911	LMV Mitchell appointed supervisor of infectious diseases (fever wards). Continues at Culduthel after 1917 (see also below).[201]
1913	Alex. Reid (-after 1939).
1914	A Fraser Lee (-1917).
1919	RD Campbell (-1945) becomes ophthalmic surgeon, David Dickie 2nd specialist surgeon (-1928 died 1930).
1920	George Hunter (- 1921) ophthalmologist, LMV Mitchell (-1927) becomes 1st bacteriologist.[202]
1924	W J Bethune (-1948) anaesthetist from 1930.
1925	Louise Fraser (-1934) anaesthetist from 1930.
1926	AJC Hamilton (-1962) succeeds James Luke.
1927	Theo Chalmers (-1954) ophthalmologist (with RD Campbell).[203]
1928	TS Slessor (-1931), EG Collins ENT (-1936), Stuart Garden (-1946),[204] Hugh Miller (-1950s) succeeds David Dickie,[205] RG Bannerman (-1935)

1928	bacteriologist/pathologist succeeds LMV Mitchell who stays as physician (-c1950),[206] JC Macdonald appointed full time radiologist (succeeding D MacFadyen who stays as physician).[207]
1930	JC Tainish (- at least 1939) full time radiologist.[208]
1932	J Allan (- 1948), MDL Proven (-1945) both dental surgeons.
1933	A Greig Anderson, Aberdeen first consulting physician (-1938).
1935	HJ Kirkpatrick (-1960) succeeds RG Bannerman, Janet Fraser (-1939 at least) anaesthetist, ?Dr Taylor resigns.
1936	I Seex (died 1961) succeeds EG Collins ENT.[209]
1937	Dr Bell Nicol - monthly skin clinic.
1938	Dr Leys (left 1946) succeeds A Greig Anderson,[210] W McWilliam (Med Super Craig Dunain) psychiatrist.
1942	Dr Gotleib covering for Dr Tainish. Appointed Radiologist in 1946.
1944	Miss MB Barr appointed almoner.
1945	OH Gossip dental surgeon.
1946	DC Wilson succeeds S Garden.; AJ Duncan replaces TN MacGregor and is soon succeeded by Dr Hay & Dr Chalmers.
1947	Stanley Alstead consultant physician succeeds Dr Leys (pages 76-7 and 86) but becomes professor at Glasgow University within the year.[211]
1948	Dr Anderson monthly skin clinics, J Bryant succeeds Dr Alstead, J Ronald succeeds J Bryant, DC Wilson physician specialises in rheumatology.[212]

RNI endowed beds

Endowing a bed was a popular way of fund raising and for benefactors to donate to the hospital. The table on the right shows the distribution by ward and below is an edited list of the dedications

Ward	Endowed beds
York	20
3 and 4	24
5 and 6	17
7 and 8	15
9 and 10	22

The Tanera Bed	Warrior's Bed	A Friend	Attadale
Children's Bed	Glenurquhart (2)	Parish of Croy	The Avoch Bed
Lochalsh Memorial	Eilean a Cheo Bed	Seaforth Highlanders bed	
Aird & Strathglass	Aigas Bed	The Killilan Bed	Sports Bed
John Mackintosh	People of Kiltarlity	Catherine MacRae Mackintosh Bed	
Parish of Petty October 1928		Lochcarron Estate Bed (2)	
John Kinnaird Memorial Bed 1920		WG Dick Memorial Bed	
Memory of Frasers of Abertarff 1925		Memory of Ida Gertrude Ogden	
Ewen and John Macrae Bed		James Forbes Jamieson Bed	
Burgh and Parish of Dornoch Bed		Alexandra Rose Day 1942 Bed	
John Murray of Clava 14th June 1939		Royal Burgh of Tain Bed	

Mary Stewart-Mackenzie of Seaforth 1920	Fortrose and Rosemarkie Bed
John and Christabel Irwin Smart	Peace Bed 30 September 1938
Seaforth Highlander War Memorial Bed	Rosskeen Bed by Mr AT Gill
Inverness Building Trades Operatives	In memory of Eileen Aldam.
In memory of Kenneth Gillies MA MC CM surgeon and member of medical staff for over 16 years. Died 13th June 1928.	In memory Angus Alex. Mackintosh of Mackintosh Captain 'Royal Horse Guards' Died 14 October 1918.
Mrs Mowat Firthview Inverness in memory of Doctor John W Mackenzie.	Memory of James Luke surgeon for 21 years. Died 24 March 1927.
In memoriam Patrick Houston Shaw Stewart Born 17th August 1888. Killed in action in France 30 December 1917.	Founded by Tavish and Christine Macmillan Glen Urquhart in memory of their little boy Alexander Duncan.
George A Macdonald memory of mother Mrs Helen Macdonald Gladstone Terr.	In loving memory of Moira daughter of David and Mary Young.
Bequest of Mr Ewan MacLennan for the sick poor of the parishes of Kintail and Glenshiel.	'Charlie's Cot' in memory of Charles A Gordon Shaw only son of Duncan Shaw WS Inverness 1899-1908.
Memory of my husband John M Macdonald Lochardil Inverness.	Memory Sir Ewan Cameron KCMG by his wife & children 1908.
Mrs Hughina Fraser memory of husband Alexander Fraser Tomnahurich Street.	Duncan Macleod of Skeabost, Isle of Skye in memory of the sons of Skye.
Dr John Wilson Black by Miss Elizabeth Georgina Black 'Evelix' Drummond Rd.	In memory of Lucius Montrose Cuthbert 1856 – 1915.
USN Mining Squadron in memory of American participation in North. Barrage operations and in remembrance of many kindnesses by people in the Highlands.	Mrs Catherine Macfarquhar memory of Roderick Thomas, Annie and Catherine Macfarquhar of Balnagaig, Rosehill Cottage, Ballifeary, Inverness.
Miss MA Fraser 57 Lochalsh Road in memory of her brother Bailie James Sargant Fraser.	In Memory of the officers, NCOs and men of Cameron Highlanders who fell in the Great War.
Alex. & Janet McKay Bed (natives of Drumsmittal, Knockbain, Ross shire) by their son the late Mr John Mackay 265 Golfhill Drive Glasgow.	Cot by Aird & Strathglass branch Northern Infirmary Ladies Auxiliary Association in memory of Edith Evans lost in SS 'Titanic' 1912.
Highland Railway by WH Cox of Snaigow, Chair & the Right Hon. Lord Invernairn, Director.	By the late DS Chisholm, Clerk and treasurer of the Infirmary in memory of his brother William Chisholm.
Duncan Macdonald of Kiltarlity Bed by Mrs Mary Agnes Mackie in memory.	The Strathspey Bed by Miss Helen MacBean Nethybridge.
Victory bed a thank offering to God for victory and deliverance from the grave	Relatives of the late John Couper Viewmont, Helmsdale for the benefit

99

peril which threatened our country in the World War 1939-1945 John MacCulloch, Derina Lodge Fortrose.	primarily of patients from Helmsdale or any other part if the parish of Kildonan.
John & Marjory Paterson Bed in loving memory by their sons & daughter.	Ewan MacLennan's bequest for sick poor of Kintail & Glenshiel.
Gifted by John Alexander Dewar Baron Forteviot of Dupplin & Margaret his wife.	The George Inglis of Newmore Bed by Mrs Catherin S Inglis 1933.
Devoted memory of my beloved husband Duncan Fraser passed away March 1924.	Prov. Donald Macdonald, Scorguie in memory parents & sister Annie 1933.
This bed was named in 1939 by past and present nurses of this Infirmary.	By Miss Mary J Sime in memory of her brothers John and William Sime.
Margaret & Charles Fraser, Gollanfield and Inglewood, Crown Drive Inverness.	Memory of Dr James MacNee for 34 years a member of the medical staff.
Memory Catherine & Margaret daughters of William Sutherland Waterloo Place.	In memory of Mr Simon Chisholm for many years a generous donor.
Memory Francis Squair Sheriff substitute of Stornoway and sister Jessie Catherine Squair by their sister Elizabeth Hood.	Elizabeth Ponton Howden Bed re bequest of 200 guineas and other contributions and legacy.
Memory of Mrs Edward H Litchfield of New York and daughter Madeline Sands.	
Dowager Lady Congleton, London memory of Margaret Peter Dove Eilean Aigas.	
Miss Justina Jessie Anderson in memory of her father, mother & brother George Anderson FRSE Mary Mackenzie Cobban, George Cobban Anderson.	
Memory of Chas Kennedy superintendent of stores Highland Railway and wife Harriet, 5 Ardross St. Parents of Mrs Elma M Kennedy Bridgend Drumnadrochit.	
Kintail & Glenshiel Bed by Lt Colonel & Mrs Macrae-Gilstrap, Eileen Donan in memory of Farquhar & John D Macrae & fallen of Clan Macrae. Great War 1932.	
Memory of Edward Davis of Cheltenham Donation of £1,000 allocated from a bequest to Scottish hospitals by his executors Alice & Alfred Davis Glasgow 1913.	
Mrs JM Stewart (of Garth) Rydal Mount, Simla, India Is Gradh Dia (4 beds). To the dear memory of (i) my beloved sister Chris Stewart who died in India, (ii) my beloved sister Catherine Sinclair Stewart, (iii) my beloved husband Frederick Stewart who died in India, (iv) my beloved sister Kate Stewart who died in India.	
Memory of Alexander Grant FRCS Surgeon-major Bengal Army, Hon. Surgeon to HM Queen Victoria and surgeon to Marquis of Dalhousie, Governor General of India having the interest of the Northern Infirmary deeply at heart Surgeon-Major Grant, with other members of his family contributed largely to the endowment funds of that institution. He died on 3rd January 1900.	
Elizabeth Ponton Howden bed for the treatment of patients in terms of her bequest of 200 guineas and in acknowledgement of other contributions made and legacy left by her to the institution.	

Bona Convalescent Home
Bona 1894

By the 1880s, the Infirmary had, for some time, felt the need for a convalescent home.   In 1882, the Northern Counties Convalescent Home was established in Nairn and the Infirmary established a fund to send Infirmary patients there although, by the late 1880s, a site closer to Inverness was being investigated.   In 1892, the ladies' committee[i] petitioned the Infirmary managers to erect a suitable house and, the following year, the managers committed £600 to its Convalescent Home Committee.   By then, several other Scottish hospitals had founded convalescent homes, the first being in Edinburgh in 1867.[213]

In 1894, the Infirmary managers purchased Bona Lodge[ii] on Loch Ness (1904 OS map overleaf) for £975 and they reckoned they needed to raise

---

[i] Most voluntary hospitals established such committees which looked to the comfort of patients including visiting, linen supplies and fund raising.
[ii] It consists of 2 semi-detached houses built in 1880 for MacDonald, Painter, Bridge Street, Inverness who lived in one half and let out the other (Mr JFM MacLeod).

£1,500 in total. Miss Keir, senior nurse in the Infirmary, was appointed matron along with a maid and part time gardener.[i] A new management committee normally chaired by the Provost began weekly meetings. After some alterations which are likely to have included connecting doors in the front and upper hall and in the kitchens in the rear wing,[ii] the Home opened on 29th November 1894 with the opening ceremony in early December.[214] Altogether, the Home had 12 main rooms and there was also a lean-to along the rear of the house which acted as the laundry.[215]

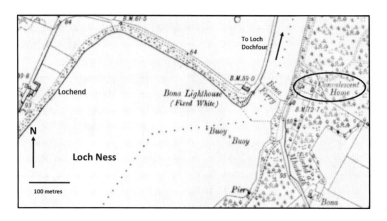

The Committee controlled applications to the Home, resisting the attempt by Infirmary medical attendants to refer patients directly. Patients were mainly from the Infirmary and there was also a small number of paupers whose weekly fee of 12/-, the same as for other patients, was charged to the Parochial Board. Patients had to make their own way there, by boat to the pier at Aldourie (lower centre of map above) and then on foot to the Home (circled on map above). In 1903, after a patient had fainted en-route it was agreed that they would not be expected to set out in poor weather and would be met at the pier by someone from the Home.

---

[i] There was an additional nurse by 1911.
[ii] The doors are now blocked off but the architraves, in the style of the original house remain.

Infirmary medical staff attended in two month blocks on rotation and the house rules were the same as that of the Infirmary. In 1895, a Ladies Committee was formed and Mrs Baillie of Dochfour, Mrs Forbes of Culloden and Mrs Fraser-Tytler of nearby Aldourie became patronesses.

The Home was funded separately from the Infirmary with separate accounting and fundraising. In 1896, the managers applied for and received £350 from the estate of the Earl of Moray.[216] In 1900, the Infirmary invested a legacy of £1,000 from Surgeon Major Dr Alex Grant and used the interest 'for the benefit of poor patients' which included assistance after they left the Home to 'tide over their first difficulties'. The investment was doubled the following year from the estate of his sister Miss Jessie Grant (page 80) also to be used to assist poor patients discharged from the Home. The following year, Miss Grant bequeathed a further £500 for this purpose.

As with other public institutions, attempts were made to be self-sufficient. In March 1895, the paddock was ploughed up by the farmer at nearby Dares[i] Farm to grow potatoes. In August 1895, Mrs Fraser-Tytler of nearby Aldourie Castle donated money to erect a piggery with a pig to follow when the piggery was complete. The pig was ready for sale by October. A Mr Walker donated a poultry house which was built at the end of the stable. In 1902, upgrading to water and sewerage was completed but water still had to be carried from Loch Ness. In 1907, the Home acquired a new water supply from nearby Aldourie Estate which saved the staff considerable work.[ii]

Annual patient numbers

Year	In-patients		Year	In-patients
1898	119		1902	86
1899	105		1903	112
1900	114		1904	116
1901	85		1905	89

---

[i] Not to be confused with Dores which is further away.
[ii] Possibly still pumped. A water pump remained in the back kitchen in the 1930s.

In March 1895, it appears the capacity of the Home was 4 males and 4 females but, from at least 1909, it had increased to 13 beds which is likely to have been an internal reorganisation since there is no evidence of an extension at this time. The table above shows the annual patient numbers which remained fairly steady. In the first 18 months there were around 100 patients and, from a range of monthly returns and census results, it seems that the Home had typically anything from 3-8 in-patients. At the 1911 census, there were 7 male and 4 female in-patients of which 5 were under 20 and 4 over 60 and all working class.[217]

In August 1914, the Home closed, partly due to the matron going on war service. In 1915, it opened for three months for nine patients but closed in December due to a staff shortage. In 1918, the Home was used for two months but, by then, a more 'elevated and accessible' building[i] was desired and it was decided to sell the property. Bona Lodge reverted to residential becoming, once more, two semi-detached houses which remain to this day largely unchanged.

During this time, Nairn Convalescent Home was used once more and, by 1917, had allocated four beds to the Infirmary and, in 1918, received 19 patients from there. By 1921, the managers reckoned that they had £4,000 to spend and were looking for another property. They considered a proposal to rent or acquire all, or part, of the Nairn Convalescent Home but this did not happen. Despite periodic calls for the development of convalescent facilities to relieve the pressure on hospital beds, there seems to have been no subsequent development and the Infirmary continued to use the Nairn Convalescent Home[ii] until the end of the 20th century.[218]

Matrons

1894 - 1900	Miss Keir
1900 - 1902	Miss Munro[219]
1902 - 1908	Elizabeth Massie
1908 - 1914	CM MacFadyen

---

[i] Fresh air and an open aspect were thought beneficial to recovery.
[ii] Despite the fact that Nairn Convalescent Home was not included within the NHS.

Inverness Military and Wartime Hospitals

The earliest description of an Inverness medical hospital is the one in Cromwell's Fort and there are 18th century references to other small scale military hospitals (page 3). Fort George was completed in the 1760s and held over 2,000 personnel. It would have been standard practice to include a hospital in the new fort and, in 1862, plans for its improvements show 4 wards each designed for 8 patients and accommodation for a surgeon (map page 152). It still had 32 beds in 1899.[220] In 1886, the new Cameron Barracks opened and included a separate hospital built on the west side at some distance from the main buildings. Brigade Surgeon Grant was in charge until at least 1907. By 1899, the Inverness Military Hospital, as it was called, had 17 beds.[221]

The Infirmary always accepted military cases but the first wartime connection appears to be in 1899 when the War Office requested that 10 beds be set aside for Boer War casualties but they were not required. Wartime needs for field doctors seriously reduced the availability at home. Many volunteered or were called up. The photograph above is of James Luke (centre), later surgeon to the Infirmary. Arms folded, he is grouped with his attendants in his Boer War field hospital which illustrates the basic conditions there - note the oil lamps for light.[i]

The First World War (1914-18)
As Highland's main hospital, the Infirmary was inevitably affected by the First World War. At the outset, the Navy requested beds and 100 were

---

[i] He would later often operate in more basic premises across the Highlands.

set aside[i] and later split with the Army when it made a similar request. The Infirmary admitted serious cases from the large hutted army camp at Cromarty but naval cases predominated.[ii] In 1915, of the 676 annual admissions, almost 40% were armed forces although this was less than had been expected. That year, 92 patients were transferred to the 'Naval Hospital'[iii] and, by 1916, the numbers had greatly reduced to 52 Navy and 16 Army cases. By then, Red Cross auxiliary hospitals such as Hedgefield had opened (see opposite). In 1917, when Culduthel Hospital opened, the Infirmary's redundant fever wards were used for naval wounded particularly for electrical treatment.[iv] That year, the hospital agreed to admit patients from wartime timber camps near Nairn and Aviemore[v] which required language interpreters to be on hand. By 1918, the hospital was admitting discharged disabled servicemen.[222]

Like other hospitals, the Infirmary suffered a lack of staff when several of its doctors and nurses, including Matron Philp, were called up. Its Convalescent Home at Bona closed when Nurse MacFadyen was called up. Getting a house surgeon was challenging and relied at one point on word of mouth to find anyone qualified, or near qualified (page 57).

Cameron Barracks held many volunteer recruits and also returning wounded and demobilising soldiers. In September 1915, it increased its hospital beds by 36 and had 140 men convalescing. That year, Lt Col Munro Moir, MO in charge, made a public appeal for donations. The Red Cross supplied VAD nurses (page 107) there in 1917.[223]

---

[i] Marquees in the grounds were planned but apparently not required.

[ii] Listed as a naval auxiliary hospital in the distribution of free tobacco by the Red Cross in 1916.

[iii] It is not clear where this was. Invergordon's hutted hospital was apparently started the following year but there may have been an earlier facility. The naval hospital at Strathpeffer Spa Pavilion was apparently not opened until 1917.

[iv] Used for muscle stimulation.

[v] In Nairn, Canadian Forestry Corp 107 Company was at Keppernach and 120 Company was at Kinsteary. 110 Company was at Glenmore and Nethybridge and 121 Company was at Loch Morlich. There were other nationalities such as Finns at Nethybridge. Prisoners of War were also involved.

Details on medical care at Fort George are sparse but there would certainly have been a need. Up to 9,000 trainee troops were stationed at the Fort with a further 20,000 in nearby camps.[224]

The Voluntary Aid Detachment (VAD) movement had been established in 1909 and run by local Red Cross associations. During the First World War this was now utilised to run Scottish Red Cross auxiliary hospitals for military personnel, set up and run by the local branch. They were usually in public buildings or large houses loaned by their owners for the duration of the war. A Red Cross commandant was in charge and each had at least one fully trained nurse and a local doctor who attended gratis. Most of the staff were Voluntary Aid Detachment (VAD) nurses who were volunteers with a basic training in nursing.[i] Patients were convalescing military personnel or those with relatively minor injuries. VAD Hospitals, as they were commonly known, received government support but, initially, at least half of their funds and much of their supplies were raised by voluntary donations. As well as Inverness, there were VAD hospitals at Nairn, Fort Augustus and at several large houses in Ross shire such as Fairburn, and Novar.

By September 1914, the local Red Cross branch was using the Northern Meeting Rooms as the Highland War Hospital Supply Depot for assembling donations.[225] The chair of the branch was Mrs Mackintosh of Mackintosh who, at her own expense,
leased, fitted out and ran Hedgefield House (photograph above) as a

---

[i] In 1915, 15 Voluntary Aid Detachment (VAD) nurses started work at the Infirmary. As well as volunteering, this was seen as part of their training.

107

VAD hospital. It opened in August 1915 when it received 20 wounded Scottish soldiers. Its medical officer, Dr Reid, and matron, Miss Mary Agnes Sinclair were in post for its entire existence. By October, it had expanded to 24 beds and was described as 'admirably fitted up and altogether a model of what a small auxiliary hospital should be.' It continued throughout the war remaining open until March 1919, the last of the area's Red Cross hospitals to close.[226]

In April 1917, Leys Castle, to the south of Inverness was loaned by its new owners Mr and Mrs Ogilvie of Delvine[i] who furnished the castle and gifted 100 guineas. It was fitted out and run by the local Red Cross with a substantial donation from Mrs Mackintosh of Mackintosh[ii] and opened in August 1917 with 50 beds (soon reduced to 40). Its first matron was Miss Ellie Black Davidson who came from Cullen VAD Hospital and who moved to Gordon Castle VAD hospital, Fochabers, later in the year. It closed in January 1919 when Miss BM Robertson was matron.[227]

In 1918, the US Navy was involved in laying the Northern Barrage - a line of mainly US mines, strung across the North Sea to contain German shipping. 2,000 mines a week were shipped across the Atlantic to Corpach, Fort William and via the Caledonian Canal to Inverness (Base 18) which was at Muirtown Basin. The Glen Albyn Distillery was taken

over as an assembly plant and, although US Naval personnel used the Infirmary for serious cases,[iii] they took over the nearby Muirtown Hotel, 90 Telford Street[iv] (photograph on the left) initially as quarters and later as a sick bay.[228]

---

[i] They had already loaned a house in Keith as an auxiliary hospital!
[ii] Who also met the matron's salary.
[iii] In 1929, US Navy personnel sent 1,000 guineas to endow a bed in the new Infirmary wards.
[iv] Beside the swing bridge at Muirtown.

The Second World War

During the Second World War, the existing military hospitals continued their work. Fort George contained both army and navy personnel. It had an eye specialist attached there in 1940[229] and is listed with 70 wartime beds in June 1945 (map page 152).[230] Cameron Barracks seems to have played a lesser role than in the First World War. A VAD nurse, who was accommodated there with seven others, recalls that it had 'a small hospital for minor ailments such as scabies.'[231] In 1945, it is not listed as a military hospital in official documentation but the source is not necessarily accurate.[i]

As in the First World War, large houses became convalescent auxiliary hospitals. Achnagairn House, Kirkhill (now the hotel) was loaned to the Red Cross as an auxiliary hospital by Mr. C Ogden the US tobacco baron who, with his wife, normally used it in summer. By October 1940, it had 35 patients who seem to have been mainly officers. It received convalescing military patients from Raigmore. The sketch above is from a postcard which seems to be signed on the back in 1945 by the VAD nurses.[232]

---

[i] It is not listed in Crewe (see references) but Crewe's list may not be complete as it includes Onich with 50 beds which was mothballed in 1941 and omits Glencoe which certainly continued throughout the war.

In March 1940, Leys Castle (see page 108) was loaned as an auxiliary hospital by its owner Mr. FW Walker.[233] The hospital seems to have closed by September 1945, when the Department of Health offered the local Health Board first option to buy surplus furniture from there. Altyre House Auxiliary Hospital near Forres was fairly closely linked to Raigmore Hospital in terms of the transfer of patients and was still operational in late 1946.[234]

In 1916, everywhere north of Inverness became a Special Military Area and people, including locals, required a pass to move around the area. During both World Wars, large parts of the Highlands were used for military training. Inverness was an important control point so that many large houses were taken over by the military for billeting or for administration. As far as can be ascertained, no buildings other than the ones described in the above pages, had a wartime medical care function.

The experience of the First World War and the development of enhanced weaponry by the 1930s suggested that military casualties in any war would be immense. Also, it was considered difficult to repulse enemy bombers and large amounts of civilian casualties were anticipated. It was expected, correctly, that enemy bombers would target cities and this pressed the need for additional hospital space in areas remote from them where hospital facilities would also be required for city evacuees.

Therefore, the Government planned for a large increase in hospital beds as well as other Emergency Medical Services (EMS). In Scotland, this came under Secretary of State, Tom Johnstone,[i] and was administered by the Department of Health which, for the first time, became a hospital authority directly administering nine base hospitals and 62 auxiliary/ convalescent hospitals across Scotland. By the early 1940s, these wartime hospitals were also admitting civilian patients, other than chronic cases, from waiting lists[ii] which had been seen as too long for at least 20 years although less so in the Highlands.[235]

---

[i] A shrewd, far sighted politician who also set up the Hydro Board.
[ii] It was essential to have a healthy wartime home workforce.

The EMS scheme in relation to hospitals was developed in two phases. Phase 1 involved setting aside beds for military use in existing hospitals which received payments from the Department of Health for the beds created. Thus, in 1939, the RNI became a base hospital and 120 patients were evacuated by transferring elsewhere or by sending them home. The hospital bed complement increased from 205 to 271 with the addition of 60 additional war emergency and 6 reserve beds. In the first two years of the War just over 20% of admissions were armed forces personnel. Given that bed numbers had increased by over 30%, to a large extent normal service for the civilian population continued and a government grant for the emergency beds compensated for the interruption to fund raising. The war time difficulties for the RNI were rather shortages of supplies and the disruption to staffing, when nurses, doctors and other staff were called up. There was also some additional building expense such as fitting blackouts. The Tweedmouth Chapel was used as a first aid post for casualties and staffed by the RNI and the out-patients department was fitted out as an ARP[i] first aid post. A mobile surgical unit was also established in the hospital grounds, somewhat of a misnomer for a time because the van which transported it refused to move because of a mechanical fault. In 1942, a decontamination centre[ii] was constructed in the grounds.

With the opening of Raigmore in 1941, the RNI received fewer armed forces admissions but it continued to receive specialist cases.[iii] By the first half of 1942, the proportion of armed forces patients had declined to 10% and, from 1943, was normally under 5%. By 1944, military beds were no longer reserved. By mid-1942, Raigmore was admitting civilian patients including those from RNI waiting lists which had over 200 cases in the late 1930s.

Raigmore Hospital was part of Phase 2 of Emergency Medical Services (EMS) development when entire new EMS hospitals were built. There

---

[i] Air Raid Precautions later called Civil Defence.
[ii] To cleanse personnel in the event of a gas or chemical attack.
[iii] Culduthel received military fever cases but apparently not in large numbers.

were seven in Scotland, the others being at Stracathro, Bridge of Earn, Killearn, Law, Ballochmyle and Peel. In Scotland, the total number of beds produced by the entire scheme (including Phase 1) is shown in the table below.

Second World War - total beds in Scotland for wartime use[236]

General Hospitals		Convalescent	
Type	Beds	Type	Beds
New Hospitals (7)	7,038	Country Houses (60)	3,426
Hospital Annexes (24)	8,526	Miscellaneous	527
Converted Hotels	910	Total	3,953
Other	100		
Total	16,574	**Scottish Total**	**20,527**

Some thought was given to post-war needs since Scotland had been deficient in hospital beds from at least 1920. The shortage of beds was not so acute in the north but the planned 600 beds at Raigmore made a substantial difference. The table below shows the number of beds for the whole north of Scotland before the Second World War. Raigmore increased this capacity by 50%.

Hospital accommodation in the Northern Region 1938[237]

	Number of Hospitals	Number of beds
Local Authorities	22	666
Voluntary	18	501
Total	40	1,167

Raigmore Hospital[238]
1941

'Raigmore Hospital has a future comparable to no other hospital similarly placed' [239]

Matron MS Savege prophesised the above in 1946 when Raigmore was under five years old with a barely completed collection of poorly insulated brick huts with an anticipated life of 40 years and built for a war which had just ended. Across Inverness stood the highly successful RNI which had dominated medical specialist services in the Highlands for the previous century and a half. It is not certain what inspired Matron's comment but earlier that year the government had announced that the emergency wartime hospital was to continue under Department of Health[i] administration until the NHS was formed.

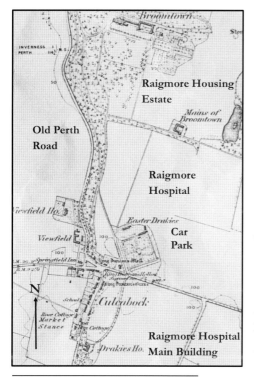

Old Perth Road

Raigmore Housing Estate

Raigmore Hospital

Car Park

Raigmore Hospital Main Building

The 1870 OS map (left) shows the Raigmore area with some present features labelled. Lachlan Mackintosh made his fortune in India and moved here from Meikle Raig near Tomatin. He built the 3 storey mansion Broomtown, later renamed Raigmore House, which stood north of the present Raigmore housing estate shop (top of map). The belt of trees across the map still forms the boundary between the housing estate and hospital and can be clearly seen in the photograph on page 115 which views this area from the north east.

---

[i] This central administration is seen to have influenced the structure of the NHS.

113

The photograph above shows Raigmore House probably in the late 1930s. The Mackintoshes were prominent supporters of the Infirmary in the nineteenth century. Lachlan Mackintosh was an original subscriber and, in 1808, sent back a substantial donation from Bengal (page 47). Aeneas Mackintosh contributed much especially in the 1860s. The bequest of Julia Mackintosh financed a children's ward in 1903 (page 75).

By 1939, the Department of Health had a regional administration and Dr Russell Martin, its local officer, played a leading role in the establishment of Raigmore. Secretary, later Chief Clerk, Miss A (Nancy) Whyte recalled Dr Martin opening a letter in late spring 1940 which confirmed the decision to erect a hutted hospital. Dr Martin and Dr AS Fraser, MOH for Inverness-shire[i] had evaluated several sites for the new EMS Hospital including Culduthel Hospital and Lentran House but the level land of the Raigmore area, which was close to existing services, 'chose itself'.[240] In 1940, a 40 acre site was requisitioned but it was not until 1956, after protracted negotiations, that 65 acres were purchased for £6,000. By then, Miss Mary Mackintosh, the last of the Raigmore family, had died.

---

[i] He became senior administrator to the new Health Board in 1948.

The site extended only as far as today's north entrance where the wall of the former garden defines part of the main car park. Near here was the last of the original buildings on the hospital site - a gardener's cottage and coach house (below) which were demolished in 1983.[241]

In 1941, Raigmore House was taken over by RAF Fighter Command 13. A nearby bunker tracked enemy aircraft, one of seven such bases across Britain. The House was HQ, officers' mess and probably also accommodation. Armed forces personnel were accommodated in nearby huts[i] which were later occupied by civilians. From 1948, the Royal Auxiliary Air Force ran the House and its bunkers as an Air Defence Unit and it was an aircraft control centre until this was centralised at Prestwick in 1950. In 1957, it became Royal Observer Corps HQ until its demolition around 1965.[242] The photo below shows Raigmore House in the right foreground, the new hospital in the far left and, between them, RAF huts at the edge of the woods near present day Raigmore Primary School. Cameron Barracks is at the top of the photo and Broomtown Farm is lower left. On the lower right is the railway.

---

[i] At the 1951 census, Raigmore Hutted Camp had 13 families (61 people) and was still occupied in the late 1950s. In February 1949, some huts were dismantled and their occupants - illegal squatters - were evicted and forced to camp in the woods.

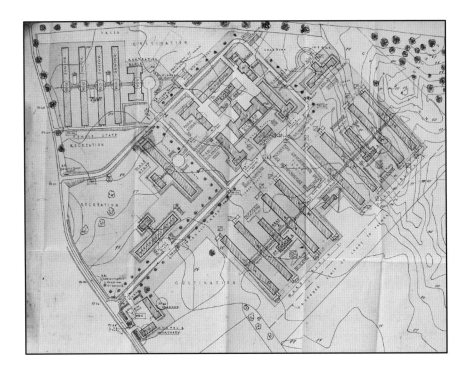

The above plan was drawn by the Department of Health in May 1940. Despite wartime austerity, flower beds and staff recreation areas were included. By late autumn, Jas Campbell & Sons, Tomnahurich Street, one of the largest builders in the north, and joiners MacDonald of Friars Lane had started work. Most of the wards were constructed in about six months at an estimated cost of £250,000 - supervised by the Ministry of Works. At one point, around 600 bricklayers worked 12 hours a day although, despite this urgent wartime need, there was no Sunday working. There was a shortage of steel and timber was forbidden as a structural material so that brick and concrete slabs with a minimum of steel reinforcement were used. The photograph opposite (top) shows a later ward under construction around 1945.[243]

The first wards opened on 5th September 1941 and the first patient was a Canadian from the Carrbridge based Canadian Forestry Corps.[244] Few records remain of this early stage, probably due to wartime secrecy which seems to have prevented any press reports. There was no official opening but there seems to have been an inaugural ball in the Caledonian Hotel in 1942.[245]

From the outset, Raigmore Hospital contained a unit run by the military (Scottish Group 11/48). It had 24 men commanded by a Major Ogg in the early 1940s and it dealt with the welfare of military patients who differed from civilians, for example, they had to be fully recovered before returning to duty unlike civilians who could be sent home to convalesce. This, and the need for military discipline, influenced patient management. The unit's management merged with the hospital quite some time before it was disbanded in late 1946. The photograph below is from 1951 but gives a good impression of Raigmore at this time.[246]

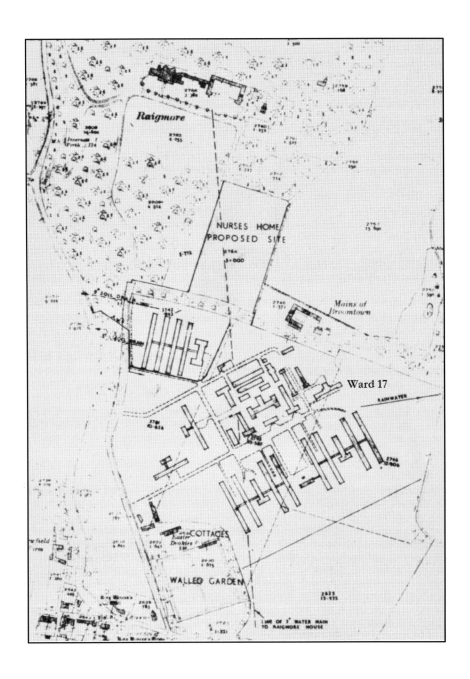

EMS hospitals were complete hospitals, built to a standard design. The above photograph and the map opposite are both from the early 1940s and show approximately the same area. North is towards the top in both. Top left is Raigmore House, near present day Mackintosh Road and the local shop. Staff quarters for nurses, sisters and domestic staff appear as lighter coloured blocks at the top left. To the right, the central units held services and administration, including matron's quarters, laboratories, kitchens, dining rooms and later the nurses' training school. The separate ward block next the strip of woodland was the isolation block Ward 17, labelled on the map, which was converted to maternity in 1947 and to the children's ward in 1955. Middle right are sixteen, 40 bed wards, separated for wartime safety into two-ward blocks. Block A (left) next to the walled garden was surgical and, from 1951, maternity. Block B was orthopaedics (moved from A in 1944) and medical. Each block had an operating theatre. In between them was the square, as it was called, where helicopters occasionally landed (page 132). In the left foreground is Culcabock. The walled garden marks the present day car park.

 The separate wards were quite inconvenient especially in winter when staff and visitors arrived cold with grit and mess brought in with their feet. The open walkways[i] between wards (left) were not popular in Inverness winters when trying to keep uniforms tidy in the snow filled northern winds but were an improvement on early days when wellington boots were required between some ward blocks. Walkways and grounds seem to have been unlit until at least 1948[247] which made moving between blocks quite hazardous and several nurses have memories of pushing trolleys with the help of a porter from a ward to the mortuary which was beside the ambulance station. One nurse remembers a windy night when the inadequately attached cover over the body flew up causing the porter to bolt in terror. The land between the blocks grew vegetables during the War[ii] and, although this added to potential hazards in the black-out, the resultant potatoes made excellent stovies for the nurses on cold nights. These were not the only disadvantages of working in Raigmore. In the 1940s, Drakies and Culcabock were small rural settlements well outside Inverness. The nearest bus stop was beside the Fluke bar and there were no buses at night although staff could hitch a lift on army lorries in the early morning and late evening.

Internal corridors were left open because of a brick shortage and each ward was heated by three slow combustion, dusty, cast-iron stoves[iii] which required a number of stokers to fuel them with coke. A huge

---

[i] They remained open into the 1950s.
[ii] The 1940 plan (page 116) has areas labelled 'cultivation'.
[iii] The operating theatres had steam filled radiators.

mound of coke sat in the hospital grounds supplied by Inverness Gas Works until it closed in the mid-1960s when coke then came from Wick. From 1949, the stoves were replaced by centrally heated radiators and, in the 1960s, coke was replaced by cheaper and cleaner oil. Each ward also had a boiler for hot water and a paraffin stove provided hot water in the ward kitchen.[248]

The original design allowed for 672 beds but only 532 were created. Wards were designed for 40 beds but this was rather crowded and they

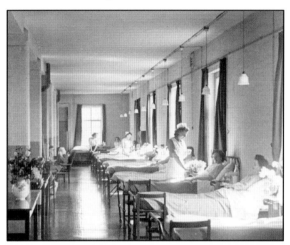

had a maximum of 32 beds by the mid-1940s. Even then, there was just room for a patient's locker between each bed. Wards were Nightingale pattern as shown in the 1950s photograph (left) and, from the mid-1940s, each had a side room for seriously ill patients.[i] Note the highly polished floor which was very difficult to maintain especially in orthopaedic wards when plaster flaked off from the casts on patients' limbs. Also, the wheels of the beds sank into the bitumen flooring in hot weather.

In 1947, the isolation ward was converted to maternity. Isolation facilities were then provided by forming 4 cubicles in Ward 11. In 1958, this was further developed into a modern layout (three 6 bed wards, two 3 bed, one 2 bed and 4 singles)[ii] as part of a study across several hospitals. This was a considerable advance but finance prevented other wards being similarly developed.[249]

---

[i] Known by the staff as the 'private' ward.
[ii] Later partly used as the Intensive Care Unit (page 131).

Raigmore Hospital was not universally well received. Many local people said 'it just didn't look like a hospital' and some referred to it as 'The Stable'. Dr Johnston,[i] first medical superintendent, described his first impression as 'mud and dreary brick walls'. The hospital was, of course, starting from scratch. As well as creating the complexities of a modern hospital, it required team building but, being a wartime establishment, many staff were transferred[ii] rather than choosing employment there and this also must have made it challenging to generate an esprit de corp.[250]

Colonel AES Irvine,[iii] third[iv] medical superintendent, seems to have been particularly skilled at this. He had a good rapport with staff and was a good communicator especially with visiting press and dignitaries. He helped stir the Xmas pudding which, by the late 1940s, had become a tradition (he is on the left in the photograph left). He developed recreation facilities, launched an internal magazine and arranged film shows in the wards.[v] In 1950, Major General Paton of the RNI became first medical superintendent of Inverness hospitals and Raigmore no longer had its own. In 1974, the post was abolished.

The recreation hall[vi] (photo opposite) was an important social and recreation focus and former staff have warm memories of films, social

---

[i] Was depute MOH for Inverness-shire and medical superintendent of Culduthel.
[ii] For example, in 1941 a group of nurses were posted from Creagdhu Auxiliary Hospital near Fort William which had been requisitioned but soon mothballed.
[iii] He joined the Royal Army Medical Corps in 1905 and awarded the D.S.O in the First World War. He was in Raigmore Hospital from 1944 and retired 1950.
[iv] He was preceded by Col Patrick Hannafin (1942-44).
[v] His own film footage of the hospital was rediscovered several years ago.
[vi] It was built by the Canadian Forestry Corps as a thank you with materials supplied by the Department of Health. It was replaced in 1970.

evenings and dances.[251] Hospital volunteers in the early 1940s wore a badge (below). The HH stood for Hospital Help and the badge allowed access to recreation facilities and to the shop. The 1950s photograph below, following a nurses' presentation ceremony, shows the detail of the hall's log frontage. The photograph includes Matron MacBride (centre right), Major General Paton, Medical Superintendent RNI (far left) and at the back, RNI surgeon AJC Hamilton.

In 1943, a Welfare Committee was formed 'to care for the welfare of patients and staff' and it received profits from the YMCA canteen in the recreation hall. It supplied amenities such as Christmas treats and newspapers and rapidly expanded to support recreations such

as badminton, cricket, whist drives and dances. In 1967, it financed silver jubilee celebrations and replaced the recreation hall in the early 1970s with an assembly hall. By then, the present recreation hall had also been operational since the 1950s

In its first year, Raigmore admitted 4142 patients and continued at this level for the rest of the 1940s.[i] There were ample beds[ii] and, by 1943, half were occupied by civilians. In May 1944, in advance of D Day, civilian admissions stopped and non-urgent cases were moved to auxiliary hospitals or sent home. From August 1944, Red Cross trains brought casualties north, mainly orthopaedic patients,[iii] including evacuees from London hospitals partly because of V2 rocket attacks. Inverness was not necessarily the most convenient location for wartime casualties. One former soldier describes how, having been wounded on 3rd August, he arrived around a week later after journeying in the top bunk of a railway carriage in the summer heat. He spent many weeks in Raigmore and was then transferred to Achnagairn Auxiliary Hospital (page 109) until April 1945 when he was sent south to a Ministry of Pensions Hospital near Portsmouth, his home area.[252]

In 1944, six trains brought around 200 patients each including German and Italian prisoners of war and there was a fresh wave of casualties in spring 1945. By November 1945, there were around 300 in-patients 90% of whom were military personal but this proportion fell away rapidly to around 10% by 1947. All in all it seems that there were thankfully fewer casualties than had been anticipated. By 1946, armed forces personnel and civilians occupied the same wards although the armed forces patients were distinguished by their standard issue[iv] blue suit of clothes.[253]

One of the main benefits brought to Highland by Raigmore was its new specialist posts. EMS Hospitals had planned specialties. Raigmore's were maxillofacial trauma and orthopaedics although the former was quite small and initially shared a ward block with physiotherapy. There

---

[i] By July 1949, there had been 34,642 admissions.
[ii] 2 wards were used for recreation and as a gym. The officers ward originally had a sitting room/area. Unlike the others, its beds were curtained off.
[iii] There were hospital trains from the start of the War, primarily designed for civilian casualties. Each of nine vans held 270 stretcher cases and had medical and food supplies on board. Each train was staffed by 1 doctor, 3 fully trained nurses, 10 nursing auxiliaries and eight male orderlies (Inverness Courier 26 June 1940).
[iv] Initially all military patients wore regulation blue pyjamas.

is little information on the early classification of patients but the table below shows the operations performed in the first half of 1943.

Operations November 1942 – May 1943

	Number	% of total
General Surgery	607	40
Orthopaedics	578	39
ENT	224	15
Gynaecology	95	6

By 1942, there was a resident orthopaedic consultant and soon much of the work was on tuberculosis osteomyelitis, a bone infection found in TB sufferers.[i] Until then, there had been no organised orthopaedic[ii] service in Highland but, in 1943, Raigmore became a base orthopaedic hospital for the Highlands and Islands with the appointment of consultant, Mr Richard Murray. He initially set up out-patient clinics in the orthopaedic operating theatre using the anaesthetic room as a waiting area and, from 1944, held weekly clinics at the RNI, monthly clinics at Forres, Nairn and Fort William, (by 1946) quarterly clinics in Wick, Thurso and Golspie and visited Skye every four months where he had three venues – Broadford Hospital, Portree High School and the doctor's house at Dunvegan. He made annual visits to the Western Isles.

Raigmore Hospital cases January 1947

Orthopaedic	83	Gynaecology	14
Medical	59	Antenatal	6
General surgical	23	Infectious disease	6
ENT	1	Skin	1

Although operating facilities were more basic and more portable than now, there must have been considerable work involved in the regular clearing of the Raigmore operating theatre for out-patient clinics.

---

[i] It was virtually eliminated by the late 1950s.
[ii] There was no orthopaedic specialist in the RNI.

However, there were other more drastic changes such as in October 1944 when the whole orthopaedic department moved from Block A to Block B to make way for prisoner of war patients. In 1944, most orthopaedic cases at Raigmore were armed forces personnel but, by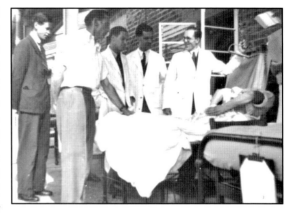
1946, they were nearly all civilian and, by then, Raigmore had two well-equipped operating theatres and 75 orthopaedic beds. The table on page 125 illustrates the dominance of orthopaedics.[254]

Mr Murray had an assistant surgeon and two house surgeons.[255] The photograph above from the mid-1950s shows Mr Murray (on the right) and orthopaedic surgeon Mr Frew[i] (3rd left) consulting over a patient on a ward veranda. Tuberculosis osteomyelitis patients spent many weeks in plaster and, by 1948, both the male and female wards had verandas where they could be outside in shelter[ii] (below[iii])[256]

---

[i] In Raigmore from 1946-81. Late, consultant orthopaedic surgeon
[ii] Fresh air was part of TB treatment and verandas were used into the 1960s.
[iii] Note the cultivated land in the foreground next to the ward.

126

Although the RNI was the main out-patient's centre for Inverness, by 1943, there were clinics for orthopaedics, surgery, medical and gynaecology at Raigmore. However, Mr Murray made frequent complaints about provision for out-patients and, in 1951, a review of facilities in Inverness found them sadly lacking. It was recommended that most clinics should be held at the RNI, being the most convenient location for patients, but that orthopaedics and gynaecology continue at Raigmore.[257] In 1956, a new Raigmore out-patient department was opened by Captain John Macleod MP for Ross and Cromarty.

A 'skin' ward seems to have been initially planned but there were insufficient cases and they were incorporated into medical wards. A skin specialist, Dr Eric Cohen, was in post from 1942-45 and he also worked at the RNI. There was no specialist between 1946 and 1950 but, by 1951, eight beds were set aside for dermatology (the first in the Highlands).[i] In 1968, dermatology moved to a larger ward at Culduthel Hospital (page 186) and returned to Raigmore in 1985 to a new nine bed unit.[258]

From 1946, Raigmore became a General Training School for nursing initially with 12 students. The training school blazer badge (left) is

thought to have been designed by Nurse Mackay a member of the first Raigmore class. The Gaelic motto *Daonnan deasail* translates as 'Always Ready', and the motto was apparently also used by the military wing of the hospital. When the Central School of Nursing building opened in 1970 two new badges were used.[259]

---

[i] Although the RNI had reported on skin diseases separately since at least 1900.

The first class of just four students to qualify are shown left. Sister Mairi Smith,[i] who held badge number 1, is on the left and tutor Miss L Skinner is centre. By 1951, two sister tutors ran Raigmore's training unit which contained a large well equipped practical room, three private study rooms and a classroom.[260] From 1950, preliminary training was delivered at Eden Court jointly with RNI staff (page 90). By 1950, there were nearly 80 nurses in training at Raigmore helping to combat an extreme shortage of nurses which had led, that year, to admissions being reduced to 250 patients.[ii]

In 1970, centralisation was complete when the Inverness Central School of Nursing[iii] was opened by Dame Muriel Powell, Chief Nursing Officer of the Scottish Home and Health Department (page 91). In 1971, its library was merged with that from the RNI which formed the basis of the present Highland Health Science Library. In 1973, the Post Graduate Medical Centre was established and, in 2007, all were demolished to make way for the Centre for Health Science where they are now located.[261]

Inverness was the only health region in Scotland without a teaching hospital and it was not until 1968 that a system of training placements for Aberdeen University medical students was established. It steadily expanded and, from 1983, students were accommodated on site at Fraser Noble Court. By the mid-1990s, there were around 60 undergraduates placed at Raigmore.

---

[i] Became Sister Smith of the out-patient department and retired in 1982.
[ii] This general shortage also precipitated the closure of Cromarty Hospital.
[iii] Later the Highland and Western Isles College of Nursing and Midwifery.

In 1941, staff quarters lagged behind some other developments and the first matron, Miss Sarah MacDougall, was boarded for three months in nearby Culcabock schoolhouse. Accommodation for resident medical officers and nurses was very basic

for many years. Sisters had larger single rooms (photograph above) but some nurses and domestic staff shared.[i] Toilet and wash facilities were communal and there were no wash basins in the rooms. In some of the nurses' accommodation the original dividing walls stopped two feet short of the ceiling, apparently due to a shortage of bricks when built. As elsewhere in the hospital, heating came from two coke stoves.[ii] One advantage of the accommodation was the easily opened windows of the single storey blocks which seem to have been frequently used by nurses coming home late at night. Plans for a nurses' home were made in the late 1940s (see map page 118) but, like later improvements to the

accommodation, they were never executed. Eventually, new nurses' quarters were built on site in the 1960s (photo page 134) but well into the 1980s nurses were still living in the original isolated EMS blocks (right).[iii]

---

[i] More than half the domestic staff and all nurses were residential in 1946.
[ii] Central heating was installed in the hospital in the early 1950s.
[iii] Raigmore Primary School is in the extreme left background. Nurses can remember the snow being halfway up the windows during some winters.

The Infirmary had established a children's ward in the 1870s and, in 1929, its York Ward was the flagship of its new development (page 75). By the mid-1940s, Raigmore also had a children's ward of 20 beds. However, paediatrics had not developed as a  specialist area and, in 1953, MOH Fraser suggested a paediatric unit. The following year Dr Patrick Macarthur started Highland's first paediatric service and, in October 1955, Captain John MacLeod, MP for Ross and Cromarty, opened the new paediatric unit (photo above)[i] which also

 accommodated out-patient clinics (photo left). At first, the ward seems to have had an average of 25 in-patients but this quickly settled to around 15. By comparison with other departments, the wards were spacious and a veranda allowed children's beds to be taken outside in good weather.[262]

---

[i] Consultant Dr MacArthur (right) is shaking hands with Captain MacLeod MP. Others are (from left) William Hall, Mrs MacLeod and Colonel Mackintosh.

Raigmore bed allocation

	1951	1963
Dermatology	8	8
Medicine	109	113
General Surgery	50	49
Orthopaedic	140	120
ENT	26	-
Gynaecology	15	30
Obstetrics	60	60
Paediatric	-	22
Sick cots	-	10
Oral Surgery		4
Total	408	416

The table on the left shows the bed allocation in late 1951 compared with 1963. In the early 1950s, ENT was centralised at the RNI and, in 1963, gynaecology was centralised at Raigmore to make way for ophthalmology expansion at the RNI (see pages 91 and 139). Oral surgery began in the early 1960s.

Although the building structure changed little in the 1950s and 60s, there was a gradual development of facilities, some accompanied by official ceremonies and others significant but unlauded. Catering had always been challenging. Transporting food to the separate wards was difficult and it was hard to keep it sufficiently hot. Initially, cooking was done on Esse stoves fuelled by dusty coke and piped gas did not arrive until around 1960. Nevertheless, in 1951, a menu system was introduced which was in advance of many other hospitals.

Many Raigmore wards seem to have had a relaxed social atmosphere. 16 year old Brian Sturrock spent a year as an orthopaedic patient in the late 1950s and his extensive diary illustrates the positive and friendly rapport between patients and staff.[263] As elsewhere, patients listened to radio but, in 1959, complaints were received about 'profane and noisy programmes on the Sabbath'. Despite finding no problem, the Health Board eventually yielded and banned Sunday radio and TV in the wards but this of course also included religious programmes. After quite a heated correspondence in the local press the ban was relaxed and partially solved by introducing headsets for each bed (see also page 87).[264] No chapel had been included in Old Raigmore except in the mortuary and a weekly religious service was held in the recreation hall. Religious services were, however, held in the wards. The present chapel was opened in 1986 as part of the new building. In 1970, hospital radio started as a weekly request programme from its studio in the RNI.[265]

In 1969, an Intensive Care Unit was established with three beds. Interestingly, it had no coronary care beds until 1972 when two such beds were added but these cases soon dominated. In 1985, the Intensive Therapy and Coronary Care Unit, as it was now called, moved to the new building, and by then coronary care patients made up 70% of the total.

In 1948, clinical photography (the photographing of patients' conditions) began when Mr Charles Hunt, a press photographer, was appointed to the Inverness hospitals. Later he also took ECGs. Around 1970, a medical illustrator and AV technician were appointed and, in 1978, the department was renamed the Department of Medical Illustration.

Ambulances were provided by the Red Cross until 1946 when it joined with the St Andrews Ambulance Society. After 1948, the Scottish Ambulance Service was formed, funded by the Scottish Office. Given the dispersed nature of the Highland population, the advantages of an air ambulance were soon apparent and, in 1933, a service started in West Scotland.[i] By 1946, there was an air ambulance service from Inverness to North Uist and Benbecula and also to Shetland.[266] It is not certain when helicopters first landed at Raigmore but nurses remember landings from the 1940s or early 1950s.[ii] The photograph below shows a Dragonfly military helicopter in 1955. It was based at Lossiemouth and was small and fairly limited. In January 1956, it carried out possibly its first night time operation when it

[i] Mr Sword, owner of Midland and Scottish Air Ferries Ltd set up a service between Campbelltown, Belfast and Islay. By July 1933, the company had taken 3 cases from Islay to Glasgow hospitals and it approached HIMS suggesting a non-profit air ambulance service. HIMS agreed but routes were not feasible and were withdrawn at the end of 1934. Mr Sword continued to maintain a 6 seater twin engine de Havilland Dragon aircraft at Renfrew for the air ambulance service.
[ii] William Browne (see references) thought it was not until 1954/55.

brought in a maternity case. From 1963, Whirlwind helicopters were in use. Helicopters landed between the ward blocks and caused considerable disruption to the wards if the windows were open. Mrs Pat Ross, a nurse at the time, remembers an incident when dahlias and earth from the flower beds next the ward were blown over a patient sleeping next to the window who work up suddenly and, thinking he was about to be interred, cried out 'I'm not dead yet'.

In 1948, the new Health Board reaffirmed the need to centralise hospital facilities. An earlier plan to use the large Culduthel site (page 184) had been abandoned and there was insufficient space at the RNI. By 1953, Raigmore was the preferred site and, by then, the inadequacy of the separate wards was increasingly apparent.[267] In 1955, it was noted that 'little had been done to improve the interior of the building in terms of plastering and decoration' and that the hospital was substandard and, unlike other former Emergency Hospitals, had not been upgraded.[268]

In 1966, work started on a new 'Inverness Central Hospital' under architect J Glease and Phase 1 was opened in 1970 by Mr DJ Macdonald, Chair of the Board. It had cost £1.42 million, and included radiotherapy, physiotherapy, occupational therapy, pharmacy, out-patients and records. Pathology and haematology were transferred from the RNI (bacteriology had been transferred in 1949). Later that year, A&E was transferred from the RNI and a department of electrocardiography set up. The name 'Inverness Central Hospital' was used initially to distinguish it from existing Inverness hospitals (which included Raigmore) but, in 1983, after a consultation, the new development was officially called Raigmore Hospital. In March 1976, a four bed haemodialysis (renal) unit was established (right) and ran until the new unit was ready in the late 1980s.

The above photograph from the early 1970s looks SSW and shows the new Phase 1 buildings near the top left. Drakies housing estate lies along the top. In the foreground is Raigmore Housing estate and, in the middle, is Old Raigmore separated by a belt of trees which has existed for over a century (map page 113). The walled garden (top right next the road) and the pond (bottom left), features of the original Raigmore grounds, can still be seen. The small car park has now extended into the walled garden area. The ambulance depot is the white building towards the top right and below it – also white - are the first blocks of the new nurses' home. The block on the lower middle left (and left of the road) is the new Inverness Central School of Nursing and Post Graduate Medical Centre. A particular benefit was the new entrance on Perth Road (top middle) which, among other things, enabled the public bus service to enter the grounds.[269]

By the 1970s, the brick wards were showing their age. In 1970, a private patient[i] from South Africa described her room in her letter of complaint as 'very

primitive'. She was possibly correct in her judgement. The wards were frequently over-crowded, beds were close together with only half having bed screens, wards had no day room and had poor facilities for ambulant patients. Each ward had only one bath to serve 30 patients.[270] The need to replace the old wards was urgent and, in 1978, Phase II started. The photograph above shows the new tower block going up beside the old wards. It was opened for in-patients in March 1985 and the first patients to transfer from the old wards were orthopaedic. The new hospital was officially opened by the Queen and Duke of Edinburgh[ii] on 15th August (photograph on page 137).

Its main feature was the tower block with 500 beds, a renal unit, intensive/ coronary care unit, a new A & E and nine operating theatres. It cost £30 million and was described as 'bright and cheery' by the local press. In the early summer of 1985, acute services from the RNI began to be transferred and, in December 1987, after £1m had been raised within 5 years, a CT scanner suite was opened by the Duchess of Kent.

---

[i] The NHS allowed few private patients and, by the 1980s, only 2 in Inverness. However, there were amenity beds in RNI (10) and Craig Dunain (8). The NHS had these from the start - single and double rooms which were not bookable but, if available on admission, could be occupied for a fee (HHB Newsletter April 1983).
[ii] The new maternity wards opened in January 1988 - officially on 31st May.

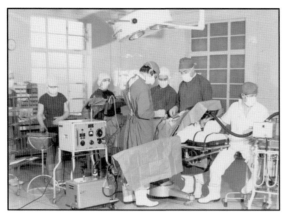

By 1988, all units had been moved from the RNI.[271]

Originally, the theatres were in individual isolated brick buildings similar to the wards. The picture (left) shows Mr ATR Hamilton's surgical team at work in one of these theatres. The facilities of the old wards became quite outdated and, in the 1970s, they were replaced by prefabricated modular theatres which were an improvement, for example they had dedicated recovery rooms. They are shown in the picture below from the mid-1980s when the old brick huts (seen behind) were being cleared. Staff accommodation is shown behind. Surgeons continued to operate in both the RNI and Raigmore theatres until 1985 when, over just one weekend, everything moved to the new Raigmore operating theatres. This move was a substantial change for theatre staff. Not only were the operating theatres state of the art and comparable with the best in the UK, but there were nine side by side. In addition, the RNI and Raigmore staff were merged into a much larger team, now working in close proximity and within the same building.

In 1990, the last remnants of the EMS hospital were removed after the completion of the new isolation unit. However, one significant piece still remains – the present recreation hall which was upgraded around 1990 and continues to be a well-used facility. On 7 October 1991, a new cytology unit was opened by retired consultant pathologist Dr HG Richmond - the first of many developments after 1990 as Raigmore continues to expand its range of medical services.[272]

Date	Matron	Notes
1941-5	Sarah MacDougall	Later matron Ballachulish Hospital.[273]
1945-7	Marguerite Savege	Left to be married (quote on page 113).
1947-50	FM Miller	Became matron Glasgow Western Infirmary.[274]
1950-58	Bethina H McBride	Became matron at Roehampton.
1958-71	Janet Brimms	Retired.
1971-81	Maisie MacDougall	Retired. In 1973 the matron's post changed to Senior Nursing Officer.

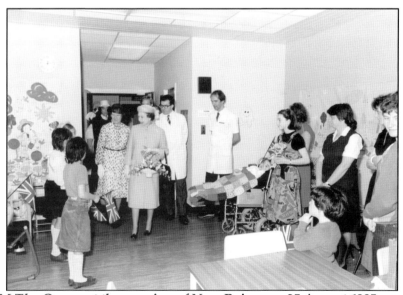

HM The Queen at the opening of New Raigmore 25 August 1985

Some early Raigmore staff

The table below gives details of some staff other than those mentioned in the text. By the late 1940s many were on the staff of both Raigmore and the RNI (page 98). Unless otherwise stated the year listed is the date of appointment with the year they stopped in brackets. It is by no means a complete list.

Date	Staff
1941	Dr T Scott (consultant from 1946) (1975) and Mr Watt are the first resident doctors followed closely by Marion Pearson (1943) resident orthopaedic surgeon and Dr Forrai – haematology. Dr Forrai was a Hungarian refugee and pathologist by 1949. Robert Mackay was chief pharmacist and Eileen Macmillan chief radiographer. Dr Gottlieb (1949) is first radiologist followed by JC Wood.[275]
1945	Archibald Duncan (1946) obstetrician.
1946	Andrew Hay (1978) consultant obstetrician. Mr Frew (1981) orthopaedic surgeon. Consultant by mid 1950s.
1946	Miss Dick -pharmacist. Retires as chief pharmacist around 1970.
1947	Dr Bruce consultant biochemistry. Dr Mitchell orthopaedic surgeon? [276]
1948	Andrew Lyon (1977) succeeds Nancy Whyte as chief clerk.
1948	J Ronald and DC Wilson (1975) consultant physicians.
c1949	Leslie Ledingham (1973) consultant obstetrician. Died soon after retiring and remembered through annual lecture.
1949	Bacteriology under Haig MacPherson (1951) transferred from RNI. Hector M Urquhart (1980) consultant ENT.
1950	AAN Bain (1966 died) consultant radiologist.
1951	Harold Williams succeeds Haig MacPherson. T Smith (1953) succeeds T Chalmers obstetrics/gynaecology.
1954	Maeve Rusk (1980) consultant ophthalmologist.
1955	AJ Sangster is consultant radiologist. RL Richard is consultant ophthalmologist. Appointment dates unknown.
1957	NAM Mackinnon's post upgraded to consultant dermatology.
1962	J Knox (1987 died) consultant physician. Dr Greir (1986) consultant ENT.
1964	GS Anderson (1980) consultant surgeon. AD MacIntosh obstetrician.
1967	Brenda Gray (late 1970s) consultant pathologist.
1968	A Morrison (1986) consultant orthopaedic surgeon succeeds R Murray. Mr Morrison was on the staff from at least 1955.
1970	Murdo Smith chief area pharmaceutical officer.
1971	James Bruce (1978) consultant biochemist since 1947. Transfers from RNI.

The Merging of Inverness Hospitals

In 1940, when Raigmore was built, cooperation between voluntary hospitals had been discussed for two decades but had made little impact on service development. Over the years, the local authorities and the RNI had difficulties in agreeing service delivery, maternity being the most recent example at that time (page 143). More stark was the separation of Craig Dunain from the other hospitals. Although it used the RNI for surgical cases, it managed its own medical, fever and TB cases rather than using Culduthel. From 1941, Raigmore Hospital relied on RNI laboratories and its laundry facilities and there was sharing of specialist staff.

The sharing of personnel does much to bring organisations together and Knox[277] considers that joint staffing began in 1942 with the appointment of Dr Tom Scott, Raigmore, as depute to Dr Leys, physician at the RNI. By 1942, obstetrician Dr MacGregor was coordinating maternity hospital cases in the three hospitals involved (RNI, Rosedene and Raigmore). By the following year, anaesthetists were shared and, from 1944, Raigmore's Richard Murray ran orthopaedic clinics at the RNI. In 1945, the RNI received an X-ray therapy unit for skin diseases from the Department of Health on condition that the facility was shared with Raigmore.

The arrival of the NHS in 1948 allowed coordination of medical services facilitated, from 1952, through the Inverness Hospitals Board although Craig Dunain remained separate. There had been a growing demand for pathological, biochemical and bacteriological services. These were well established at the RNI but it had insufficient space and, in 1949, bacteriology was transferred to Raigmore. The following year, both hospitals shared Eden Court's Nurses' Preliminary Training School.

By 1962, RNI ophthalmology waiting lists were long and, to allow expansion, RNI gynaecology moved to Raigmore (pages 92, 131). However, this displaced some Raigmore surgical patients (paediatric and orthopaedic) who were moved to Culduthel although the surgery still took place at Raigmore - not ideal for children who often had to endure long waits for ambulance transport. By 1962, most specialties were centralised although paediatrics was spread over three hospitals (table below).

From 1970, all laboratory facilities, A & E and nurses' training were centralised at Raigmore as were all the RNI's acute services in 1986. By then, modern medicines had much reduced the incidence of infectious diseases and Raigmore had sufficient capacity to take the remaining cases from Culduthel which closed in 1990. The development of a community hospital at RNI along with other changes finally allowed the Health Board to close the outdated Hilton Hospital in 1987.

Psychiatric services continued to develop separately but the rapid trend towards voluntary rather than committed patients at Craig Dunain meant that their physical ailments, such as infectious diseases were more likely to be treated in the other Inverness Hospitals rather than in Craig Dunain although in-house treatment continued.

Inverness hospital in-patients 1962

	RNI	Raigmore	Hilton	Culduthel
General Surgery	96	49	-	-
Orthopaedic	-	120	-	20
ENT	30	-	-	-
Ophthalmology	28	-	-	-
Paediatrics	10	22	-	20
Sick Cots	-	10	-	-
General Medical	60	113	-	-
Chronic Sick	-	-	80	-
Dermatology	-	8	-	-
Tuberculosis	-	-	-	48
Other Infectious Disease	-	-	-	34
Gynaecology	-	30	-	-
Obstetrics	-	60	-	-
Oral Surgery	-	4	-	-
Total beds	224	416	80	102

Maternity

The development of maternity services in the Inverness area seems to represent a long struggle between child welfare reformers, backed by enabling acts of parliament, and local authorities reluctant to spend money on a service for which they had increasing responsibilities. Although local authorities' laisez faire policies were not confined to maternity, there seemed to be, by modern medical standards, a particular disregard of high infant and maternal death rates which extended well into the 1930s. Edinburgh opened a lying-in hospital[i] in 1793 but the idea was not adopted by Inverness hospital managers. Traditionally, births were at home which was fine where there were no medical complications. Comfortably off families could afford to pay a doctor's fee and, by the 1920s, nursing homes were increasingly used as an alternative to home births. Poor families traditionally relied on local contacts, family and district nurses. The destitute and 'illegitimate births' often had only the Poorhouse. From 1846, the Poorhouse received maternity cases but conditions in Dunbar's Hospital were such that, in 1859, the Inspector of the Poor noted that unmarried mothers refused to enter it even though this meant losing parish support.[278]

The Infirmary was slow to establish maternity facilities. In 1906, it was decided that 'no women requiring lying in were to be admitted'.[279] By 1914, 'difficult' obstetric cases were received but a proposal to form a ward was rejected on the grounds of space and it is not clear how many, if any, patients were actually admitted at that time. Despite some exhortations from groups such as local nursing associations, little subsequent development took place.[ii] In 1923, a proposal to create a

---

[i] Later the Edinburgh Royal Maternity and Simpson Memorial. 'Lying in' was up to several weeks of rest thought to be required after giving birth.

[ii] In 1953, Dr Theo Chalmers recalled 'Maternity cases were admitted into the general surgical wards where difficulty was expected and continued to be so until Dr. Fraser said this was to stop. Most maternity work was done in the patients' homes or in nursing homes.' (courtesy of Dr David Bisset)

maternity ward was turned down in favour of an eye ward and, while a maternity ward is clearly shown in the proposed plan for the new Infirmary in the late 1920s, it somehow never came to pass. In 1932, the hospital appointed an obstetrician, Dr Garden, to receive 'cases of difficult labour' and some attention was given to labour room facilities but the emphasis was gynaecological rather than on obstetrics. Numbers of maternity cases were low and there were just two dedicated maternity beds (table on page 83).

The Notification of Births (Extension) Act and the Midwives (Scotland) Act of 1915 gave local authorities powers to make provision for mothers and children.[i] From 1906, the Burgh had used two jubilee nurses as part time health visitors and, subsequently, volunteers of the British Women's Temperance League. From 1911, it employed its own full time 'lady health visitor' but still gave some support to local maternity and child welfare organisations such as the Bowmont Centre (page 153) and the Northern Counties Infants Home (page 159). In 1922, a modified Child Welfare Scheme unified the work of Inverness volunteer agencies. Throughout this period there seems little evidence of any dialogue with the Infirmary over the issue. This was despite increasing public awareness of the mortality rate in childbirth, both of mothers and infants, and increasing expectation that some action should be taken. The tardiness of Inverness is further emphasised by noting that maternity wards were opened at the Ian Charles Hospital at Grantown-on-Spey in 1923 and at Nairn Town and County in 1933.

The growth of Inverness nursing homes possibly allowed the local authorities to take their collective eye off the ball. By the 1920s, the Ida Merry Home was dedicated to maternity and other homes such as Viewhill and Rossal became prominent providers in the 1930s. In 1934, the MOH thought that their total of 27 maternity beds was sufficient for the area. However, unlike the Infirmary which aimed to serve the poor, they were mainly for the better off who could afford the fees.

---

[i] Local Authorities had to maintain a register of midwives whose qualifications were also regulated by the 1915 Act.

The 1937 Maternity Act and the need to provide for wartime evacuees precipitated urgent action from the Burgh and County by then working together as the Joint Hospitals Board. From late 1937, there were ongoing discussions with the RNI over maternity beds. The local authorities proposed a unit of 20-25 beds linked to the RNI[280] and, by 1938, there was agreement in principle but disagreement over its actual form. The RNI was reluctant to take the initiative, reasoning that the local authorities had taken no action on maternity which was their responsibility and had made no payments to the hospital for treating maternity patients. In 1939, the issue was referred to the Department of Health which, 'due to the extreme urgency of the situation', appointed obstetrician, Dr TN MacGregor to Inverness primarily in the interests of evacuees and effectively to force the local authorities to implement the 1937 Maternity Act. The local authorities thought the RNI was essential for serious maternity cases and wanted Dr McGregor based there. In late 1940, the RNI was quite clear - it had no space for maternity beds, it already had 2 gynaecologists on its staff and it already treated 'abnormal maternity[i] cases'. Meanwhile, in January 1939, Mrs Merry had offered her maternity home to Inverness Burgh and it was thought that it could be run in conjunction with Rosedene but, by mid-1940, negotiations had failed and Rosedene became the sole council run maternity facility.[281]

After this, various events including a dispute over a maternity case sparked off a series of discussions and apparent misunderstandings between the local authorities, Department of Health and the RNI managers. In spring 1941, a meeting between the RNI managers and the Department of Health seemed to link the resumption of the RNI's £5,000 p.a. grant from the Department to the resolution of the maternity issue and, by the end of the year, Dr MacGregor[ii] was appointed to the staff of the RNI and beds were allocated to him. In 1947, the issue was overtaken by the opening of a temporary maternity unit at Raigmore Hospital which later expanded into Highland's main maternity hospital.

---

[i] It treated 94 such cases in 1939 and 86 in 1940.
[ii] He ran monthly clinics at Fort William, Dingwall and Forres as well as twice monthly clinics at Wick and Thurso (Scottish Hospital Survey).

By 1957, Raigmore maternity was oversubscribed whereas units in other Highland hospitals were typically only half full and many were later reduced or closed (table on page 166).

The following pages document the development of each of the establishments concerned with maternity and child welfare in the Inverness area. It begins with a review of nursing homes which have contributed in no small way to this and to other areas of community health care albeit mainly for Inverness' middle class.

Nursing Homes

By 1900, there was an increasing demand for a flexible supply of trained nurses to fill temporary gaps in hospital staff, to work in private homes during family illness or confinement and to assist local authorities deal with fever outbreaks. Inverness had a growing number of private nurses who worked mainly independently. In 1873, only four are listed but, by 1899, this had grown to around 20.[282] By the early 20th century, district nursing associations had been established but there were also privately run nursing institutes often associated with a nursing home. The advent of the National Health Service made many nursing institutes, agencies and associations redundant - certainly in the early 1950s.

After 1900, nursing homes began to appear in Inverness and they filled an important niche in the provision of medical care to the community. The larger ones treated a range of cases and had a labour room, operating theatre and a visiting medical practitioner. Their staff would normally include midwives, fever trained and theatre trained nurses. Around 1940, there were an estimated 12 maternity beds in Inverness nursing homes. As well as maternity and medical cases, some homes offered a range of operations such as tonsillectomies and appendectomies as well as more serious cases such as amputations. After 1948, operations and maternity were largely subsumed into the NHS as was geriatric care and many Inverness homes were closed by the 1950s. It is only in the 21st century that the process has moved full circle with, once again, private nursing homes playing a key role in health care. The following are some of the more prominent early homes in Inverness.

Craigside Nursing Home & Trained Nurses Institute, Craigside Lodge, Gordon Terrace seems to be the first nursing home recorded in Inverness and was opened around 1904. Its Lady Superintendent was Miss Wallace Ross who, by 1910, had transferred the business to nearby **Viewmont Nursing Home & Trained Nurses Institute**, 10 Culduthel Road, which seems to have been the only nursing home in Inverness for the next decade. At the 1911 census, Miss Ross was assisted by a nurse, probationer nurse and two servants. A 1917 survey notes that it normally had a pool of 12 nurses and served the whole of the north.[i] It provided nurses to work in people's homes including maternity and hired out nurses to local authorities and hospitals when required. In 1918, Miss Ross died and Miss J MacFadyen took over and the home seems to have continued as before. In 1923, it had D MacFadyen as its surgeon. Around 1927, it became the **Isobel Fraser Home of Rest** which was run by the Aged Christian Friend Society. Despite having had an extension in 1921, it became overcrowded and moved to a new build, designed by architect Leslie G Thomson, in Mayfield Road where it remains. Costing £10,000, it was opened by Mrs Mackintosh of Mackintosh in August 1938.[283]

Around 1918, Miss J MacFadyen (above) opened **Ness House Nursing Home, 1 Bishops Road**, (now the Highland Hospice). Like Viewmont, Ness House had a nursing agency and, by 1927, had a 'large staff of nurses for outside cases'. However, it seems to have closed the following year when it became the Grosvenor Hotel. In 1935, the building was purchased by the RNI as accommodation for pathologist Dr Kilpatrick and later for Major Paton, Medical Superintendent (page 85).[284]

By 1918, Miss MacFadyen had apparently cornered the Inverness market in nursing home provision. However, around 1920, Mrs Margaret Ross opened the **Yewbank Nursing Home & Association of Trained Nurses** at 24 Southside Road. The association nurses were also hired out as infectious diseases nurses. It had closed by May 1927 when its goodwill was purchased by Viewhill (overleaf).[285]

---

[i] The same survey found 15 private nurses in Inverness, all with maternity training.

Viewhill Nursing Home & Association of Trained Nurses, 1 Old Edinburgh Road, a former girls' school,[i] opened on 1st May 1927 with two listed matrons - Miss Ellis and Miss Hay. Miss Hay seems to have been sole matron in 1930 when she was succeeded by Miss B MacLean. Viewhill ran as a limited company which had around 80 shareholders mainly in Inverness, many of whom were nurses, teachers and unmarried ladies. In August 1929, it acquired the goodwill of Ness House Nursing Association (see page 145). Its staff appear regularly in records of other establishments for example Miss Moodie was appointed matron to the Ida Merry Home in 1930, a nurse was hired to the Mackinnon Memorial Hospital in Skye in 1934 and Nurse Cameron became acting matron at Nairn Fever Hospital in 1935. It carried out operations and, by 1934, had 5 maternity beds. Despite its success, most years it ran at a loss and, in 1937, it closed being up for sale as a dwelling house by the following spring. By 1942, it was a youth hostel. When the home closed, the matron, Miss B MacLean, founded Rossal Nursing Home (opposite).[286]

Also opened in May 1927 was **St Margaret's Nursing Home,** 35 Southside Road which had 12 beds and was run by trained nurses - the four Miss Mackintosh sisters. It received surgical, medical and maternity patients and charged a minimum of 5 guineas per week. Around 1930, an extension was added which contained a new operating theatre. By 1934, it had around 13 bedrooms which included 6 maternity beds. By then there were only three Mackintosh sisters. In early 1947, the remaining two sisters gave up the business and a new matron was appointed – Miss Spalding of the Belford Hospital, Fort William. A new limited company[ii] acquired the home and continued its work. As well as St Margaret's itself, the home also owned Clifton Lodge on Culduthel Road as a nurses' home. In 1949, the company sold this and acquired nearby Glentarff at 33 Southside Road instead. In the year to June 1948, the hospital had 240 patients with an average of nine in-patients. Like other homes, it suffered when the NHS started and, two years later, had only 134 patients (who stayed an average of 17 days). This was not

---

[i] It had been the house of Victorian engineer and writer Joseph Mitchell.
[ii] One of its directors was Dr LMV Mitchell.

financially viable and the company went into voluntary liquidation in July 1950. The property was up for sale later that year and was considered by the Health Board as a nurses' home but the building upgrade costs were thought too high. It is now residential.[287]

In late 1937, **Rossal Nursing Home** Ltd, 31 Island Bank Road, was formed to treat 'maternity, medical, surgical and other cases'. It had five directors and around 20 shareholders. It opened the following March and registered as a maternity home receiving cases from across the Highlands. Miss Barbara MacLean, matron at Viewhill (see opposite), was involved in setting up the company and became matron. However, in 1939, she died suddenly and was succeeded by Miss J Ross. Rossal's facilities seem to have exceeded those found in many small Highland cottage hospitals. It had 18 beds - contained in six single, one 5 bed, one 4 bed and one 3 bed ward – as well as a nursery and labour room. It had an operating theatre with separate anaesthetic and sterilising rooms and a local doctor performed the operations. It had ample staff accommodation including separate staff dining room and sitting room. It is likely to have been adversely affected by the introduction of the NHS and, although it certainly had maternity cases up until 1952, it was up for sale well before then and the company was dissolved in late 1953. The Health Board approved its acquisition as an ENT unit but stood aside to allow Inverness Burgh to purchase it in 1953 as a residential home and it continued as such into the 1980s. The purchase of Rossal allowed the Burgh to move all its ambulant cases out of Muirfield thus freeing up space there for chronic sick cases (page 35).[288]

Willowbank Nursing Home, 11 Island Bank Road, opened around the same time as Rossal and also had Miss B MacLean as matron although it is not mentioned in Rossal's surviving company records. Births there are announced in early 1938 but not thereafter and there seems to be little remaining documentary evidence of its work. It closed around 1944.

The Carrol Medical & Neurasthenic[i] Nursing Home, 29 Island Bank Road, was open by 1936 with matron Helen D Robertson although Miss Robertson soon moved to Calvine (see below) and the home was up for sale by public roup (auction) in April 1938. Miss Jessie Maclennan, now matron, purchased the home for £4,000 and was still matron in 1943. It was described as having 12 beds with staff accommodation and was still active in 1950. In 1958, it was purchased by the Highland Orphanage as a 20 bed children's home and replaced their Culduthel Road premises the following year. By the 1980s, changing social policy away from large institutions substantially reduced resident numbers and, in 1983, it closed and later became a guest house.[289]

Calvine Nursing Home for Medical & Convalescent Patients, 4 Annfield Road ran from 1938 until 1947. The proprietrix was Helen Deane Robertson formerly matron at the Carroll Nursing Home. There is no evidence of it having maternity beds.[290]

There were several other homes which were smaller or for which records are not readily available. In 1934, Mrs Flora Palmer, **93 Church Street** had four maternity beds. Mrs Jeannie Gibb **42 Castle Street** had four maternity beds in 1935 and Mrs Gill, **19 or 11 High Street** registered a maternity home in 1936 which was still operating in 1939.[291] Following the Registration Act of 1938, Miss Ann Kennedy registered **Struan, 14 Ness Bank** as a nursing home as did Miss Morag Maclean at **47 Harrowden Road** for three beds.

It has been reported that **Raigmore House** was a maternity home but no evidence of this can be found. In January 1946, there was much discussion over future provision of maternity beds (page 163) and Dr Russell Martin, local Department of Health officer, noted that Raigmore House 'may be a possibility' and this along with a reference in an architect's file may be the origin of the belief (see photo page 114).

---

[i] An obsolete medical term describing chronic fatigue or ME.

Families Maternity Hospital[i]
Fort George Ardersier 1913

Traditionally, families lived with troops in the barracks at Fort George. There was a military hospital in the Fort (page 105) but no community nurse and, by 1900, as local nursing associations became established, the disparity in family welfare between military and civilian life would have become increasingly apparent.   In 1899, Mrs Douglas Campbell (right),[ii] an officer's wife, visited Fort George and found family medical care  provided by an untrained woman in nearby Ardersier and 'an old doctor whose advice in illness was 'Keep your windows shut' '.

Fort George was the Depot of the Seaforth Highlanders who, in 1906, invited the Soldiers' and Sailors' Families Association (SSFA) to appoint an Alexandra[iii] nursing sister. A SSFA Nursing Committee was formed which Mrs Douglas Campbell chaired until 1910. In 1907, SSFA spent £400 on building a nurse's cottage and, in 1909, the Seaforths held their first Torchlight Tattoo in Inverness to fund a bathroom for it with a second tattoo the following year. The military married quarters were then very basic and the Fort's MO considered them unfit for childbirth. He and Mrs Campbell, with her husband's agreement (he was now Battalion CO), identified a site, drew up plans and persuaded the War Office to provide maternity facilities. In 1912, a Montrose firm erected a two bed maternity hospital costing £800 although, by then, the regiment, and Mrs Campbell, had moved elsewhere.[292]

---

[i] Technically, a nursing home rather than maternity hospital (footnote page 161).
[ii] The Honourable Violet Averil Margaret Vivian, daughter of a baronet married Lt Col Douglas Campbell later Brigadier-General and 20th laird of Douglas of Mains.
[iii] With the RAF in 1918, it became the Soldiers', Sailors' and Airmen's Families Association (SSAFA). It supplied nurses to areas of need with a local commitment to fund raising. Queen Alexandra was SSFA's first president and their nurses, from 1892, were called 'Alexandra Nurses'. Not the same as Queen Alexandra's Imperial Military Nursing Service - the Army Nursing Service from 1902.

The hospital – the only such SSFA facility in Scotland - was situated beside the nurse's cottage outside the ramparts just to the east of the Ravelin Gate Bridge (map page 152). It had its first two cases in July 1913 and, the following year, of the nurse's 72 cases, 28 were maternity. This level of maternity cases continued and, in 1916, SSFA enlarged the hospital to a third bed which was funded by the 'Officers of the Depot'. The above photograph is from around 1917 and shows the original nurse's cottage on the left, the hospital on the right and the connecting 1916 extension behind the central group of figures.

Nurse Hutchinson was in post when the hospital opened but, in 1912, she was posted to Egypt and was succeeded by Nurse Jessie Owen[i] who brought her mother as cook. In 1934, Nurse Owen and her mother retired having delivered 353 babies. Her second delivery, in 1913, had complications and the case went to Nairn Hospital but it is not clear if Nairn or other civilian hospitals were used at other times. Miss Owen seems to have been well regarded, for example, she was guest speaker at the Ida Merry Home AGM in 1930. The picture opposite, from around 1920, shows her with her mother Mrs Bowden[ii] at the hospital.[293]

---

[i] Mrs Campbell was closely involved in recruiting her and said she looked far and wide for someone with special qualities for life at Fort George.
[ii] Mrs Bowden reached 100 years old in 1942. Nurse Owen died in 1948.

During the hospital's first decade, SSAFA gave an annual grant of up to 60% of costs but, by the 1930s, this was normally around 25%. The hospital also apparently received a small government grant. The remainder came from ongoing local fund raising mainly by the Seaforth Highlanders and other regiments stationed at Fort George. From at least the early 1920s, much of the funding came from a large annual fete which continued into the 1930s and 1940s. There were also annual dances in the 1930s.[294]

By the 1930s, it was known as the Garrison Family Hospital. In 1938, a trust formalised an executive committee and confirmed that the hospital was for the wives of soldiers deployed at Fort George, wives of civilians working there,[i] and wives of soldiers from other regiments living locally. In 1939, the trust funds[ii] were transferred to the Seaforth Highlanders Regimental Association and, from then, the committee was entirely made up of officers rather than their wives as had been the case initially.[295]

It seems to have closed during the Second World War but reopened thereafter. After 1949, with services now available from the NHS, SSAFA no longer financially supported the hospital. This prompted renewed local fund raising and a hospital fee was charged although the main funding came from the Depot using profits from the Fort George

---

[i] The local minister's wife gave birth there in 1925 (Scotsman 19 June).
[ii] In 1966, transferred to Seaforth Highlanders Family Welfare Fund in Aberdeen. By then, the Depot was in Aberdeen and the maternity unit had closed.

piggery.[i] In 1954, a fete raised over £1,000. The voluntary committee continued to run the hospital as well as maternity and child welfare clinics. Up to 90 children attended the welfare clinics and there were around 12 births each year but records of births cease after October 1956 when Nurse Wemyss was in post.[ii] The hospital closed in November 1956 although the local authority continued clinics for antenatal and other cases for a time. The hospital then became residential before being demolished around the late 1960s.[296]

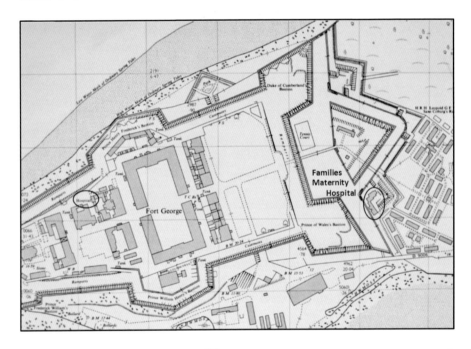

The above plan of Fort George[297] shows the Families Maternity Hospital on the eastern (right) end of the fort (circled). Also on the map is the location of the military hospital (also circled) to the west (left) (see pages 105 and 109).

---

[i] Two pigs were champions at Nairn Show in 1950.
[ii] In post from the 1940s.

Ida Merry Maternity Home and
Bowmont Child Welfare Centre
101 Church Street and Craigmonie, Annfield Road

The Ida Merry Home, unlike other nursing homes in Inverness, was solely for maternity. Mrs Ida Merry of Belladrum[i] (left) was a prominent supporter of health care. She was involved in many local organisations such as a Ladies District Aid Committee to the Infirmary which she set up and chaired in 1911. She was later one of the Infirmary's managers and, in 1918, unsuccessfully petitioned them to support a Child Welfare Centre. Around 1919, she and others purchased and converted a house at 101 Church Street Inverness 'for the purpose of giving advice to mothers about their own and their children's health'. Lady Roxburghe donated £720 through the Children's Jewel Fund[ii] and the Centre was named after her son, Lord Bowmont.[iii] [298]

The Mothers Welcome or Bowmont Child Welfare Centre had 'large numbers of mothers each Tuesday' who, free of charge, consulted local doctor Dr J Mackenzie and presumably the matron who also did home visits.[iv] Matron was a fully qualified nurse and there were one or two probationers. In 1925, there were 15 births in the Centre and, by then, it contained a three bed maternity ward, labour ward and isolation area. The maternity ward cost £4 per fortnight, which was the length of time mothers were expected to stay, although mothers requiring financial

---

[i] Hon. Ida Helen Lizzie Chetwynd (1860-1950) married Archibald Merry, son of James Merry MP a Glasgow industrialist who purchased Belladrum in 1858.

[ii] The Children's Jewel Fund began in London in 1917. Wealthy women donated jewellery for child welfare. When it stopped in 1920 it had raised £700,000. Lady Roxburghe has no obvious Inverness connection and her gift is likely to be the result of a social connection with Mrs Merry.

[iii] Title of the eldest son of the Duke and Duchess of Roxburghe.

[iv] In the mid-1920s she apparently made over 3,000 visits annually.

assistance could have their fees reduced. Cases requiring medical intervention were not admitted and were more likely to use the Infirmary. The facility was for the wives of working men and it seems to have set fees to suit families who would not have been able to afford Inverness nursing homes. [299]

The Centre received a grant from the Scottish Board of Health and, as part of the voluntary scheme of child welfare, received a grant from the Burgh (£60 in 1924). However, that was about to change. There was apparently a power struggle over control of child welfare between the Centre and the Burgh (represented by Dr MacDonald, MOH). The Burgh wanted the Centre to keep records of cases according to the Burgh's format and wanted the Burgh health visitor to attend the Centre weekly to ensure sufficient coordination between her work and that of the Centre, especially the conduct of matron's home visits. The MOH also required to inspect the Centre premises. The Centre had agreed to most of this but communications broke down, apparently over the management of the matron's work, and the Bowmont Centre handed over its child welfare service to Inverness Burgh Council which, in 1926, transferred the service to the Forbes Dispensary (page 189) as part of its

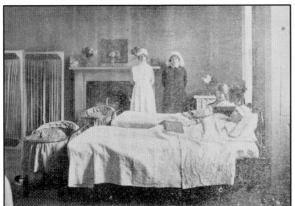

Child Welfare Scheme. The loss of child welfare was a considerable change for the Centre which, in 1923, had actually considered closing its maternity wards to make room for the expanding child welfare. [300]

In early 1925, the Highland Maternity and Child Welfare Union[i] had issued an appeal for funds towards a proposed 12 bed maternity hospital in Inverness. It is not clear if this was intended to be at 101 Church Street but, with the loss of child welfare, the Centre was refurbished, a ward was added and it re-opened as the seven bed Ida Merry Maternity Home (photograph opposite). As before, the Home was for the wives of working men in Inverness. Unmarried mothers were admitted if there was space although it appears that the policy was to keep them apart from married ones. There was a private (single) ward which, at £4 per week, was double the cost of the other ward, but was said to be 'very successful'. By November 1926, there had been 28 cases in the Home

including one unmarried mother and five private patients. Staff consisted of matron, nurse and probationer nurse but demand increased and, around 1930, a midwife was appointed. By then, patients came from as far as Perthshire and Sutherland.[301]

In 1924, the Home had 5 trustees – Mrs Merry and '4 gentlemen' - and was 'managed by a committee of ladies' (there were 11 of them in 1926). There was much fund raising among the small number of subscribers towards a £10,000 endowment fund. While the target seems ambitious, the venture was supported by a large number of prominent people. In 1928, the Duchess of Somerset opened a well-attended fete at Belladrum (to which the Queen sent a gift) and, by August 1929, the endowment fund had reached £4,000.[302]

Given the increasing funds and patient numbers, a larger house was required and, in 1931, the Home[ii] transferred to Craigmonie[iii], Annfield Road which Mr Merry had bought for £2,400, receiving £600 from the

---

[i] Duchess of Sutherland president, Lady Lovat vice president, Mrs Merry treasurer.
[ii] Its former premises at 101 Church Street became a youth hostel in 1932.
[iii] Now the hotel.

155

sale of the Church Street premises. In September 1931, Craigmonie was opened by Lady Bertha Dawkings, Lady in Waiting to the Queen, who delivered the Queen's personal message. The photo on page 155 shows Ida Merry on the left with Lady Dawkins. The number of cases continued to rise (table below) but more cases were sought including those who could afford only a small contribution towards the fees. This suggests a desire to broaden the clientele and partly explains the need for regular fund raising although evidence also suggests that Inverness nursing homes were not very profitable.[303]

The Home was now a much larger establishment which required more maintenance and more staffing. In the mid to late 1930s, there were usually four nurses employed along with matron, maid, cook and gardener. Fund raising was remarkably successful and the Home continued to benefit from the support of those prominent in local affairs. For example, in 1935, an appeal was made by Sir Murdoch Macdonald MP and a garden fete at Belladrum was opened by Mrs Mackintosh of Mackintosh. In 1937, the Home topped the BBC radio appeals. However, despite all this effort, there was an ongoing deficit of over £100 p.a. By 1937, the accumulated deficit was over £600 and Mrs Merry was now in her late 70s which did not bode well for the future development of the Home.[304]

Ida Merry Home number of cases (selected years)

Year	Cases	Notes
1926	28	
1930	56	4 beds are now endowed.
1934	80	Now 10 beds.
1935	89	
1936	116	Cases from Banffshire, Perthshire, Ross-shire & Sutherland.
1937	132	
1939	115	Said to have about half of Inverness confinements.

In January 1939, Mrs Merry, now mainly living in London,[i] offered to transfer the Home to the Burgh. The Burgh[ii] was in difficulties because, as well as fulfilling the 1937 Maternity Act, it had to provide 29 beds for potential wartime evacuees and discussions with the RNI on taking maternity cases were not going well. In August 1939, the Burgh met with Mrs Merry who had 'no objection to accommodation being provided for unmarried mothers at the Ida Merry Home provided they were kept separate from married women.' She also wanted the Burgh to name a ward 'the Ida Merry Ward' in any future Maternity Hospital and that the ward be solely for married women. The Burgh, due to the 'extreme urgency of circumstances', provisionally agreed to take over the Home from 1st October 1939 and subsequent admissions to it were apparently through the Burgh MOH with the aim of a joint administration along with Rosedene Maternity Hospital. However, as well as requiring refurbishment there were difficulties over the Home finances and, as a result, the Burgh pulled out of the negotiations. By then, the Home was £800 in debt and in, August 1940, it was decided to close it until this debt could be cleared. There was considerable local concern since there appeared to be no alternative,[iii] Rosedene being only for serious cases. Local organisations, including the local British Medical Association, appealed to the Burgh and to Mrs Merry who agreed to keep the home open for three months to allow a rescue plan. It continued beyond that but, despite further fund raising, the Home, with a debt of over £2,000, finally closed on 16 December 1941.[305]

Matrons[306]

1925-29	Miss Mackenzie - retires.
1929-31	Miss Moodie – came from Viewhill.
1931-4	Miss Cruickshank.
1934-41	Miss Brydie.

---

[i] She was still a director of the Infirmary in the late 1940s.
[ii] Along with the County.
[iii] The other nursing homes were too expensive for ordinary families.

The Role of Women in the Hospitals of Inverness

To a large extent, women are absent from the early annals of the Inverness Hospitals. Their roles are confined to nursing and housekeeping neither of which was afforded a high status in 19th century Inverness and both roles were subservient to male doctors and managers. No women appear as managers of the Infirmary in the 19th century and Ida Merry is conspicuous as one of the very few women managers in the 20th century although even her influence was not sufficient to persuade the Infirmary managers to develop obstetric facilities. TD Mackenzie's photograph (below) of the Infirmary managers – probably from the 1930s - speaks volumes on the exclusion of women[i] in medicine.[307] This situation is not unique to Inverness. Although Edinburgh University admitted female medical students in 1870, it refused to allow them to graduate and it was not until 1878 that the first women doctor practised in Edinburgh and not until the late 1880s that Scottish universities allowed women to graduate in medicine. The Infirmary did not have its first female house officer until 1917.

In Inverness, a small number of women were influential as managers and entrepreneurs in child welfare and maternity and in establishing nursing homes. While Ida Merry is the most prominent, Miss Wallace Ross (page 145) established what seems to be the first nursing home and others such as Miss J MacFadyen (page 145) and Miss B MacLean (page 146) were worthy successors.

---

[i] There were, however, women GPs in 1920s Inverness such as Dr Janet Fraser (page 160).

Rosedene
2 Drummond Crescent

Rosedene's first use as a care establishment was to look after infants[i] whose mothers could not cope. In 1916, the Scottish Mothers Union[ii] had opened the Northern Counties Infant Home at 106 Castle Street under a matron with Dr John Macdonald MOH as honorary medical officer. It accommodated six infants up to one year old and was staffed by young girls being trained in child care. It received a grant from the Burgh and charged 5/- per week, admitting patients free where they could not pay. The training of girls was quite formal and, by the 1930s, the Rosedene School of Nursing was advertising training sessions costing £20 with quarterly intakes. It noted that most trainees obtained posts on leaving.[308] Demand was high and, around 1918, it moved to larger premises in the Old College[iii] in Ardross Street. By the early 1920s, the home had 12 babies and five girl trainees in child care.

---

[i] The Highland Orphanage opened in 1882/93 at 71 Culduthel Road. In the early 20 th century it contained around 70 children. It did not admit infants.

[ii] Formed in 1889, it was mainly Episcopalian and Church of Scotland mothers.

[iii] Now Highland Council HQ, the Northern Counties Collegiate College opened in 1873 and in 1921 became the Inverness Royal Academy War Memorial Hostel.

The Home required more space and the situation was solved when Mrs Frances Lilian Day of Hilton House donated Rosedene as a memorial to her own daughters and, in 1923, the new home was opened by Lady Mackenzie of Gairloch for 20 infants. It was normally quite full. In 1928, 7 came from Ross and Cromarty, 2 from Sutherland, 2 from Moray, 3 from Inverness-shire and 6 from Inverness and, by the 1930s, it had up to nine staff. The local authority gave an annual grant and councillors sat on its committee. Honorary physician was Dr Janet Fraser. Children usually left around 3 or 4 years old to return home or to be adopted. In 1939, its capacity was 25 children accommodating 22 on average and it had assets of just over £3,000. By then, it was known as the Rosedene Baby Home.[309] The photograph above from 1930 shows Matron, Mrs Maclennan, with the entire staff, trainees and infants.

In 1940, progress was halted when, due to wartime needs, Rosedene was requisitioned as a maternity hospital and leased to the Inverness Burgh and County Joint Hospital Board on a yearly basis at £150 p.a. with the proviso that it be returned to the Trustees a year after the war ended. At that point, the children had to return home or be adopted.[310]

In 1939, Dr TN MacGregor, obstetrician, and MOH Dr Fraser, arranged the conversion of Rosedene to a 16 bed maternity hospital with delivery room and operating theatre. It cost around £1,000, partly met by the Department of Health. Rosedene received its first patient on 15ᵗʰ March 1940 and, in May, was formally opened by Lady Hermione Cameron of Lochiel. It was Highland's first maternity hospital and was reserved for 'difficult or abnormal cases of confinement' requiring 'highly specialised medical or surgical aid' thus complementing rather than supplanting local nursing homesⁱ such as Rossal and St Margaret's.[311] Patients, who were charged 3 guineas per week, came from the Northern Counties and Moray & Nairn. The Inverness Joint Hospital Board initially thought that, along with the Ida Merry Home, it would provide 'adequate maternity services for the whole of the North of Scotland' which says much about local authority thinking and public expectation at the time.[312]

The layout of the building was difficult. Clinics and administration were on the ground floor and the four small wards were on the upper floors. A former nurse recalls 'We had no lift and this meant we had to carry women up and down stairs on stretchers.' The operating theatre was also used as an infants' nursery. Heating was by open fire and laundry was sent out. It was staffed by matron and 4 midwives during the day and 2 at night. There were 4 domestic staff. Staff lived in but accommodation was 'cramped and unsatisfactory'. Matron and sisters had attic rooms and others small cubicles. Later some staff stayed at the RNI.[313]

Dr MacGregor was based at Rosedene initially and immediately set up out-patients clinics which, by 1941, had at least 100 attendees per month. The following year, gynaecological clinics started at the RNI and Raigmore which also had antenatal clinics. There were 352 admissions in the first year and numbers grew quickly. On average, 13 beds were occupied but, at times, there were up to 20 patients and such levels continued throughout the 1940s. Around 75% of cases were from Inverness Burgh and County.[314]

ⁱ A maternity hospital differed from a maternity home in the degree of medical services and staffing available. However, the distinction may be more apparent than real. Some nursing homes – like maternity hospitals - had surgical facilities with trained staff and surgeons on call.

By late 1940, the hospital was full being too small for the rising demand and some patients were sent to the Ida Merry Home but, by 1941, it was running down. Other nursing homes were approached and attempts were made to acquire additional accommodation including Carrol Nursing Home, Eden Court and Ach an Eas, then occupied by the army, but to no avail. Eventually, by mid-1946, there was an arrangement with Rossal Nursing Home to take local authority maternity cases.

When the War ended, the Rosedene trustees affirmed their intention to sell it. This prompted urgent discussions with the Department of Health which resulted in the conversion of one ward at Raigmore into maternity (page 163). In 1946, a new build at Eden Court had been recommended but, in 1951, further Raigmore Maternity Wards were converted and Rosedene patients were transferred there in mid-April.[315]

Rosedene Matrons[316]

1940	Miss M Doull.
1940-9	Miss Isabella Nixon.
1949-51	Miss Campbell. Transfers to Raigmore with patients.

Despite requiring substantial upgrading, the health board considered Rosedene as a nurses' home and also as their HQ before returning it to its Trustees in 1952.[i] The photograph on page 159 dates from around this time. The 1948 Children's Act had made local authorities responsible for any child who could not be cared for by its parents and Rosedene was purchased by Inverness County and opened in 1953 as the Northern Counties Children's Home accommodating 30 children from both the Burgh and County.[ii] In 1968, it was taken over by the newly formed Social Work Department and continued as a children's home until the early 1980s, later becoming a women's refuge, a business centre and now a spa and dental clinic.

---

[i] Rosedene funds were apparently split equally between the Infirmary, Orphanage, Isobel Fraser Homes, Forbes Dispensary and Queen's Nursing Association. In 1952, the Forbes Dispensary Trust was anticipating its share of the residue of Rosedene.
[ii] Until then, children were still being placed, albeit infrequently, in Muirfield.

Raigmore Maternity Hospital
1947

The Inverness local authorities had dragged their feet over providing for maternity in terms of the 1937 Act (page 142) and, as a result, the need to provide for evacuees and the rising demand for hospital births caused somewhat of a panic. As early as November 1940, the Joint Hospital Board was in discussion with the Department of Health on providing additional maternity beds which, in January 1942, they agreed to make available at Raigmore provided the local authorities agreed to costs of converting existing wards. This they did but arrangements dragged on.

The lease for Rosedene Maternity hospital ran out in 1947 and the lack of maternity facilities elsewhere in Inverness was extremely concerning. In mid-1945, the Department of Health noted the need to create 45 maternity beds at Raigmore and, in May 1946, the Secretary of State consented and detailed plans were drawn up to convert four wards. The possibility of a purpose-built new maternity hospital at either Eden Court (owned by the RNI) or Raigmore was also explored but, in the immediate post war, there was not the capital, materials or manpower available. The cost of converting the Raigmore wards was estimated at £45,000 as against £100,000 for a new hospital and the Raigmore wards were thought to have a life of 20-30 years. Accommodation for additional nursing and domestic staff was required and the RAF Camp huts at Raigmore House (photo on page 115) were considered but never used.[i]

By mid-1946, the Rosedene trustees wished to sell their building as soon as possible and the Department of Health put its 4 ward conversion on hold in favour of converting only one ward (the original isolation ward) which was faster and cheaper at around £1,000. Meanwhile, further concern was caused by the temporary closure of St Margaret's Nursing Home (page 146) leaving Rossal as the only maternity home in Inverness. Rosedene was now handling over 50 cases per month and, in May 1947,

---

[i] There were nine timber huts and 12 Nissen huts. Nissen huts were tunnel-shaped and made of corrugated iron with a cement floor.

 the Inverness Joint Hospital Board cancelled the arrangement with other local authorities to send patients there.

On 5 September 1947, the Raigmore 12 bed maternity unit opened, receiving its first case from Grantown-on-Spey. In these pre NHS days, there was a charge for a maternity stay in hospital. The Department of Health set its charges based on the costs of developing Raigmore which worked out at 15% higher than for Rosedene. Therefore, local authorities[i] and doctors tended to avoid the Raigmore unit so that it averaged only 14 cases per month initially although this later increased. After much debate, the Department reduced its rates but, by then, the introduction of the NHS was imminent and the issue was swept aside. Maternity was not, of course, new to Raigmore. By 1942, Raigmore's female surgical ward (Ward 6) was admitting antenatal and gynaecological cases and, in 1943, there were around 160 gynaecological operations.[317]

However, the issue of Rosedene's imminent closure remained and more facilities were required for the post war baby boom. In January 1949, the conversion of four wards at Raigmore began[ii] and, in March 1951, they were opened by Dr TN MacGregor former consultant obstetrician.[iii] The photograph above was taken at the opening. Dr MacGregor is centre flanked by Raigmore's Matron McBride and Miss Campbell, head of the maternity unit.

---

[i] Ross and Cromarty did not participate and used the maternity unit at the Ross Memorial Hospital, Dingwall.
[ii] This was a major development for Raigmore being about 25% of the existing beds. However, at the time the hospital had at least that amount of spare capacity.
[iii] He had moved to Edinburgh in 1946.

There were 50 beds in wards of 1, 2 and 4 beds which contrasted with the traditional Nightingale layout of

the rest of the hospital. It included sitting rooms and a premature baby unit[i] described as 'impressive' at the time which had 7 rooms for mothers. Rosedene closed and its matron, Miss Campbell, took over the new facilities as superintendent midwife. Raigmore (photograph above) was quite a contrast to Rosedene and one sister did her ward rounds with the aid of a bicycle. The first baby born, in April 1951, was Ian, son of Mrs Campbell of Spean Bridge (photograph below) who received a silver cup from Miss Campbell. Raigmore's catchment area was the North of Scotland and, by 1955, it had around 1200 deliveries p.a. Ante and post-natal clinics were held twice weekly.[318]

By 1956, the unit had 2 part time consultants, 1 senior registrar, 2 house surgeons, 26 nursing staff and 18 domestic staff. Compared with

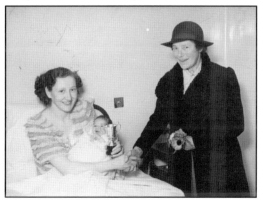

Rosedene's 11 nursing staff and 18 beds of a decade previously, maternity provision had indeed been transformed. By the mid-1950s, Raigmore dominated maternity provision in Highland in occupancy as well as capacity. Other centres were usually less than half full whereas

[i] A new 'special baby care unit' with 20 cots was opened in March 1977.

Raigmore was normally oversubscribed. As the table below shows, Highland had many small maternity units in the early 1940s. All the outdated former poorhouse labour wards were closed by 1948. Other centres were expanded but the growing recognition of the benefits of nearby emergency facilities prompted centralisation. In May 1988, the maternity wards became the last major facility to move out of Old Raigmore into a new maternity unit which allowed the health board to re-designate all remaining maternity beds in Dingwall, Nairn and Grantown-on-Spey hospitals leaving maternity facilities at four centres - Inverness, Lochaber, Skye and Caithness.

Maternity capacity (number of beds) in Highland before and after the NHS
(comparing 1941 and 1957)

Hospital	1941	1957	Note
Raigmore, Inverness	-	50	
Ross Mem. Dingwall	3	17	Maternity stopped in 1990.
Henderson, Wick	8	10	Closed 1978. Cases to Dunbar Hospital, Thurso and Caithness General, Wick.
John Martin, Uig	7	9	Closed 1965. Cases to the new Portree and Broadford Hospitals.
Town & County, Nairn			Maternity stopped 1991.
Dunbar, Thurso	3	6	Maternity to Caithness General in 1986.
Pope, Helmsdale	-	4	Closed 1938-49 and from 1977.
Ian Charles, Grantown	(5)	(5)	Not part of Highland until 1976. Maternity ceased 1987.
Rosedene, Inverness	16	-	Closed 1951.
Cromarty	8	-	Underused. Closed 1953.
Muirfield, Inverness	2	-	Former poorhouse. Later Hilton.
Arthurville, Tain	2	-	Former poorhouse.
Ness House, Fortrose	4	-	Former poorhouse.
Swordale, Bonar Bridge	2	-	Former poorhouse. Now Migdale.
T&C Home, Latheron	2	-	Former poorhouse.
Total	62	101	
In 1965, the new Belford Hospital opened with 20 maternity beds.			

Infectious Diseases Hospitals

Infectious diseases have been around since time immemorial and the need for an isolation facility, such as for leprosy,[i] had been apparent for many years. As Inverness grew in size, diseases such as typhoid which originated from poor living conditions and inadequate sanitation became more apparent as did the potential for transmitting other diseases such as smallpox. Indeed, conditions in Inverness were especially poor. A survey of 1842 found an unusually large number of destitute many of whom lived in low, damp, poorly drained houses beside the river, many with middens in the back yard and some with animals such as pigs the house. The survey quotes Dr John Nicol (page 199) who wrote:-

'The people (of Inverness) are, generally speaking, a nice people, but their sufferance of nastiness is past endurance. Contagious fever is seldom or ever absent; but for many years it has seldom been rife in its pestiferous influence. The people owe this more to the kindness of Almighty God than to any means taken or observed for its prevention. There are very few houses in town which can boast of either water-closet or privy; and only two or three public privies in the better part of the place exist for the great bulk of the inhabitants. Hence there is not a street, lane, or approach to it that is not disgustingly defiled at all times, so much so as to render the whole place an absolute nuisance. The midden is the chief object of the humble; and though enough of water for purposes of cleanliness may be had by little trouble, still the ablutions are seldom – muck indoors and out of doors must be their portion. When cholera prevailed in Inverness, it was more fatal than in almost any other town of its population in Britain.'[319]

There seems to have been no attempt to form a fever facility in Inverness before the nineteenth century and, after 1804, the fever wards of the new Infirmary were thought to be sufficient. However, the arrival

---

[i] There appears to be no documentary evidence of any leper hospital in the Highlands but there continues a tradition of there being a facility at Bruchnain between Clachnaharry and Bunchrew between the 13th and 15th centuries. The disease died out and the last indigenous Scottish case, from Shetland, was recorded in 1798.

of Asiatic cholera in 1832 caused a rethink. Not only was this a highly transmittable and deadly disease, it affected all classes regardless of living standards including those of the Inverness establishment. The 1834 epidemic forced the Burgh to consider specific accommodation (page 18) and, after the formation of parochial boards in 1845, there was an increasing expectation that they and the Burgh would take action against such outbreaks.[320] There was, however, no immediate action on emergency hospital provision. The cholera outbreak of 1849 appears to have been relatively easily contained, the Burgh seems to have been fairly impoverished at this time and rural parishes generally did not have the resources. The area had, of course the fever wards of the Infirmary which surprisingly was still admitting smallpox cases in the 1870s although never cholera cases.

However, in August 1866, three 'well known and respected' Inverness citizens died suddenly apparently of cholera and this sparked off a period of intense activity during the remainder of 1866. A subsequent meeting of the Public Health Committee identified a storehouse at the harbour as a potential hospital but, after receiving a petition against it, the site was rejected as being too close to everyday commerce. The suggestion of using a wing of the Infirmary was also rejected, the main reasons being that it would discourage people from attending the hospital and the potentially harmful effluent would enter the river too high up in its course. Later, the possible use of a ward in the Poorhouse at Muirfield was also dropped. Instead, a cholera hospital was started on a site at Capel Inch[i] near the harbour and it may indeed have been used. However, it was abandoned after a petition against it received 300 signatures. It was thought to be too close to houses, Merkinch School,[ii] a drying green and a public road.[321] There then seems to have been a lull in proceedings for the next decade until premises became available at the Citadel.

---

[i] Capel Inch is the area of foreshore which lies between the railway bridge and Thornbush Quay on the west side of the river i.e. opposite the Citadel. At the time, much of it – from Madras Street downstream was backed by fields.
[ii] Merkinch School then sat next the river at the end of Madras Street.

The Citadel (Common) Hospital
1877

By the mid-19th century, the Burgh owned a range of storehouses at the Citadel. One was occupied by a hemp (rope) factory which, along with others, was destroyed by fire in 1865.[322] However, the nearby Artillery Volunteers drill hall[i] escaped and this building became vacant when, in 1873, the Volunteers opened a larger hall in Margaret Street (now part of the Spectrum Centre). In 1874, the Infirmary signalled its intention to stop taking smallpox cases given the risk of infection spreading in the hospital[ii] and a meeting between the Burgh and the Parish occurred soon after when the Citadel was apparently first suggested as a site.

In 1877, the old drill hall was converted into the Citadel Isolation Hospital for cholera and smallpox patients. It was virtually rebuilt. Its three original storeys were reduced to two, the walls being reduced in height from 20 to 12 feet, and it received a new slated roof. Its interior walls were re-lined and there were new windows, new doors and two new fireplaces. A separate block containing wash house, coal cellar and

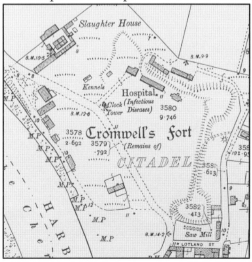

'dead house' (mortuary) were added. The architects were Matthews and Lawrie and it cost over £800.[323] The harbour location allowed the local authority to meet the ever present danger of infectious disease brought by visiting ships. The hospital is clearly shown on the 1902 OS map (left) with what appears to be the wash house block on its right.

---

[i] Possibly part of the original barracks of Cromwell's Fort (Macdonald 1919).
[ii] The 1867 Public Health Act had encouraged local authorities to make provision.

The hospital is also shown on the photograph above[324] which dates from around 1890. Cromwell's Tower[i] is on the extreme left, the large building on the right is the harbour master's office and, behind it, protruding to the left of the central sycamore tree, is the Citadel Hospital. It had two 6 bed wards, a nurses' sitting room and a kitchen. The loft above was unused. There are few records of the hospital's use in the 19th century. In 1881, two nurses were employed when a smallpox case was removed from a ship. In 1892, during a cholera scare the Burgh agreed that any cases of cholera in soldiers from the Cameron Barracks could be admitted if required and a decade later agreed that they could erect tents nearby if the hospital could not accommodate all the patients. This was never required.[325]

It was always difficult to staff small emergency fever hospitals since both the need for and supply of nurses were unpredictable. Like some other isolation hospitals, it had a resident caretaker.[ii] In 1891, it was Annie

---

[i] Mid-18th century and not part of the original Cromwell's fort.
[ii] As part of their contract, caretakers could be expected to immediately vacate the premises in the event of a fever case and to assist with caring for the patient.

Gould, who appears to have been 75 years old at the time and who died there around 1902. She was later described as having been a 'very pawky' lady who was there for a long time. The post continued until the facility was more intensively used.[326]

In 1893, local solicitor James Mitchell returned from London and died of smallpox the following week. Although his household was isolated in the Citadel, an outbreak was feared and the Burgh ordered the erection of a second building to be used as a reception for smallpox contacts. It was a 70 x 18 feet (21 x 5.5m) wooden and corrugated iron building with two wards, each with 5 or 6 beds,[i] and a small kitchen. It appears to be the building shown to the left of the original hospital on the map on page 169. After 1900, smallpox and cholera declined although the danger was still present. In 1904, a seaman with smallpox from a visiting ship infected a local groom who, with his family, was treated at the Citadel.[327]

Improving national standards required local authorities to provide suitable disinfection and, in 1902, a pressure steam disinfector was constructed near the hospital and a van provided to transport clothes and bedding – all at a cost of nearly £600.[ii] The disinfector was in constant use not only by the Burgh but by others such as nearby Districts and the Military Hospital at Cameron Barracks. It was still in use in 1940 and, until then, had bedding transported by a horse ambulance which was housed at Falconer's Garage on Tomnahurich Street.[328]

The Infirmary fever wards were often under pressure and, from 1904, the Citadel was available for overspill of scarlet fever and diphtheria cases. It is not clear how often it was used for this but, in 1911, a scarlet fever case certainly went there when the Infirmary refused her, not apparently because of her illness, but because she was heavily pregnant.

---

[i] In 1918, it had 3 beds in each ward.
[ii] The MOH noted that this did not obviate the Infirmary from having a suitable one. Its poor disinfection was an ongoing issue for its fever wards (see also page 61).

In 1908, the MOH reported that both the cholera and smallpox hospitals[i] were in good order[ii] and could be opened at short notice. From then, the Citadel appears to have been used more often. The government had been exhorting local authorities to have emergency isolation facilities and, from 1908, the Aird District of the County was allowed the use of 3 beds. In 1911, a request from Nairn to access the facilities was refused.

The 1911 census, lists a nurse, caretaker and one patient but patient numbers expanded when, in 1912, the original building was fitted out for advanced cases of phthisis[iii] and Nurse Roy from the Infirmary was appointed matron.[iv] A second nurse was appointed soon after and there was a porter and maid. The wooden building became nurses' accommodation. From 1913, tenders were put out for supplying the hospital with food and fuel which suggests regular use. By 1914, it had a telephone and, in early 1915, it upgraded its bedding and screens.

In the first 6 months of this new TB facility, it treated 14 patients of whom six died and it continued with normally around five beds occupied although numbers varied from 0 - 9. By 1915, it was receiving cases from as far away as Skye. In 1916, it was approved for national insurance purposes[v] for 14 beds although the MOH noted it had only six beds in each of its two wards. Using one of the buildings for nurses' accommodation reduced flexibility but one ward was used at times for cerebro-spinal meningitis and, in March 1916, it was given over to cases of measles, and later mumps and chickenpox, from the naval base at Invergordon. By then, and until 1920, a ward at the Poorhouse was also used for TB (see also page 29).[329]

The opening of Culduthel Hospital in 1917 reduced the need for the Citadel and, by then, the building required refurbishment to the extent

---

[i] By then, the wooden building was for cholera and the original one for smallpox.
[ii] Although it seems that the wooden building did not have piped water until 1912.
[iii] Possibly in response to the National Insurance Act of 1911 (see page 193).
[iv] The matron post also incorporated Culduthel when it opened (see page 187).
[v] This indicates it had reached a certain national standard.

that the Navy, in need of fever facilities, decided not to use it. The need to ensure immediately available isolation facilities for cholera and smallpox was reaffirmed nationally and, from early 1919, the hospital reverted to its original purpose and TB cases ceased.[i] Nursing staff were no longer required although the wooden building continued to be set aside (but unused) as staff accommodation until at least 1930. A caretaker was appointed although attempts to secure a residential one failed. In the 1920s, it seems to have been little used. In the mid-1920s, a 'tinkers camp' sprang up nearby and was allowed to remain provided it moved if the hospital was occupied. Given the logistics of this, it was probably thought unlikely that the hospital would be required.[330]

In early 1929, an inspection by local and national officials considered it unsuitable for scarlet fever and diphtheria and it was not used in the fever outbreaks of 1928-29 when Culduthel Hospital was severely pressurised. It was thought to be suitable if the building was reconditioned but its redundancy at this point is confirmed by the fact that it did not come under the new Inverness Joint Hospitals Board but was retained by the Burgh which continued essential maintenance. In 1934, the MOH wrote, enigmatically, that 'The Smallpox Hospital at the Citadel, consisting of 12 beds, is quite suitable for the area for which it has to cater'. However, in July 1937, it closed and the caretaker was given notice. The Joint Hospital Board purchased bedsteads and other materials from the Burgh for £2 for use in Muirfield. In February 1938, the Scottish Youth Hostel Association tried, but failed, to purchase it and the Burgh continued to maintain the building. From late 1937, it was used for air raid training in preparation for war and, in October 1940, it was agreed to use it to store petrol. By requisition, it was let for £21 p.a. to the Air Ministry in April 1941 and, after the War, it was used to kipper (cure) herring. It was demolished sometime in the late 1940s and evidence suggests that the second building[ii] was also demolished at the same time.[331]

---

[i] By then, Culduthel was open (page 175).
[ii] A contributor to Inverness Our Story remembers acquiring corrugated iron from the building close to the old fever hospital.

The Evolution of Infectious Diseases Legislation

Infectious diseases hospitals mainly evolved through local authorities having to respond to successive legislation. Below are listed some of the key Acts of Parliament and how Inverness local authorities responded.

	Act of Parliament	Inverness
1832	Cholera (Scotland) Act enabled the Privy Council to make orders for the prevention of cholera. Powers lapsed after 1834.	Dunbar's Hospital was set aside to treat cholera victims.
1866	Circular from Board of Supervision on dangers of cholera. Precipitated need for local authorities to make hospital provision.	Discussions began which led to the Citadel Hospital.
1889	Infectious Disease (Notification) Act led to Local Authorities needing to provide fever hospital accommodation. In Highland, only Inverness and Wick had separate fever hospitals before this. Ross shire used the Ross Memorial Hospital.	Much negotiation between Northern Infirmary and Inverness Burgh on payment for treating infectious diseases.
1897	Public Health Scotland Act confirmed local authorities as responsible for public health and empowered them to provide infectious diseases hospital accommodation and to employ nurses to nurse people in their own homes. It increased the powers of the Local Government Board (LGB).	LGB was increasingly critical of the Northern Infirmary fever wards. Eventually Inverness Burgh purchased Culduthel House.
1906	Local Government Board Circular made pulmonary tuberculosis (TB) an Infectious Diseases.	Northern Infirmary and (later) the Northern Asylum each constructed a TB sanatorium.

Culduthel Hospital
1917

Culduthel House restored (photograph 2013)

By 1900, the Infirmary fever wards which had served the Burgh and County well (page 60) were unable to keep up with increasing national standards and were seen as too small. The Burgh also needed access to a larger sanatorium for tuberculosis cases[i] and, by 1912, it seemed to be moving towards partnership with the County over the use of Invergarry Sanatorium but this fell through.[332]

By early 1914, the Burgh and the nearby County Districts had plans drawn up for a new joint infectious diseases hospital (page 62-3). However, in March, the Burgh agreed to purchase Culduthel House[ii] from JP Grant of Rothiemurchus.[333] By early 1915, tenders were being received for adapting the main house and for erecting in the grounds three pavilion blocks for scarlet fever, diphtheria and typhoid. Each

---

[i] The only available local facility was the Infirmary and the Citadel (page 61, 172)
[ii] Culduthel House was built in the 1780s. The Burgh paid £3,000 for it.

block had two wards and together totalled 39 beds (photograph below). At this point, because of an outbreak of measles amongst Inverness troops, the mansion house was being considered for use for emergency military cases but this seems not to have happened.

By late 1915, the hospital was nearly complete but it did not open until Christmas Eve 1917. By the following February, all Burgh patients[i] had been transferred from the Infirmary Fever Wards and were later joined by County[ii] patients.[334] Culduthel was administered by the Burgh and the County contributed 40% of the standing charges. Craig Dunain had its own separate fever and TB facilities (page 221, 223-4).

In early 1919, MOH Dr MacDonald described Culduthel as having an isolation hospital and sanatorium and indeed it seems that phthisis cases were removed there from the Infirmary. However, it is not clear where

---

[i] A former patient recalled being transferred from Culduthel to the RNI fever wards suggesting a period of flexible use of both facilities (Inverness Our Story Bk 1).
[ii] Just from the nearest 2 Districts. Badenoch and Strathspey continued to use Meadowside near Kincraig and Lochaber used the Belford Fever Hospital

they were accommodated and it was not until January 1923 that a separate 24 bed phthisis pavilion (photograph below) costing £10,000 was opened by the Provost Petrie.[i] It had central heating and also had eight cots. By 1924, a considerable number of children were in the TB wards and concern was expressed about their education. A sand pit was constructed for them in 1925. The pavilion was the standard design for the period. There was a central nurses' block and two wings. The wards straddled the block allowing a through flow of fresh air in all weathers - part of the treatment for tuberculosis at the time. The veranda was also to provide sheltered fresh air treatment but it had no awning until at least 1927. There was also no covered walkway[ii] from the kitchens in the main building which made delivery of hot meals problematic.

---

[i] This brought accommodation to 63 beds for the remainder of the 1920s.
[ii] Although the local authority appeared to approve it in 1922 it was never built.

In 1927, electric lighting replaced gas and, in 1929, central heating was installed in the three original pavilions. That year, the fever ambulance,[i] based at the hospital, was replaced (the other St Andrews ambulance was at the Infirmary). Although it had a small laboratory by the 1930s, Culduthel continued to use the RNI's laboratory and radiology facilities and subsequently relied on Raigmore for similar services.[335]

Culduthel Hospital cases 1923-28

	1923	1924	1925	1926	1928
Scarlet Fever	29	82	37	103	104
Diphtheria	27	12	11	29	245
Tuberculosis	54	42	46	64	41
Measles	-	50	12	2	-
German Measles	-	-	-	14	-
Erysipelas	2	1	4	10	-
Puerperal Fever	2	1	-	4	1
Typhoid	2	4	6	7	4
Others*	5	1	9	7	-
Total cases	121	193	125	240	395
In hospital at 31 Dec.	25	33	34	38	84
*mumps, neonatal conjunctivitis, chickenpox, meningitis, pneumonia					

Scarlet fever and diphtheria cases dominated (table above) and, indeed, from 1918-1928, the hospital treated 456 cases of scarlet fever and 640 of diphtheria. Isolation was the main requirement in most cases but many homes could not provide this and hospitalisation was essential in preventing epidemics. Medicines such as antibiotics which we now take for granted had yet to be discovered and this meant long stays in hospital while the body healed itself. In 1924, the average stay was 47 days for scarlet fever, 36 days for diphtheria, 21 days for measles and 108 days for tuberculosis. The hospital's accommodation was thus utilised for a relatively small number of cases by modern standards. Patients must have had a long, monotonous stay but this was relieved slightly in 1927 when two wireless sets were gifted.

---

[i] A horse ambulance was used until 1921.

The number of cases varied greatly (table opposite). 1928 was particularly challenging with outbreaks of both diphtheria and scarlet fever. At one point, the hospital accommodated 67 cases of scarlet fever. Later, there were 40 cases of diphtheria - double the capacity of its 20 bed diphtheria pavilion - and four nurses and a maid became infected. Towards the end of the year, the number of cases in the hospital rose to 97 and further admissions were refused.[i] It was clear that more accommodation was required and that the hospital needed to be able to treat a range of infectious diseases without tying up a whole ward for a single case as often happened e.g. meningitis. Even so, cross infection continued - patients with diphtheria caught scarlet fever and vice versa. This had been a problem in the Infirmary fever wards a decade earlier. Two 10 bed wooden cubicle wards were planned but the Department of Health suggested a larger permanent capacity and eventually, in October 1937, Lady Hermione Cameron opened the £12,000, two storey, 24 bed cubicle block with operating theatre[ii] (photograph above). The operating theatre reduced the need to send patients to the RNI[iii] for surgery.[336]

---

[i] There was no alternative and patients would have had to be treated at home.
[ii] Initially, it appears to have been infrequently (used 9 times in 1938). By 1970, it was used only for endoscopy.
[iii] In the 1920s, the Infirmary had eight beds for TB surgery but there was much demand. Patients frequently died on the long waiting list (MOH AR).

By the mid-1930s, the original pavilions had been expanded to 56 beds and these, along with the 24 bed cubicle block and 24 bed sanatorium, brought hospital capacity to 104 beds. The map below shows the layout of the hospital which was set in extensive wooded grounds.

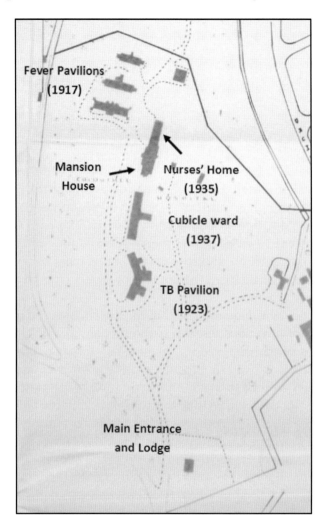

The 1929 Local Government Act abolished district councils and Inverness County Council became a unified health authority. Along with the new Town Council it formed a Joint Hospital Board thus paving the way for centralising the treatment of infectious diseases across mainland Inverness-shire at Culduthel. It also combined the county and burgh MOH posts but created a new assistant MOH whose post included the medical supervision of Culduthel and Muirfield hospitals. Existing medical officials competed for fewer posts and, in 1930, Dr LMV Mitchell, Culduthel medical superintendent from the start of the hospital, lost out to Dr Broadfoot. From at least 1943, Culduthel also had a resident medical officer (see table page 187).

**Location of treatment of
Inverness TB cases 1934-35**[337]

Hospital	%
Culduthel	50
RNI (surgical cases)	33
Invergarry Sanatorium	6
Elsewhere	4
Seaforth Sanatorium	3
Grampian Sanatorium	3
Invergordon Hospital	2

The centralisation of infectious diseases treatment at Culduthel can be illustrated by the TB figures. As the table above shows, half were treated at Culduthel and surprisingly few were treated at the 20 bed County facility at Invergarry. The Grampian Sanatorium (later St Vincent's Hospital) at Kingussie was privately owned and Invergordon was Ross and Cromarty's fever hospital. The Seaforth at Maryburgh was for child and youth sufferers. 'Elsewhere' includes mainly city specialist facilities including Robroyston and Mearnskirk in Glasgow and Southfield in Edinburgh. The figures do not include patients at Craig Dunain which had its own sanatorium (page 221).

In comparison with some other hospitals, Culduthel seems to have been fairly well staffed from the outset. The census of 1921 shows 12 staff and nine patients.   As capacity and patient numbers increased so did staff.   By the early 1930s, staff consisted of matron, 3 sisters, 3 fever trained staff nurses and 11 probationer nurses and, by 1938, there were an additional 4 staff nurses.   In 1938, all but two of the nursing and the 12 domestic staff lived in.   Initially, staff accommodation was in the mansion house which, in 1928, was supplemented by a six bed wooden building to accommodate the additional staff required during outbreaks of scarlet fever and diphtheria.   Both buildings were thought inadequate and, in 1935, an 11 bed extension to the mansion house was opened costing just over £1,600.   In 1941, tenders were sought for a nurses' home extension which was finally completed in 1947 costing about £13,000 – twice the original estimate.[338]   The nurses' home is attached to the left of the mansion house in the photo below which dates from around 1965. There was a training programme for nurses from the 1930s but, by the late 1940s, there were few qualifying. This, and the lack of support for students, for example no tutor sister, resulted in the hospital losing its separate training status in the early 1950s (see also page 90).

The hospital kitchen was located in the basement of the mansion house and, by 1938, its replacement was seen as urgent. The hospital's heating was also well below standard but neither of these were substantially improved until the late 1940s. In the early 1950s, a new staff dining room was built.

In the 1930s, the range of diseases treated at Culduthel increased as shown in the table below (compare it with that on page 178), the cubicle block being essential in facilitating this diversity by helping combat cross infection. Patient numbers continued to be variable. Scarlet fever remained by far the most common and came in a series of epidemics. TB cases were also high and these became more dominant in the 1940s and early 1950s as other diseases abated. Puerperal fever (infection of the uterus around childbirth) is now very uncommon as is erysipelas (a skin infection). Typhoid cases, which had necessitated a separate pavilion in 1915, had become relatively rare by the 1930s as domestic housing conditions generally improved. In 1939, Dr Fraser MOH assessed that around 30% of Culduthel's total case load was children.

Culduthel Hospital
Main infectious diseases cases 1930s (selected years)

	1934	1935	1936	1938
Scarlet Fever	304	225	319	216
Tuberculosis	62	69	73	63
Measles	59	25	11	21
Diphtheria	8	7	15	38
Erysipelas	9	16	15	14
Pneumonia	1	12	13	11
Puerperal Fever	7	12	12	7
Tonsillitis	0	16	1	10
Typhoid	3	5	7	1
Others*	8	18	2	0
Total cases	461	405	468	381
In hospital at 31 Dec.	69	51	76	38

* conjunctivitis, cerebro spinal fever, nephritis, eczema, laryngitis pediculosis, dysentery, septic abortion, meningitis, polio.

In April 1939, a survey of hospital facilities in Inverness Town and County found a serious deficit in hospital beds especially for geriatric and maternity cases. Neither the Burgh nor the County had been proactive in establishing maternity beds (see page 141) and the wards at Muirfield, the only geriatric facility, had for years been overcrowded and under-resourced (see page 30-31). It was also thought that Culduthel required more TB beds.[i] The Culduthel site had around 30 acres - ample room for expansion - and it was planned that it would take geriatric cases from Muirfield and also become the area's maternity hospital. The hospital board plan provided for an additional 60 'sick poor' (geriatric) beds to replace those at Muirfield[ii], 40 TB beds (thus doubling capacity), 30 orthopaedic[iii] beds, 30 maternity beds and an additional 70 staff beds. These developments would create a hospital of over 200 beds and around 100 nursing and domestic staff, about the same size as the RNI. However, the start of war delayed the plans and, in 1941, Raigmore was opened with a potential capacity of 600 beds so that the Culduthel expansion was not required.[339]

TB beds in Highland 1950

Hospital	Capacity	Staffed*
Culduthel	24	24
Invergarry	26	11
County, Invergordon	64	44
Cambusavie, Sutherland	12	8
Town & County, Wick	10	9
Craig Dunain	34	34
Grampian Sanatorium, Kingussie	30	30
Total	200 beds	160 beds

*Post-war nursing shortages prevented some wards from opening.

---

[i] A later survey considered that there were ample in Highland.
[ii] Muirfield's official capacity was 40 sick beds but often had over 60 in-patients so that wards were frequently overcrowded (page 33).
[iii] There was no orthopaedic at the RNI.

Dermatology ward from 1969

In 1949, Dr E A Johnston, medical superintendent, had a regional remit for TB and, in 1950, he surveyed Highland's capacity for treating it (table opposite).[340] TB was still a major concern and cases had continued to rise after the Second World War. Fresh air was still part of the treatment with outdoor shelters in people's homes but, by the mid-1950s, new antibiotics including streptomycin drastically reduced the number of sufferers. Culduthel's TB capacity had not changed since the 1920s but it remained full unlike some other centres where the post-war shortage of nurses reduced capacity. Invergarry was seriously outdated and about to close. Patients went outwith the area to access more specialist treatment or where there was insufficient capacity locally and it was common for TB sufferers to go to hospitals in the cities especially if a relative lived there.[i] The Grampian Sanatorium at Kingussie continued to be privately run but the NHS paid for 30 beds.

---

[i] In 1934, a government survey noted that in the Highlands 'TB is regarded as a scourge to be feared and a stigma to be concealed'.

In the 1960s, as infectious disease and TB declined,[i] other medical wards were created. In 1962, as part of a local reorganisation (page 139), the children's surgical ward transferred from Raigmore to Ward 1 (nearest building in the photo on page 176). In 1975, its capacity was 16 beds and four cots spread across two wards. A play area was fenced off outside. The children had to attend Raigmore for procedures and ambulance journeys often caused delays and discomfort. In 1969, dermatology was transferred from Raigmore to the 12 bed Ward 6 (photograph page 185) and later that year severe pressure on Hilton Hospital forced the formation of a geriatric ward of 20 beds at Culduthel.

Culduthel Hospital bed capacity in the 1960s[341]

	1962	1966	1969
Orthopaedic	-	20	20
Non Respiratory TB[ii]	5	5	-
Respiratory TB	63	43	15
Infectious Diseases	34	34	15
Dermatology	-	-	12
Geriatric Long Stay	-	-	20
Chest Complaints (not TB)	-	-	20
Total	102	102	102

In the 1980s, the expansion of Raigmore Hospital allowed all acute beds to be transferred from the RNI which, in 1987, received long-stay geriatric patients from Culduthel. Infectious diseases were now so reduced that they could be accommodated in the new chest unit at Raigmore as could all other Culduthel cases. Therefore, Culduthel Hospital closed on 2nd September 1989. The site was subsequently cleared of all wards leaving only the original mansion house as residential accommodation and the surrounding large site for new housing.[342]

---

[i] In the first half of 20th century, apart from TB, infectious diseases declined steadily probably due to improved social conditions and health care as much as to inoculation and, later, antibiotics.
[ii] TB affected all parts of the body especially bones. These cases had been previously treated in Raigmore (see pages 125-6).

Matrons[343]

From early 1915, the post of matron at the Citadel incorporated Culduthel. In 1914, Citadel Matron, Miss JJ Roy, was called up and Miss Asher became Acting Matron. In 1917, Miss Roy resigned, having never worked in Culduthel. Miss Asher was therefore in charge from the opening of the hospital.

Dates	Matron	Notes
1917-40	Miss AM Asher	Retired.
1940-45	Miss Mary Catto	From Aberdeen.
1945-49	Miss SL MacDonald	
1949-66	Miss ED Noble	Assistant from 1944. Retired.
1966	Miss MT Hadden	

Medical Superintendents[344]

1917-30	LMV Mitchell	
1930-4	J Broadfoot	Had been in practice at Dingwall.
1934-41	Dr EA Johnston	Moved to Raigmore (page 122).
1941-3	Dr EA Mills	
1943-50	Dr EA Johnston	In 1950, the post was combined with other Inverness hospitals.

Early Resident Medical Officers (where known)[345]

1941-3	Alice Mackenzie	Called up for war service.
1943	Dr Cecil Bell	
1944-5	Dr Hilda Broda	
1945-?	Dr JE Tillotson	
1947	Dr Melville	
1948-50	Dr Ray Penny	Left to be married.
1948	Dr GK Mackenzie	

Auchbain Farmhouse
Daviot
1893

In the early 1890s, the Highland Railway Company built the railway line between Carrbridge and Inverness. There was much fear that disease would break out amongst the many navvies employed and, in 1893, Mackintosh of Mackintosh made a small farmhouse at Auchbain[i] available to the county as a smallpox hospital. In 1893, it was furnished, had a caretaker appointed and was ready for use. It had two wards each with two beds and staff quarters but, like many similar establishments elsewhere, there is no evidence of it ever being used. It continued to be maintained as a temporary smallpox hospital until at least 1900. From the early 20th century, the County districts next to Inverness relied on the Burgh's Citadel hospital for cases of smallpox, cholera and plague which were very rare.[346]

---

[i] Close to the present A9 just south of Daviot.

The Inverness (Forbes) Dispensary
Huntly Street 1832

Scotland's first dispensary, the Edinburgh Royal Public Dispensary, opened in 1776 and, by the 1830s, several Scottish towns had one in place. In October 1832, the Committee for the Interests of the Poor on the Green of Muirtown opened a Dispensary at 44 Huntly Street[i] which became very important to the health care of the poorer people of Inverness having made over 100,000 treatments by 1925. The Dispensary was 'for bestowing medicines gratuitously to the sick poor' and also targeted those such as tradesmen and labourers who risked destitution when they fell ill. It carried out vaccinations and minor operations. It also received donations of food and other necessities which it distributed to impoverished families.

When the Dispensary opened, it employed a 'resident porter/attendant'. His job was to assist a local medical practitioner who carried out regular surgeries and home visits and gave his services free of charge.[ii] The attendant also dispensed medicines. By 1836, there was an assistant

---

[i] Street numbers changed over the years - it is listed as at 37 Huntly St in the Inverness Directory of 1873. It seems to be the same site as today.
[ii] An honorarium was usually granted.

porter but this post may not have continued. In 1837, a paid medical attendant was appointed but seems to have been discontinued in the 1840s because of funding difficulties.

There was a large initial demand. In the first year there were 1159 treatments of which 27% were visited at home and 28% were surgical. Over 60% of the patients were female and, interestingly, only 14% were over 60 years old perhaps reflecting the relative short life expectancy of the poor at this time. 34 children were inoculated with cowpox[i] and this level continued for many years. The Dispensary opened in time for the first cholera outbreak (that same year) and it was later said to have taken 'the principal charge of the medical arrangements' during the 1834 outbreak. Then, it had 30 dispensers of medicine at 16 stations across the Burgh and was open day and night[ii] for 8 weeks during the outbreak. It treated 533 cholera sufferers of which 47 died.[347]

The Dispensary was initially managed by a committee of 15 subscribers, three taken from each of five districts the idea being that they would know the potential clients and be able to recommend them for treatment as well as be a focus for collecting subscriptions and donations. This system of collection seems to have only lasted for a few years at most although it was revived several times without much success. The management structure also seems to have changed and, by 1840, the local MP was patron, a senior minister was president and all the councillors, magistrates, clergy etc. of the Burgh were managers. In 1843, there was a committee of 32 although it appears that, after a few years, few attended the AGMs which were very small gatherings. This lack of interest extended elsewhere, for example, the clergy seemed unable most years to persuade their congregations to donate.

After the Dispensary opened, the out-patient dispensary service at the Infirmary reduced considerably (page 50). Like voluntary hospitals elsewhere, the Infirmary welcomed this development which reduced

---

[i] An early vaccine against smallpox.
[ii] From the start there was an on-call service at night.

their expenditure. At the first AGM, the Dispensary managers stressed that they were not in competition with the Infirmary[i] which was too far away from most of the potential clients of the Dispensary especially in winter.[ii]   Over the years, the Dispensary promoters were careful to regularly highlight its distinct contribution to the health of the Burgh – unlike the Infirmary it had a drop-in facility and made home visits. Later, the promoters stressed the financial saving to the Parochial Board of helping to combat pauperism.   However, this did not prevent some unfavourable comparison with the Infirmary from some members of the Burgh council over the years.[348]

It is apparent that, in the stratified society of 19th century Inverness, the Dispensary dealt with many cases which would not have been considered by the Infirmary. However, the potential funding came from the class which would not have required the Dispensary's services and, even with the nominal support of the Burgh establishment, it was hard to secure funding in the 1840s. For a number of years, the Dispensary was on the point of closing. It accumulated debts, meetings were poorly attended and the collection system broke down. Eventually, in 1849 (the same year as the return of cholera), the Burgh rallied. Subscriptions and donations were collected including substantial church collections which put the Dispensary on a more even keel from then on although there were still some financial difficulties in the 1850s. Unlike the Infirmary where ongoing medical advances were costly to implement, the Dispensary's facilities and staffing were essentially stable and remained that way.

Initially, the Dispensary rented its accommodation but, by the 1860s, it was seeking new premises. The accounts showed a surplus and, in 1861, a donation of £500 provided sufficient funds for a new building. In 1868, the new Dispensary was built apparently on the same site which had also been recently occupied by Mr Whyte, photographer. Architects were Matthews and Lawrie and contractors were Anderson - builders from

---

[i] The Dispensary regularly referred patients to the Infirmary.
[ii] Unlike the Infirmary, the Dispensary confined its work to the Burgh and Parish.

Grantown, Mackenzie - carpenter, Russell - slater, MacKay - plumber, Cameron – plasterer and Ross – painter. The consulting rooms were on the ground floor with the resident attendant's flat above. It cost £700 and was funded entirely by subscriptions and donations.[349]

Out-patient numbers	
1835	1,642
1841	418
1848	476
1854	474
1860	558
1864	626
1870	973
1873	930
1892	2,517
1894	3,642
1895	3,418
1898	2,200
1900	1,942
1904	1,433
1906	1,703
1910	1,861
1913	1,774
1920	1,644
1923	950
1929	787

In 1880, Dr George Geddes Forbes[i] endowed £6,000 to the Dispensary on condition that it be named the Forbes Dispensary in recognition that the Dispensary had been 'founded chiefly' by Dr Forbes' brother, William Welsh Forbes.[ii] The endowment was to pay for qualified medical staffing and Alexander Mitchell,[iii] pharmacist from Portree, was appointed resident dispenser. Until then, the resident dispenser was not required to have any medical qualification although, by the mid-1860s, a knowledge of dispensing medicines was required along with the ability to speak Gaelic and someone with a military background continued to be preferred. The position of a local doctor as honorary medical attendant continued (table page 195) but it seems that an honorarium was now paid (£100 in 1880) and there was often a competitive annual election for medical officer. Under Dr Forbes' endowment conditions, a trust was formed with the Inverness Provost, four bailies, the local MP and the minister of the West Church as trustees. There was provision for six trustees elected from the contributors but, after a time, none put themselves forward. From then on, the Dispensary seems to have been largely financially secure although it continued to receive voluntary donations.[350]

---

[i] Surgeon Major Forbes of Millburn (died 1881) served in the Bombay Army and also donated the Forbes Memorial Fountain on Ness Bank to the Town.
[ii] Highly praised for his work during the cholera of 1834. In 1855, his MD dissertation was on Asiatic cholera. He was a Burgh magistrate and died in 1864.
[iii] He had gone bankrupt in 1877 possibly the reason for the move to Inverness.

As the table opposite shows, out-patient numbers declined in the 1840s but had increased to around 12 per week by the 1860s. Thereafter, they rose fairly quickly reaching a peak of well over 70 per week by the mid-1890s although numbers then fell away - a trend apparent across Scotland. After the 1912 Insurance Act, the number of patients reduced as many were referred to their panel doctors[i] and the number of vaccinations had declined in common with elsewhere. However, there were still many uninsured people - women, children and the poor - many of whom presented with diseases of a 'serious and urgent nature'.[351]

The main work of the Dispensary continued as before but it began to increase its facilities and range of treatments. In 1904, of the 1433 cases, 495 (34%) received medicines as recommended by the patient's doctor. The rest were treated directly by the resident dispenser. In 1912, 75% of patients were seen by the medical attendant who also made over 800 home visits in cases of 'grave illness'.[352]

The range of treatments at the Dispensary increased. From at least 1909, J Allan operated a dental service making around 200 extractions p.a. From 1911, it housed the Burgh's new TB dispensary[ii] with Dr LMV Mitchell, the authority's TB officer, in charge and, from then, he was also the Dispensary's medical attendant. In 1896, Dr J Wilson Black opened an eye dispensary[iii] in the Old Free North Manse at 99 and 103 Church Street which, in 1912, he transferred to the Forbes Dispensary. That year, he treated 255 cases. From 1913, Dr. J W Mackenzie ran an ENT clinic (table page 195). These developments would have put the premises under some pressure and, in 1913, an extension was added with a surgery, dark room, patients' toilet and additional rooms to the dwelling house.[353] Co-operation with other agencies continued. The Infirmary allowed the

---

[i] The Act provided medical benefit to all employed persons and voluntary contributors earning less than £160 p.a. (but not their families). It was supervised by Scottish Insurance Commission and administered by local committees which maintained a list (panel) of doctors to whom insured people were allocated.
[ii] They paid the Dispensary £50 p.a.
[iii] From at least 1900, the Dispensary had provided eye lotions for many patients attending Dr Black's eye dispensary.

free use of its electrical room for examining patients. In 1912, over 90 child cases were sent to the School Board[i] authorities for action and twenty eye clinic patients were referred to the Infirmary for treatment. The medical attendant worked closely with the Burgh's two jubilee nurses[ii] who, in 1913 and on his recommendation, made over 1800 home visits to serious cases - making daily visits to some.[354]

In 1926, the Burgh's child welfare centre was moved from the Bowmont Centre to the Dispensary[iii] (page 154) and was formally opened by Provost MacEwan. It occupied two rooms each afternoon when the Dispenser was off duty. By 1934, the clinics received over 50 mothers and over 60 infants per week and the premises were seen as too small by the MOH who wanted a purpose built centre but this did not happen and, by 1940, it was very overcrowded.[355]

In 1948, the new NHS brought in free prescriptions for all and, the following year, the trustees approached the new health board. They noted that the Dispensary had been superseded by the NHS - indeed they stated that no one at all had attended after 5th July 1948, the day the NHS started. They sought assistance to convert it to a convalescent home for Inverness and stated that Isobel Fraser Home managers had agreed to run it alongside their own. However, the Board's architects estimated it would cost £8,000 to convert it and would produce a maximum of eight beds which was not cost effective. The scheme was abandoned and, in 1953, the trust was changed to allow its resources of around £14,000 to form the still active Dr Forbes Trust which provides grants to local people towards the cost of medical treatment and equipment, convalescence, food, clothing and travel expenses to visit sick relatives. In 1955, the building was sold by public roup (auction) to the Red Cross which vacated it in 2014. It continues as offices and is still called Forbes House.[356]

---

[i] The 1908 Education Act required local authorities to medically inspect all school children. The 1913 Act required the authorities to also treat them.

[ii] The Dispensary supplied them with bandages & medicine from at least 1904.

[iii] It seems that the Burgh health visitor had already been located at the Dispensary for some years.

Medical Attendants[357]
Post holders are shown where known but the record is incomplete.

1832	Dr Rankin (until 1833) and William Welsh Forbes (until 1837).
1837	Daniel Cormick appointed first paid medical attendant at £25pa.
1837-41	Possibly has a paid medical attendant. Dr Thomas Mackintosh and William Fraser, medical student, are mentioned in 1840.
1843	Dr Chisholm, Dr Manford and Dr MacDonald.
1844	Dr Chisholm and Dr Manford.
1858-54	Dr Walker.
1854-	Dr James G Mackenzie.
1850s-64	Dr ?William Welsh Forbes. Likely to have been frequently MO.
1864 - 7	Dr Campbell (died 1867).
1868	Dr Stewart.
1873-6	Dr Clark.
1876	Dr DF Mackenzie.
1891	Dr Wilson Black.
1894	Dr Lang.
1899-1911	Dr John MacDonald and Dr Lang essentially alternate years.
1911-40s	Dr LMV Mitchell.[i]
1917-19	Dr FM Mackenzie (LMV Mitchell at war).

Additional specialist Medical Attendants[358]

1909-22	J Allan, Dentist	Later at RNI.
1912-27	J Wilson Black Physician, Eye Diseases	Also at RNI.
1913-27	John W Mackenzie ENT	Also at RNI.

Resident Dispensers[359]

1836-62	Hugh MacRae	Resident porter/ attendant (died 1862).
?-1869-81-?	Sergeant Henry Ferrier	Resident porter/ attendant.
1884-89	Alexander Mitchell	Died in 1889 at Dispensary.
1889-10	James A Mitchell	Son of Alexander. 17 years old in 1889.
1908-38	Anna B Mitchell	Sister of the above.
1938-45-?	Jeanette J Petrie	Daughter of former Provost.

---

[i] Dr LMV Mitchell OBE was the son of Alexander Mitchell resident dispenser to the Forbes Dispensary. He lived at the Forbes Dispensary and ran the Burgh TB Dispensary from there. See also page 80.

The Stone Bridge over the Ness

This sketch by Alexander Ross shows the old bridge over the River Ness which was swept away by a flood in 1849. It had a cell which was said to have incarcerated 'lunatics' but not apparently after 1780 and it is not known if there was any other such local facility until the cells in the Northern Infirmary were occupied from 1804.[360]

Mental Health[i]

Prior to the 19th century, the treatment of mental illness among the poor in Highland, in common with much of Scotland, does not seem to have been very enlightened. Society coped with those who were able to be usefully employed but was less skilled in dealing with those who required special help, especially where they were subject to violent outburst, and some form of incarceration was usually employed including a cell built into the old bridge of Inverness (opposite). From the 18th century a number of Royal Asylums were opened for the wealthier, the first in Scotland being at Montrose in 1781 followed by Aberdeen in 1800. There were a further five all of which did much to influence the treatment of the mentally ill. Scotland's first public asylum for the poor opened in Edinburgh in 1807.

In the 18th century, the voluntary hospital movement made some effort to provide for mental illness. In 1733, the projecting wings of the Town's Hospital in Glasgow had 'lunatic cells'[ii] and, later, basement cells.[361] In 1804, the Northern Infirmary was, therefore, following recognised practice when the managers claimed that '*A Lunatic Asylum is attached with accommodation for twenty but constructed in such a manner that it is not exposed to contagion from the Hospital, nor can it interfere with the quiet comfort of the patients*[iii] *in the Infirmary*.[362] This rather exaggerated the capacity of the Infirmary's two wings each of which had four vaulted cells (each 8 feet square) and a keeper's room. The second storey had three additional rooms but they appear not to have been used initially for the mentally ill (plan page 40). In February 1805, the cells were furnished and one female and two male patients were admitted. Initial numbers were low and only 21 were

---

[i] The terminology to describe mental illness evolved over time. *Lunatic* was a general term for anyone disabled by mental health. *Maniac* normally signified deranged behaviour but in the 19th century the Infirmary managers interchanged the term with *lunatic*. In terms of mental disability, *idiot* described the most disabled with *imbecile* and *moron* describing less disabled conditions. It is a complex area which we have not delved into here.

[ii] As had Aberdeen and Edinburgh Infirmaries in 1742 and 1748 respectively.

[iii] Disturbance from the basement cells had been a problem in the Town's Hospital.

admitted between 1804 and 1809 although it later increased (table page 201).[363] Initially, the gardener/porter was in charge of the mentally ill but later a specific 'keeper' was appointed.

In 1820, at the Infirmary managers' request, Dr Nicol,[i] medical attendant, reported on the treatment of mentally ill patients (picture opposite). He considered the cells unsuitable for treating the mentally ill and noted that the original intention of the cells had been merely to house those who also required medical treatment, although this was no longer the practice. In contrast to the sane in-patients, record keeping of mental cases was irregular with basic information such as admission and discharge dates omitted. In some cases the patient's full name was unknown. Dr Nicol compiled a record of patients going back to 1805 and it was noted separately that, from 1805-20, 162 'maniacs' had been admitted of which 108 were cured or relieved and 6 had died.[364] Details of earlier years were sketchy but, after 1812, there were between 9 and 24 patients admitted each year. In 1817-18, most stayed no more than two months although about 20% remained over nine months. Dr Nicol found that there was no systematic assessment on admission and no treatment according to needs. Those who could were allowed to wander in the grounds and through the building, many often ending up in the kitchen. He was particularly critical of the lunatic keeper whom he said was coarse mannered, frequently absent and who confined some patients to their cells for long periods which Dr Nicol considered injurious to health.[ii] He noted that the cells were sometimes overcrowded, smoky and inadequately heated and when they were being cleaned there was no alternative accommodation for patients.[iii]

Old attitudes to the incarceration of the mentally ill had been changing and, around this time, it was a national issue. In 1814, there had been a

---

[i] A relative of William Inglis, John Nicol (1788-1849) was born at Teawig. An Inverness doctor from 1812 and Provost (1840-3), he promoted public health (page 167). He farmed and owned Holm (woollen) Mills, on the Ness. He died of cholera while treating sufferers. His marble bust, made for the Infirmary, is now in Inverness Town House.

[ii] While it is tempting to be critical of the conditions in the Infirmary cells they were apparently much superior to some other parts of the country and better than some described by the Royal Commission which preceded the Lunacy Act of 1857.

[iii] Dr Nicol's views were progressive at the time and followed those of Jean Esquirol in Paris – a pioneer in the humane management of insanity cases.

failed parliamentary bill to establish district asylums at Inverness Aberdeen, Glasgow and Edinburgh. In 1815, a law was introduced to licence and medically inspect 'madhouses'[i] and, from 1814-16, there was a government survey of provision for the mentally ill.

In 1818, there was further local discussion on establishing a separate asylum which may have prompted the Infirmary managers concerns.[ii] Dr Nicol's report gives an impassioned and reasoned account of the humane treatment of mentally ill patients which he said should be within a structured 'family' setting, with differentiation according to their need, and appropriate activities. He showed why the treatment of lunatics in the Infirmary and the accommodation for them, solely in a cell, was quite inadequate. He also noted that the sexes were not differentiated and that there was no female attendant for the women patients.[365]

The Infirmary managers seem to have tried to rectify the situation although they would have been severely constrained by the building design. Later that year, they advertised for a man *and* a woman to 'manage the insane department' who had to have a 'temperate and gentle disposition'. From then, the 'keeper of lunatics' seems to have had a female assistant. The Infirmary regulations of 1830 note that the keeper of the insane must show the 'greatest kindness and forbearance'. He must not 'tamper with the feelings of the patients' and not show the 'least resentment when their paroxysm lead them to personal violence and abuse'. He had to have a nurse in attendance when dealing with the personal needs of female patients.[366]

From early on, there were concerns about maintenance for lunatics in the Infirmary and there were frequent cases where those recommending them for treatment were not willing to accept responsibility for the cost of their care. Later, lunatics were not admitted without a bond of 5/- per week, payable in advance, and there had to be someone to receive

---

[i] The term used for establishments which boarded the mentally ill or disabled.
[ii] Or indeed it may have been the managers who were promoting the need for a separate facility as they later did in the 1830s.

Northern Infirmary lunatic in-patients

Year	Admitted	In-pat. on 1st Jan.
1817	12	6
1822	7	8
1825	23	13
1827	27	na
1832	12	12
1835	14	8
1838	11	5
1842	9	8
1844	12	9
1846	na	15
1847	24	14
1850	18	1
1859	9	0
1863	2	1

them on their release should they be discharged not fully well.[i]

The legal aspects of detaining the mentally ill gradually evolved. In 1815, an Act of Parliament had required the signature of two doctors to detain a sufferer. Although this did not apply to hospitals, the notion seems to have spread and, by 1830, the Infirmary required a certificate of insanity before admission. From 1841, sheriffs had the power to order the detention of lunatics and the Infirmary secured its first such order in 1842. Thereafter, this became common practice.

By 1857, when members of the Lunatic Commission visited, the intention was merely to hold cases until they could be sent to southern asylums although residents could be detained for up to six months. It was also normal practice[ii] to confine 'dangerous lunatics' in the Infirmary cells rather than in prison and the Commission thought that this was worse for the individual since their subsequent removal to an asylum took longer – the sheriff confining them apparently taking little subsequent interest in their case. By 1858, only premises licensed by the Lunacy Commission were allowed to accept patients and the Infirmary was not licensed, neither were sheriffs granting warrants. However, as the table above shows, there were still patients held until 1863.

---

[i] There was a similar issue with incurable patients, particularly when, as often happened, patients were referred on behalf of the parish by the kirk minister.

[ii] It may have been the practice for many years. In the Inverness area, it was the only alternative to police cells for disruptive cases.

By the late 1850s, the Infirmary facilities seem to have deteriorated and resembled the situation in the early 1800s. In 1857, the Lunacy Commission found only four cells in each wing, two at the front and two at the back separated off from the rest of the hospital by strong doors. The cells were stone vaults with wooden floors but no heating. The windows were boarded up leaving a gap of about 3 inches at the top to let in light. The rear cell windows had no glass so the gap also let in air unless a hatch was fitted from the outside. In winter the occupant had, therefore, the option (but not the choice) of cold or darkness. The only other ventilation came through holes in the cell doors. There was no provision for washing or sanitation in the block. Each cell had a wooden trough bed with chains to restrain occupants if required. In each of the connecting buildings there was an additional room with two beds which were also used as day rooms for quieter patients. The porter/cell keeper had little time to give to the cell occupants many of whom, therefore, received very little exercise the reason being also that there were no enclosed airing courts. Although a nurse would go with him to attend to female patients, the cell keeper kept the keys to the female as well as the male cells, an issue which had been raised by Dr Nicol in 1820.

In 1836, the Infirmary cells had been extended (page 49) but managers continued to advocate a separate facility. In 1843, Inverness County set up a sub-committee of prominent land owners, chaired by Lord Lovat, to promote the erection of a Royal Northern Asylum at Inverness for 'poor[i] lunatics'. By 1845, there were around 250 subscribers[ii] from across the Highlands and funds amounted to £4,700.[367] In July 1845, the asylum committee convener wrote to potential subscribers stating that 'the erection of the building was in the course of being proceeded with'.[368] This seems to have been over optimistic. In 1846, there was some friction between Inverness Burgh and the committee although this was apparently later resolved. Finding a site was initially problematic but, by July 1849, an outline plan for a 'lunatic asylum' on a 2.5 acre site at Charleston to the west of Inverness was produced. However, later that

---

[i] This contrasted with the existing Royal Asylums which were fee paying.
[ii] Including Dr Nicol (page 199).

year, essential support from the Lord Advocate was withdrawn and, anticipating the development of state funded institutions, the scheme was abandoned and subscriptions[i] repaid.[369]

Meanwhile, disquiet about the lack of facilities continued. By 1845, the Infirmary cells had been full for some time and, in 1847, the managers, conscious for some years of the cells' inadequacies, decided to admit only short stay cases and move existing longer term cases elsewhere. The new parochial boards had to ensure care of 'pauper lunatics' within an asylum where necessary and the lack of Infirmary cells meant that more cases had to be sent to asylums in the south which was expensive. The size of the problem is illustrated by the situation in 1857 when the Northern Counties had 373 'pauper lunatics' over 70% of whom stayed with relatives[ii] or were boarded out. Five resided in local poorhouses but the rest went to Lowland asylums or licenced 'madhouses' - the journey and the location being an ordeal for them. The problem would have been almost insurmountable within the funds available at the time if Highland families had not been so assiduous in caring for their relatives at home.[370]

Representations to parliament continued to be made – especially by the Inverness Parochial Board but, by then, there was growing demand nationally for action. In 1855, the famous Miss Dix visited from America and helped promote the setting up[iii] of the Lunacy Inquiry which eventually led to the 1857 Act and to the building of district asylums.[371]

---

[i] An agreement of 1848 stated that should the Asylum scheme collapse, the funds would go to the Infirmary which eventually received over £700.

[ii] The 1857 Lunacy Commission noted the 'Highland peasantry' tried hard to care for a mentally ill relative at home. Perhaps unfairly, they ascribed this humanitarian quality to superstition (sending them away brought bad luck). They thought local authorities exploited this by underpaying maintenance. They also found a continuing belief in traditional cures including immersion in St Fillan's well at Loch Earn.

[iii] Dorothea Lynde Dix, an American campaigner for improved treated of mental health, is credited with helping to establish the first mental asylums in the USA. She is often credited as a prime mover in Scotland but, by the time she visited, there had been Scottish debate for many years including an influential book – *What Asylums Were, Are and Ought to be* - in 1837 by Dr WAF Browne (page 205).

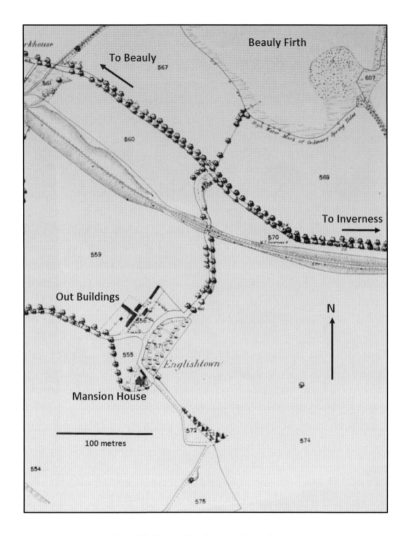

Englishton Asylum, Bunchrew

The map above of Englishton (photo on opposite page) is from the 1872 Ordnance Survey with the shores of the Beauly Firth shown to the north.[372]

Englishton House Asylum 1859

The promoters of an Inverness Royal Asylum had been unsuccessful but a non-state institution was indeed established, if rather late in the day. In May 1859, Mr William Hyslop,[i] former head attendant at Perth Asylum, leased Englishton House[ii] near Bunchrew and, in June, opened a private open asylum there for 23 male and 18 female patients using the accommodation of the mansion and the surrounding cottages.[iii] Dr WAF Browne,[iv] Commissioner in Lunacy, described it as an example of a village asylum, *'where many acres of muir have been reclaimed, where a group of houses and huts, situated on pleasant slopes and amid gardens overlooking the Beauly Firth, accommodate some thirty or forty husbandmen, who, with no other bonds, nor*

---

[i] Born 1830 in Southwick, Dumfries and studied mental health under WAF Browne at Crichton and evidently followed his teachings (see below).
[ii] 18th century house owned by Lord Lovat. Occupied by General Wade in 1720.
[iii] Rising demand saw a number of such establishments across Scotland averaging around 25 patients. Many had a poor reputation (Hamilton, The Healers).
[iv] WAF Browne was medical superintendent at Montrose Royal Asylum and then at the new Crichton Royal Hospital from 1838. In 1857, he became Scotland's first Commissioner of Lunacy.

walls, nor restriction than the will of the governor, have made a large corner of desert to blossom like the rose'. Indeed the liberty allowed to the patients was 'well in excess of that offered in similar establishments'.[373]

The mansion house held the female patients, the Hyslop family and the kitchen and laundry. Male patients lived in a converted cottage and barn. Later, another cottage was added. The cottages and barn (map page 204) were thatched and were upgraded with wooden floors, windows and stoves. Dampness was frequently a problem and dormitories could become overcrowded but, improvements to the accommodation were made and, by March 1864, the capacity had increased to 66.

The opening of Englishton allowed local patients to be transferred back from distant asylums such as at Musselburgh and Montrose and this had started by mid-1859. In June 1860, 18 of the patients were paupers from Inverness parish and the 1861 census shows 20 male and 23 female patients of working class origins with a preponderance of labourers and servants. The patients' ages ranged fairly evenly from 15 – 68 years old with females slightly younger. A large proportion of the male patients worked outdoors. There was a large walled garden and, by 1862, 5 acres were under cultivation with a large number of pigs, 2 cows, 2 horses and a number of pets – 2 foxes, a goat, a roe deer, a lamb and several cats and dogs. Other patients worked in the house.[374]

Staffing levels were consistently well above average consisting of Mr and Mrs Hyslop and at least two male and two female attendants along with two female domestic servants who also acted as attendants. Staff were described as supervisors rather than 'keepers'. At several points, discharged patients stayed on as general servants but this practice was frowned on by the Lunacy Board. The eight staff listed at the 1861 census included a carpenter/attendant.[375]

The work of the Asylum and the skill of Mr Hyslop in 'normalising' his patients received widespread commendation. Many were surprised at how well the patients presented, especially at social events which were regularly held in the Asylum.[i] Most patients spoke English and Gaelic and although the Hyslops had no Gaelic most of the attendants had. Patients came from across the Highlands but predominantly from Inverness and Ross and Cromarty. Most were pauper patients sent by Parochial Boards but there was also what was described as 'a higher class of patient'. Most patients arrived in a very poor state and few were considered curable. Lunacy Board inspectors found patients clean, if somewhat untidy in appearance. They were bathed weekly and in the nearby sea from May until September (see map page 204). They were well treated with weekly dances, games, singing classes and 'homely but amusing instrument concerts'. There were regular excursions e.g. to Loch Ness by bus in June 1860. 25 newspapers and low cost periodicals were received weekly. Normally the Asylum was full and it regularly turned away a considerable number of applicants.[376]

From 1861 on, the Lunacy Board was expressing concerns about the future of Englishton once the District Asylum opened and indeed, after this happened in May 1864, 36 pauper patients were transferred there. By July 1864, Englishton had only 12 patients.[377] From 1865, the new district asylum could also accept private patients and the Lunacy Board[ii] thought this may put Englishton further at risk. Englishton patient numbers then were around 16 mostly from Caithness with which an agreement to supply further patients was anticipated and, in June, a grand ball was held at the house apparently signifying some optimism in its future. By then, classes in the 3 R's were being held. There were still three male attendants in March but, by autumn, Mr Hyslop was selling off his stock of sheep and cattle – a necessary action since much of his labour had gone.

However, in October 1865, Caithness reneged on any agreement and decided to send all its lunatics to Montrose and this might have been

---

[i] However, because of its limited facilities, the Asylum was not allowed to receive difficult or dangerous patients.
[ii] The Board wanted patients diverted from private asylums into the new public ones. Most private establishments in Scotland did not have the high reputation of Englishton and the Board limited its licensing of them.

expected to be the final straw for Englishton[378] but, by early 1866, there were still 11 patients, the Asylum had been further upgraded to try to attract more affluent patients and there was a resident medical officer.[i] Other staff were reduced to one male and one female attendant as well as some recovered patients who had stayed on as general servants. It is not clear what finally caused a change of heart but, by June, the Asylum was closed and Mr Hyslop was receiving gifts and acclaim from grateful local people. He had already purchased another asylum, Stretton House, in Church Stretton, Shropshire which, by 1889, was run by his son Lt Col CW Campbell Hyslop.[ii] [379]

> William Hyslop seems to have been a remarkable man but an incident at the beginning of July 1859 - soon after he came to Englishton - may have raised his local esteem immediately. The four-horse mail coach was leaving Inverness westwards around 8.15 pm when the horses shied at a flood on the road which tipped the coach so that the driver, guard, and some of the passengers, fell off. One horse got free from its harness but the other three bolted over the canal bridge at Muirtown still pulling the coach. They were met near Clachnaharry by Mr Hyslop on horseback on his way to Inverness. He dismounted and tried in vain to grab the reins and was able to cling onto the coach for quarter of a mile but he still failed to reach them. He then jumped off but his own horse had galloped up and, regaining it, he pursued the coach. There then 'followed quite an equestrian feat'. At full gallop, he got alongside and 'with more than common dexterity' jumped off his own horse onto the back of one of the mail coach horses from where he easily reined it in (in true Wild West movie fashion). By then, the horses had galloped about four miles and were opposite Bunchrew but the mail coach was saved and was able to continue on its way.[380]

---

[i] By law, asylums of over 50 patients to be visited daily by a doctor.

[ii] Younger brother T. B. Hyslop (1863-1933) became superintendent of Bethlem Royal Hospital London (Bedlam) and a prominent London consultant. He had wide interests and held strong views e.g. he advocated eugenics.

Northern Counties District Lunatic Asylum
1864[381]

There they stand, isolated, majestic, imperious, brooded over by the gigantic water-tower and chimney combined, rising unmistakable and daunting out of the countryside – the asylums which our forefathers built with such immense solidity to express the notions of their day.[382]
Enoch Powell 1961

The Northern Counties District Lunatic Asylum (above) opened on 18th May 1864 on an unusually large 180 acre site.[i] Built of local whinstone and faced with Tarradale sandstone, the total cost including furnishing, fittings, equipment and residents clothing was around £50,000.[383] This was a considerable contrast from the Inverness Poorhouse which had been built three years before, with only a slightly lower capacity, at a cost of around £6,000 (page 23). Scotland was certainly trying to make amends for its previous neglect of the mentally ill.[ii] The architects were

---

[i] 100 acres were purchased in 1858 reflecting the urgency to establish an asylum. The large area was commented on favourably by the Lunacy Commissioner.
[ii] But there were ongoing concerns about costs of the Asylum.

Matthews and Lawrie[i] and it was the third asylum built in Scotland under the recent Lunacy Act. Contractors included W&G Greig, masons from Aberdeen, and it was described as the 'most perfect' of the asylums to date, the construction being supervised by Medical Superintendent Dr Aitken appointed in 1859. The care in planning as well as the investment reflects the growing interest in the scientific study of mental illness in Victorian society and the key place of district asylums in treating it.

The 1857 Lunacy Act established a General Board of Commissioners in Lunacy for Scotland[ii] and District Boards of Lunacy. The Northern Counties District included Nairn, Inverness, Ross and Cromarty and Sutherland. Caithness chose not to join and continued to use Montrose Royal Asylum.[iii] District Boards had some discretion on how they took forward their asylum and how it was run but the Commissioners gave broad guidance based on the thinking on mental health at the time. Essentially, there was little specific treatment and it was thought that instilling self-control within a secure tranquil environment with good food and accommodation would allow patients to recover. Asylums should be in a rural environment not too far from an urban area so that patients could benefit from the resources of the town but be away from the noise, bustle and polluted atmosphere - factors which were (and still are) considered to contribute to poor mental health. A beautiful view was helpful and the grounds should be large enough to allow cultivation since purposeful work was seen as beneficial. Inverness District Asylum was, therefore, considered to be in a good location although there were later worries about its windswept and cold site[iv] and, of course, its location within its catchment area. Until 1975, Inverness shire and Ross and Cromarty included the Western Isles so that the Asylum's catchment area stretched across the north of Scotland. This contributed to ongoing pressure of demand but also isolated many patients from their own

---

[i] Won in limited competition with George Fowler Jones and Peddie & Kinnear.
[ii] Replaced by the Board of Control in 1913.
[iii] As did Shetland. Orkney used Aberdeen.
[iv] Later ameliorated by tree planting.

environment and culture which can hardly have aided recovery.

The Asylum was like a large country mansion as exemplified in the early 1900s picture of the hall (right). It was in the form of a long single block with separate accommodation

for the medical superintendent. Patients mainly had single rooms as shown on the plan on the next page (the 2 separate blocks were not built) and the accommodation was split equally into male and female sides.

The first patient, Donald Donaldson from Inverness, was admitted on 19th May 1864 and, in the first year, there were 212 admissions including 158 transferred from other asylums.[i] Of these 212 patients, 46% belonged to Inverness, 37% to Ross and Cromarty, 9% to Sutherland and 8% to Nairn - proportions which broadly represented their respective populations. Initially, there was quite a turnover of staff. Wages were quite low, a male attendant received £22 p.a. and a female £10, about half the salary of a domestic servant in Inverness, and they were expected to maintain a high standard of conduct. In 1866, five attendants were dismissed – three for cruelty to patients, one for insubordination and one for drunkenness.[384]

---

[i] Most initially were from Englishton and private 'madhouses' in Central Scotland. Of the public and Royal Asylums most by far returned from Montrose with smaller numbers from Edinburgh (Morningside), Glasgow (Gartnavel) and Aberdeen.

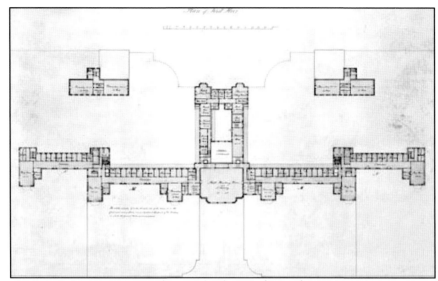

Northern District Asylum Plan

In 1865, a cemetery was opened for patients whose relatives could not take away their remains. It is said to include the grave of Colour Sergeant James Munro, 93rd Highlanders, who won the VC at Lucknow in 1857 and was severely wounded.[385] The only identifiable gravestone marks the burial of two sisters from Tain. The cemetery was full in 1895 after which Tomnahurich was used but it remains a peaceful spot (photograph below). There was also a pet cemetery nearby for ward pets.[386]

212

In the early days, the building was described as clean but bare and 'unhomelike' and exceedingly cold, blamed on too many open windows. Heating was by open fire and there was also a system of warm air vents which was supposed to distribute heat throughout the building. Although the building warmth improved, at the turn of the century dormitories were still registering freezing point in winter and, in 1902, central heating was installed. The diet was apparently much better than that found in many other institutions such as poorhouses. The food was 'abundant, of good quality and neatly served' and probably quite plain although not spartan. In 1867, each resident consumed an annual average of around 70 pints of table beer, 220 pints of milk, a bottle of whisky, 1.3 bottles of port and 1lb of tobacco. The attention paid to the wellbeing of patients continued to be praised. In 1920, the inspecting commissioner said that the condition of the sitting rooms and dormitories 'left nothing to be desired', that the clothing was 'neat and substantial' and that there was an 'ample amount of well cooked food'. Patient restraint was rarely required. In 1922, there were accusations of extravagance because 'the standard of comfort was excessively high' but these were dismissed by the supervisory Board of Control[i] in Edinburgh.

There was much emphasis on the freedom of movement of patients in and outwith the building and, in 1874, the walls of the airing courts were pulled down[ii] and, thereafter, the Asylum was remarkable in having no walls or fences.[iii] This, along with its rural setting, made it the subject of much admiration for its treatment of the mentally ill from reformers such as Dr WAF Browne (page 205) and its excellence continued to be commented on. Patients were frequently outdoors and reports comment on their liveliness compared with elsewhere. Since the district asylums were essentially a new and expensive development there was much observation and discussion on the efficacy of treatment and the causes

---

[i] The Board of Control inspected twice annually and usually reported very favourably on all aspects of the treatment of patients and on the management.
[ii] Male and female airing courts, at opposite ends of the building, contained patients during exercise periods. One can be seen clearly in the photograph on page 209. Inverness was the 2nd large asylum in Scotland to remove them.
[iii] Unlike many asylums and poorhouses, no boundary wall had been built.

of mental illness such as hereditary, cultural traits and the effect of the environment[i] such as isolation or alcohol,[ii] thus reflecting the growing interest in the scientific study of psychiatry and of mental conditions.[387]

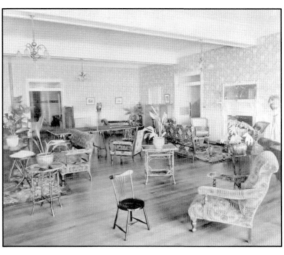

From the outset, the importance of sensory stimulation was promoted by inspectors and the initial lack of furnishings and decoration was commented on. However, it improved as shown in the photograph of the female patients' sitting room from the early 1900s (above). In 1864, following a donation of books, a library for patients was formed and periodicals and newspapers were received, some being donated.[iii] A piano was purchased at the outset.[388] Weekly activities included church services in English and Gaelic, dances and concerts. By 1879, there was an annual examination of educational progress with prizes awarded for literacy and numeracy as well as an annual exhibition of design, art and craft work. These activities became long standing traditions embedded in the life of the Asylum. From 1871, there was football, hockey and curling (the Asylum had its own curling pond) and the Asylum football and hockey teams were particularly successful.[iv] In 1909, a cricket pitch was formed, in 1912, the recreation field was laid out which included a bowling green and pavilion[v] and, in 1913, a tennis court was constructed.

---

[i] In 1898, it was considered that a third of admissions were due to the effects of heredity and a fifth due to excess alcohol.
[ii] Although some alcohol continued to be part of their diet (see previous page).
[iii] However, in 1875, Dr Aitken commented on the pernicious tone of some modern literature and thought it a bad influence.
[iv] In 1937, the football team reached the 4th level of the Scottish Junior Cup.
[v] A bowling green and cricket pitch had been first laid out in the 1860s.

By the 1920s, there was an annual sports day and an annual motor drive for women patients. There were other cultural activities such as the formation of a pipe and drum band in 1912 and a silver band in 1937.

However, the Asylum became a victim of its own success and the treatment of patients became hampered by overcrowding. It had been designed for 200 patients but, within a decade, contained 50% above that number and this constant overcrowding, and the need to find ways of overcoming it, is a dominant theme in the history of the Asylum.

Northern Counties District Lunatic Asylum in-patients[389]

Year	Average in-patients	Admitted		Discharged		Deaths	
		M	F	M	F	Number	%*
1865	200	103	109	3	5	10	5%
1875	313	38	39	16	22	21	7%
1885	410	47	59	35	32	33	8%
1895	435	71	66	44	35	25	6%
1905	654	69	71	41	55	52	8%
1915	705	109	77	77	35	80	11%
1925	674	61	62	27	31	54	8%
1935	745	81	69	28	19	71	10%
1945	844	66	59	30	48	58	7%
1955	1,004	310	354	231	288	83	8%
1963	1,090	605	495	538	411	159	15%

*% of average in-patients

As can be seen in the table above, there was an inexorable rise in patient numbers. There has been a perception that entering the Asylum was a one way process but, as shown above, patient discharges were significant. In 1964, Medical Superintendent Martin Whittet noted that, in the 99 years to May 1963, 23,354 patients had been treated of which 15,657 (67%) had been discharged. The rise in patient numbers appears to be mainly due to the constant pressure of new patients rather than the accumulation of cases. In the early days, despite most admissions being long term cases,[i] there were high hopes of curing patients especially if

---

[i] In 1889, there were still 3 original patients by then aged 77, 79 and 82.

they were admitted at an early stage in their illness. Many were discharged as 'recovered' within three months (50% in 1888) but, in 1899, it was noted that 35% of admissions were readmissions. This may have been because of too eager discharging encouraged by overcrowding although many readmissions were boarded out patients who had ceased to cope with their placement. The policy of reintegration into the community continued to be seen as the correct one and, in 1912, recovery, or reintegration, rates were reckoned at 50% - well above the national average.

It had been thought that, as with physical ailments, the introduction of hospital treatment would cure mental illness and therefore reduce the numbers of sufferers in the community. The ever rising number of admissions was therefore surprising and, in 1877, ever analytical, the superintendent concluded that there were three main causal factors – (i) the level of emigration[i] from the Highlands which left vulnerable, often older people, with insufficient family care, (ii) an asylum which was more comfortable and generated less prejudice[ii] and (iii) a change in social attitudes whereby people were less tolerant of an insane relative. On this latter point, he felt that, since society was becoming less tolerant of mental illness, 'slighter degrees of mental aberration were seen to require treatment'. From the 1890s, the increasing numbers of senile, mainly female patients were noted and, by 1929, these made up a large number of bedridden cases. The superintendent noted that these, along with many other cases, really just required care which should have been available elsewhere. Although he did not use the phrase, it was clear that he saw the asylum being used as a 'dumping ground'.

From the start, all patients who could work were employed.[iii] This was seen as therapeutic as well as economical in running costs. As with poorhouses, the trades and professions of patients were utilised where

---

[i] Emigration was being encouraged across the Highlands as part of the Clearances.
[ii] However, the reluctance during and after the First World War to place 'shell shocked' troops in district asylums underlines the stigma which still existed, a situation which was commented on at the time by Superintendent TC Mackenzie.
[iii] But not paid for their labour until the 1950s.

possible. In 1865, 60% of the 185 patients were employed[i] in a range of activities (table below). Later, a greater proportion of men would be involved in farm work and building works such as laying foundations and reservoir construction. Women continued to be mainly employed indoors. By 1870, all of the clothes and many of the shoes were made in the asylum workshops.

Number of employed patients 1865

Male Occupations		Female Occupations	
Field worker	30	Sewer	21
Household	10	Household	14
Shoemaker	3	Knitter	10
Stoker	2	Laundry	9
Joiner	2	Kitchen	4
Doorkeeper	1		
Tailor	1		
Clerk	1		
Schoolmaster	1		
Upholsterer	1		

The 1885 staff (below) included tradesmen and agricultural workers, such as ploughman and grieve (farm manager), who were essential to the ongoing craft work, construction and work on the land. As the Asylum increased its construction work and facilities, the staff included engineers. In 1912, artisans occupied nine of the Asylum staff cottages.[ii]

Full time staff in 1885

Medical Superintendent	1	Clerk	1
Assistant Medical Officer	1	Grieve	1
Stoker/Gasman/Plumber	2	Matron	1
Female Attendants	12	Cook/maids	6
Male Attendants	18	Laundress	3
Night Attendant	1		

---

[i] Such proportions continued. In 1885, 65% of men and 79% of women worked.
[ii] The 1891 census has carpenter and plumber. In 1911 - shoemaker and upholsterer.

In 1885, the 47 staff gave a patient/staff ratio of approximately 9:1. Gradually staffing levels improved so that, by 1921, although patient numbers had risen to 332 males and 324 females, there were 29 male and 65 female staff giving an improved ratio of 7:1. The improvement in staffing is further illustrated by the fact that, in 1894, 410 patients (including 70-80 in the sick wards) were looked after by two night staff[i] but, by 1898, there were eight on duty. Medical staffing was not generous. Initially, there was one medical officer, increased to two in 1904 and three from 1921 (page 236). In 1937, Dr McWilliam noted that there were still only three medical officers for a hospital of 800 patients.

Staff lived in and, as their numbers increased along with the growing number of patients, more living space was required which put pressure on the building and facilities. In 1876, two dayrooms for around 24 patients each were built on although there was still overcrowding. Workshops were removed to the farm steading and converted to dormitories. Central to the well-being of the patients was the kitchen which, in 1880, was described as 'an injury to the whole establishment'. Its replacement was opened in 1882 and was in a separate block connected by covered walkway. The block also contained a dining hall (photograph right) which seated over 350 but this was soon barely sufficient. The kitchen was renovated in 1898[ii] and was still in use in 1963 without major alteration but catering for considerably more patients. In 1904,

---

[i] These 2 staff were expected to visit each patient every hour throughout the night.
[ii] In-house baking of bread ceased allowing the bakery to be incorporated.

new dining facilities for the male hospital wards were opened (pages 222-3) which relieved pressure on the main dining hall. The original kitchen and dining room were converted into dayrooms and dormitories as were the recreation room[i] and chapel in 1892. Thereafter, the dining hall was used for recreation and for religious services.

By the late 19th century, it was clear that rising demand would continue and plans for 'extensions on a vast scale' were drawn up by architects Ross and MacBeth. The work was undertaken over the ensuing years and, as well as the developments described in pages 222-3, included refurbishments to the laundry and a new mortuary constructed in 1907.

Although the main solution to overcrowding was the continued building expansion, there were other strategies which helped. By 1893, the policy of allowing freedom of patient movement outside the building was seen as one way of dealing with overcrowding or at least of maintaining a high capacity. In 1879, an open establishment with one nurse was opened at the nearby farmhouse of Balphadrig. It housed 16 female patients who were able to live fairly independently - one of the patients being in charge of the kitchen. It was described as a convalescent facility and was seen as a novel development. However, it was later thought difficult to run mainly because of its inaccessibility from the main building and it was closed after 5 years when substantial renovations were required and when accommodation in the main Asylum building had improved.

Patients were increasingly boarded out.[ii] 24 were placed in 1907, a further 34 in 1908 and 50 in 1909. By 1910, 'within a radius of sixteen miles of the Asylum, 132 patients (51 males and 81 females) were to be found in private dwellings and specially licensed houses'. The following year, after a huge effort, 39% of asylum patients were boarded out.[iii] This eased pressure on accommodation and delayed expensive building expansion, a policy regularly lauded by Lunacy Commission inspectors.[390]

---

[i] A new recreation hall seating 400 was eventually built in 1927 costing £7,000.
[ii] Boarding out continued until at least the 1950s.
[iii] The Scottish average was 18%.

The acquisition of Kinmylies in 1903 provided more potential living space and it was used to accommodate those working at the farm, mainly males, but it took several years for the mansion house and other buildings to be refurbished. By 1905, part of the steading and adjoining cottage had been converted to accommodate 48 male patients and this freed up a male dormitory[i] in the Asylum for female patients.

Although the Asylum continued to expand, it was not meeting the needs of all the population. District asylums were primarily for the treatment of pauper lunatics. Private patients could be admitted if there was space and this was the case initially – there were three in 1866 and seven the following year. More often, they were not allowed due to the lack of accommodation and this was generally seen as unfair.[391] The only alternatives were the Royal Asylums which were expensive and poorer families who were not paupers had still nowhere to go for treatment. Theoretically, a poor but non pauper sufferer could be admitted to the district asylum as a voluntary patient funded by their parish but such cases did not attract grant support from the state and parishes were reluctant to agree to a voluntary placement. There were no voluntary patients in Inverness until 1920 (see page 230).

To ensure access to an asylum, therefore, the easiest way was to become a pauper. By 1922, the Commissioners found that 80% of pauper lunatics in Scottish asylums were not truly paupers and were greatly concerned that poor people who could not afford hospital fees were required to risk the social stigma of being a pauper whereas, if they had contracted an infectious disease, the local authority would have treated them free of charge. It was one of many bureaucratic inconsistencies. There was a further twist to the situation. Those who boarded out the mentally ill received an allowance from the parish council. In 1903, superintendent, Dr Keay, noted a rapid increase in the number of registered pauper lunatics in Lewis when the benefits of a pauper lunatic

---

[i] Actually the original recreation hall.

grant[i] were realised. Dr Aitken noted that many cases were certified in batches and for reasons which would not have achieved certification 20 years before. The 'consideration of a grant' had removed overnight the stigma of lunacy' (and also, presumably, the stigma of pauperism).

From the 1880s, there were worries about the death rate (table on page 215). Many patients arrived in poor health and, as Dr Aitken pointed out in 1889, many admissions were aged, feeble, anaemic or phthisical. Tuberculosis was a particular problem as it was generally throughout the Highlands. For example, in 1897, 15% of admissions had tuberculosis. Dr Aitken noted that longer term patients also developed the disease suggesting that there was transmission within the Asylum probably exacerbated by the overcrowding especially in the male wards.[ii]   In 1905, noting that 19% of deaths were from the disease, he suggested a sanatorium. In 1911, verandas were built at opposite sides of the Asylum and, in 1914, the wards behind were converted to provide modern sanatorium treatment for 11 male and 11 female patients. In 1936, these were replaced with a purpose built unit for 35 patients (photo above) which was used fully until the mid-1950s and later as wards until at least the 1970s. It later became converted into a Sports Pavilion which is how it is now remembered.

---

[i] From 1875, there was a grant to help maintain registered pauper lunatics outside asylums e.g. in poorhouses or boarded out. The number gradually increased across Scotland but the sudden increase in registration in Lewis drew attention to the issue.
[ii] The 1915 Board of Control annual report noted that over 50% of those dying from TB in the Asylum had been resident for over 5 years.

From the outset, the sick had been accommodated across the Asylum in single rooms but rising numbers[i] required dedicated hospital accommodation. Therefore, in 1896, tenders[ii] were accepted for a west wing extension to provide male hospital wards.

At the same time, a new main entrance was constructed to the west and this left the original south entrance as an ornamental and recreation area which provided an attractive, quiet area accessible to convalescing hospital patients. The new entrance led to a spacious hall and wide corridor to the centre of the building. New reception and waiting rooms were also created. Around the turn of the century the access road was also changed which diverted the main public road way from the building. In 1902, an internal telephone system was installed, the first of its kind in Scotland, but it did not connect all of the wards and was renewed in 1923.

Inverness Lunatic Asylum

In the 1898 sketch above, the completed male hospital wards are shown on the right. The new centrally heated wing could accommodate 88

[i] In 1897, there were 49 men and 26 women sick.

[ii] Local tradesmen were Alex Cameron, mason, Fraser and Macdonald, carpenters, Alex Thomson, plumbers and D Dallas, plasterers.

patients in a range of wards and sitting rooms furnished and decorated attractively which was believed to contribute to recovery from mental illness. Floors and wall panels were of pitch pine, the floors being waxed[i] and not washed which was thought to reduce the rate of any disease transmission especially TB. The accommodation included a 20 bed sick ward, a 20 bed observation ward, a large dormitory, around 20 single wards, a wide corridor which doubled as a sitting room, a sitting room for convalescents with access to the now secluded grounds and a range of service rooms such as nurses' kitchen and sitting room, doctors' consulting room and a padded room – the first one in the Asylum.[ii] In 1899, there were 67 patients in the male wards. The wing had its own entrance so that new patients did not have to go through the building to reach the hospital wing. The new male wards included female nurses, a new development which was successful as were the facilities generally which, in 1924, were described as 'excellently adapted'. There was never an operating theatre and patients in need of surgery went to the Infirmary.[392]

In 1901, a similar wing opened on the opposite (female) side. This included additional single room accommodation for patients and a senile patient dormitory as well as day rooms, corridor space for exercise and 'bathrooms, lavatories and every modern appliance with regard to the convenience and comfort of the patients'. Again, much attention was given to the décor to ensure 'a bright and cheerful aspect'. The new hospital wings had also improved the general dormitories by removing the sick patients. In all of these extensions, much of the work of foundation and site preparation was done by patient labour.

Possibly because of its excellent facilities and management, the Asylum largely avoided infectious disease but, in 1925, there was an outbreak of enteric (typhoid) fever and patients were moved to Culduthel Hospital. This was seen at the time as an excellent example of cooperation between the different local authorities which only goes to underline how

---

[i] All Asylum floors were waxed instead of wet scrubbed from 1888.
[ii] Commissioners' reports note that there continued to be little restraint of patients.

disjointed public health continued to be. In 1932, a serious outbreak of paratyphoid precipitated the need to re-equip the laboratory which was put under the charge of one of the medical officers. An outbreak of typhoid the following year further emphasised need for an isolation block and, in late 1935, a 20 bed unit opened which was still in regular use in the 1960s.

In the 19th century, like other hospitals, the training of nurses and attendants had steadily improved. In 1896, Asylum nurses first gained the nursing certificate awarded by the Medico-Psychological Association[i] and in-house training steadily expanded with large numbers of staff achieving certification each year. In 1929, the Asylum was approved by the General Nursing Council as a complete training school for mental health nurses, six nurses gaining the award in the first year.

However, the main issue for nurses was the lack of accommodation. The slope of the site of the 1901 female hospital wing allowed an additional storey below the patients' accommodation and this was used for a 24 bed nurses' home with a large recreation/sitting room. By then, the lack of accommodation for married men was an issue. In 1900, there were 25 married men on the staff but only 6 staff cottages in the grounds. Staff relied on getting accommodation in Inverness which was expensive and inconvenient and thought to affect recruitment. In 1910, a joiner's workshop in the asylum steading was converted to an attendant's cottage. In 1912, it was noted that of the 18 staff cottages, half were occupied by artisans and, in 1914, additional cottages for attendants were provided on Leachkin Road as well as 6 new ones built. In 1923, a house for the asylum engineer was constructed as well as 2 staff cottages and, in 1928, a further 6 were built. Again, much of this work was done by patients.

As patient numbers expanded and staff working conditions improved, the number of nurses increased putting further pressure on their accommodation. There had been some improvements in the 1920s, - the

---

[i] From 1926, it was the Royal Medico-Psychological Association and, from 1971, the Royal College of Psychiatrists.

three assistant matrons[i] had acquired a sitting room and dining room, the maids a dining room and the male attendants a recreation room. However, poor accommodation was seen as one reason for the high turnover of staff. By 1932, there were 93 nurses and maids but the only dedicated nurses' accommodation was the 23 bed unit opened in 1901 and the rest had to be accommodated across the main building which, of course, restricted the intake of patients. Bedrooms were overcrowded and many were shared – one maids' bedroom had five beds. In 1936, a new purpose built 3 storey nurses' home opened costing £28,000. It accommodated 103 staff beds (plus seven staff sick beds) and included kitchen, sitting room and recreation room.[ii]

The redundant staff quarters were eagerly absorbed into patient accommodation for around 180 additional patients, mainly senile ones, and this increased Asylum capacity to 820 beds. In 1932, there had been 750 patients in an asylum designed for 620. In 1936, for a brief period only as it happened, the 783 patients were well within the Asylum's capacity. By then, a workshop in the grounds had been transferred to the nearby farm steading and the building converted into a 40 bed accommodation unit for male working patients. Named the Villa, it opened in 1938 and was designed to be homely with single rooms.

There were other significant developments in the 1930s[iii] which can be seen as an era of asylum development comparable with the turn of the century. The construction of the sanatorium and isolation block has already been described (page 221, 224). In 1932, occupational therapy was started and led for the next decade by Miss Maclean who held an administrative post. The department received regular praise for its excellent work. The same year a small shop opened in the dining room and, in 1934, both were combined in a purpose built occupational therapy block which accommodated classes of around 20 patients.

---

[i] From 1903 there was a depute matron. Assistants were appointed from at least 1906.
[ii] By the mid-1960s, fewer staff were resident and part of it was used as flats for medical staff, offices and as a training school.
[iii] Contrast this with the lack of investment in Muirfield (pages 31-2).

Some building work in the 1930s was delayed by a dispute over the supply of electricity. The Asylum was originally lit by gas but, in 1899, this was replaced by electricity,[i] generated from a gas plant in the grounds - one of the first in the North of Scotland.[ii] All buildings were completely rewired in 1930 and a new electric plant was planned but Inverness Burgh would not initially agree to its share of the funding claiming that it would be cheaper to supply the Asylum from the town's power station at Whin Park. Subsequent analysis disagreed and, in 1935, at a cost of £25,000 the central heating and electric plant were replaced by 'the most up to date and economical in the country' and this seems to be borne out by the fact that the central heating plant lasted nearly 30 years, being converted to oil in 1963. Likewise, the electric plant lasted until being replaced by mains electricity in 1962 and its site was used for a new 20 bed isolation block built mainly to isolate typhoid carriers.

There was a further dispute with Inverness Burgh when the total cost of the mid 1930s building works (electricity plant, central heating, sanatorium and isolation block) was declared overspent by around 20%. While all the other local authorities involved (see page 210) reluctantly agreed to meet the additional cost, Inverness Burgh refused and instigated an enquiry. After a year of dispute, they too complied.

The original purchase of a large area of land around the Asylum was to provide employment for the patients, regular work being considered to be therapeutic but, in common with all such public institutions, attempts were made to be self-sufficient in food as far as possible.[iii] The original farm had 90 acres but much of it was poor hill land. Nevertheless, large amounts were taken into cultivation - 44 acres were tilled in 1876 and 76 in 1885 - and the work of clearing and drainage occupied the labour of patients for many years. However, the limited amount of cultivation meant food had to be bought in and milk, seen as of particular benefit to

---

[i] Several years in advance of the Infirmary.
[ii] In 1907, it supplied Kinmylies via a 50-volt underground cable.
[iii] Asylum farms were thought extremely useful because they provided a range of different types of work and potentially provided much to interest the patient.

226

patients, was in short supply. In 1891, the byre was enlarged as part of plans to start a dairy herd but this did not happen until Kinmylies was purchased (see below) and a herd of 40 milk cows established. Thereafter there was abundant milk. As patient numbers increased, more land was required both for employment and food. In 1902, a 12 acre croft was purchased from Dochfour estates and, the following year, the District Board of Lunacy bought nearby Kinmylies for £14,500 which included mansion house, steading, farm house, 10 workers cottages a large productive garden and 200 acres of arable land. In 1904, there were 87 patients engaged in farm work and a further 133 working in the grounds and gardens and arable land continued to be taken in from the hillside to the north of the Asylum. In 1932, the adjacent Milend farm was purchased for £4,000[i] and, in 1944, a small adjacent croft, all of which brought the total farmland to over 400 acres. Pigs were kept from an early date, the first piggery being completed in 1867, and there were beef cattle and overwintering of sheep but there seems to have been no poultry until 1932.

The supply of water in summer was an issue from the outset. The hill above the Asylum provided the catchment area and the first reservoir was constructed in 1869. Much of the work of this and subsequent reservoirs was carried out by patient labour. Despite the regular extensions, it was difficult to keep up with rising demand as patient numbers increased and, in periods of low rainfall, water was in short supply. An additional reservoir was under construction in the early 1920s but, in 1922, water had to be carried from the canal in specially made large metal tanks. In 1929, supply was severely restricted from April to August and again in 1936 and 1937. Connection to mains water was finally made in the 1960s. Shortage of water was an issue in case of fire and, in 1890, a special reservoir for fire hoses, connected to the curling pond, was constructed in the grounds. The Asylum had its own fire equipment but, in 1908, it also made an agreement with Inverness to use its service.

---

[i] Apparently because the existing farm land could not produce enough milk.

By 1939, patient numbers had risen to 852 and the Asylum was again overcrowded. To make matters worse, at the outbreak of the Second World War, 277 patients were transferred in from Kingseat Hospital near Aberdeen.[i] 60 were accommodated at the now vanished Bught House which was leased from Inverness Burgh and the rest accommodated within the Asylum but run separately – 'an asylum within an asylum'. Aberdeen staff had also been transferred through. Not only was this a difficult operation but the subsequent serious patient overcrowding was compounded by a shortage of staff. A large amount of staff were called up to war duties and a shortage of nurses continued into the late 1940s. By 1942, the staff patient ratio had almost halved. Dormitories were overcrowded, dayrooms became dormitories and corridors became dayrooms. The Villa had 93 patients – twice its capacity - who utilised dayrooms as dormitories by pushing back the beds during the day and setting them up again each night. The Kingseat patients finally left in 1948.

---

[i] On a smaller scale, in 1915, 31 patients had been transferred from Perth District Asylum when it became a wartime military psychiatric hospital.

Following the War, the Asylum was again looking for more space, this time for off-site accommodation for male nurses. Nearby Dunain House (photograph opposite page)[i] had been requisitioned by the army during the war and, in 1946, it was relinquished. In 1947, the Asylum leased it and a wing was added but, in 1951, the health board decided to purchase it for early cases of neurosis. The renovations and arrangements took some time mainly because of the need to treat dry rot but it eventually opened in December 1956 with 27 beds although its high running costs were soon apparent.[393] The table below shows patient numbers and this pattern continued with anything from 20 – 27 in-patients. It closed in the mid-1990s and became residential but fell empty and was destroyed by fire in 2014.[394]

Dunain House in-patients[395]

Year	Average in-patients	Admissions
1958	15	80
1960	17	225
1962	24	343
1964	23	121

The acquisition of Dunain House was a small event in comparison with the profound changes which began in the late 1940s and were heralded, in 1947, by a change of name to Craig Dunain Hospital. New ideas on patient treatment as well as the resources of the new NHS promoted new developments. The hospital's uniqueness and the development needs of psychiatric services in the Highlands demanded a separate management board which was formed in 1950. That year, a review of psychiatric services noted that its facilities, while later not considered good, compared favourably with similar institutions elsewhere. It was also thought that any increased provision for out-patients, then very small, would put pressure on facilities, for example staffing.[396]

---

[i] A nearby mansion built about 1780 with a wing added in 1872.

There was much emphasis on changing patient experience. A visiting dental service had started in 1947 and was now expanded. In 1951, a hairdressing service started for female patients and a catering officer was appointed. Dances and social events were revived including an asylum band with a director of music. An in-patient social club was formed and there was now a tearoom as well as a shop. By 1953, all the wards had radio and, from that year, patients were paid for the work they did and received pocket money. There was significant and ongoing redecoration and refurnishing over several years and, in 1957, Craig Dunain was complemented on its 'very lively air'. The facilities were not seen as good, but compared favourably with similar establishments elsewhere.

Medical staff was substantially enhanced by two registrars. In 1951, a neurosurgeon from Aberdeen started lobotomies[i] at the RNI and a psychiatric social worker post was created. In 1953, a consultant psychiatrist and pharmacist were appointed and staff also included a senior and two junior medical officers and senior registrar. Increased staffing allowed out-patient clinics, already established at the RNI and Fort William, to be extended to Stornoway and Wick in 1953. In 1955, an electroencephalography (EEG) department was set up.[ii]

From the outset of the Asylum, there was an emphasis on understanding and treating the causes of mental health but the work was largely confined to 'certified lunatics' and the lack of voluntary patients in Scottish asylums has already been touched on (page 220). The first 20th century voluntary[iii] patient in the Asylum was in 1920 and numbers remained very low being discouraged by social attitudes, overcrowding and, from 1939, the disruption of the war and its aftermath. However, this now changed rapidly. In 1951, 36% of admission were voluntary and this rose to 80% in 1954. Overall admission numbers also increased rapidly. In 1953, total admissions were three times that of 1949 and, the

---

[i] A psychosurgical procedure first done in the UK in 1940 and very common in the 1950s until medication and concerns about side effects made it unpopular.
[ii] Used to diagnose a range of mental conditions including epilepsy.
[iii] As opposed to fee paying private patient.

following year, had increased by a further 25%.[i] By 1950, the lack of a reception centre was felt. New cases, often mild or temporary had to mix with chronic long term patients and the large increase in admissions would have highlighted this feature. Accordingly, in 1953, two new 10 bed reception wards for voluntary patients and two new sitting rooms for visitors were opened.

It had long been thought that the proportion of mental illness in the Highlands was greater than elsewhere and, indeed, in the late 1960s, the proportion of resident medical patients in Highland was 150% of the Scottish average.[397] It is therefore not surprising that pressure on the Asylum continued. In 1951, official capacity was 930 beds but, by the mid-1960s, this had been increased to 1030 beds.

In 1864, a small chapel had been situated in the upper floor but, in 1892, it was converted to a dormitory (page 219). The following year, the visiting lunacy commissioners had strongly advocated a separate chapel but, despite the apparently small cost and the importance put on spiritual wellbeing, religious services continued in the dining room which was quite unsatisfactory. From 1927, they used the new recreation room and it was not until 1957 that an inter-denominational committee was formed which relatively quickly raised funds for a chapel. The foundation stone was laid in 1961 and the non-denominational chapel was dedicated in 1963 (middle foreground on photograph page 233).

By the 1960s, significant changes signalled the end of the work of the farm. The nature of the old Asylum had changed. Most patients were now voluntary and, although useful employment was possibly still seen as beneficial, it was no longer possible to marshal them as a large organised workforce. Patient workers were now paid which, along with the greater commercialisation of farming generally, reduced financial returns. Around 1965, the adjacent golf course absorbed 30 acres of the farm which also provided the site for Craig Phadrig (page 237). This prompted a review of the farm operation[398] and, by 1967, the land was

---

[i] By 1963, total admissions were 1100 of which over 98% were voluntary.

being disposed of with much going for amenity or for housing as Inverness expanded. Kinmylies House was declared surplus to requirements in April 1985 and put on the market the following year.[399]

The photograph opposite, from the early 1970s, looks westwards and shows how the building had extended over the years when compared with the photo on page 209. The numbers on the photograph are to help identify the different parts. The original block (1) lies to the left and was split equally and symmetrically between male and female accommodation. Behind is the dining room and kitchen (2) built in 1882 (page 218). Behind that again is the shop and occupational therapy unit (3) opened in 1934 (page 225). The end of the main block nearest the camera shows the large wing (4) containing the female hospital wards built in 1904 with the nurses' home in the lower storey (page 224). To its right lie the utilities - laundry (5), engineers' base (6), gardeners' workshops (7) - and, at the end of this, is the Villa (8) (page 225). Further right, the square building is the occupational therapy unit (9) and further right still is the mortuary (10). In the right foreground is the 1935 nurses' home (11) (page 225) and above it can be seen the 1935 sanatorium (12) (page 221). By the 1970s, this was used as ordinary wards and later still used as a sports pavilion (a sports ground (13) was laid out in front of it). To the right of the sanatorium is a block known as the Square (14) which contained farm buildings and plumbers' and joiners' workshops. Between the nurses' home and the main building is the chapel (15) opened in 1965 (page 231). By the 1970s, the extensive grounds on the slopes behind the hospital were no longer used for farming and contained a golf course (16). To the right of the golf course were staff houses (17). Staff houses were found at various locations around the hospital especially on Leachkin Drive off to the centre right. By the 1970s, farming had ceased but there was still a lot of work in the grounds which was carried out by up to 10 staff and around 40 patients. In addition to the grounds in the photograph they managed extensive gardens just off to the centre left which produced flowers for the wards and fruit and vegetables for the kitchen. There were also productive gardens at Kinmylies House (page 227) and Craig Phadrig (page 237).

Patient numbers 1970 - 2000[400]
(selected years)

Year	In-patients
1971	950
1977	895
1989	480
1989	450
1992	385

By the 1960s, the role of large asylums and their organisation began to be questioned. The appropriate care and treatment for mental illness and conditions were seen to require more specialist, differentiated, smaller scale and community based facilities. However, an inspection by Department of Health officials in 1970 made no mention of this but commented on the lack of links with the new social work departments and with the community. It also found the hospital dull and institutionalised and, although facilities were improving, there were still 100 patients with neither chair nor locker. The hospital was considered overcrowded and the Department felt that developments in psychogeriatric care could reduce numbers significantly.

In the 1970s, the development of specialist facilities elsewhere, particularly at Craig Phadrig, allowed the numbers of in-patients to be reduced. Facilities for senile dementia (Timbury type units) were developed across the Highlands at St Vincent's (Kingussie), Migdale (Bonar Bridge), Wick Town and County and at Invergordon. There was also a policy of promoting supported independent living where possible. Therefore, from the 1970s, Craig Dunain was gradually run down as shown in the table above and, from 1980, the policy of Care in the Community accelerated this decline in patient numbers. Craig Dunain finally closed in 2000 and is being developed for residential accommodation.

Matrons

	Asylum		Kinmylies
1864-5	Miss Probyn		
1865-9	Isabella Ross[401]		
1870-5	Annie MacLaurin		
1876-81	Isabella Donald		
1881-87	Miss MA Macdonald		
1887-88	Mrs Manson[402]		
1888-94	Maria Robinson	1902-4	Miss Wilson
1894-1910	Annie Gass	1904-11	Miss Patullo
1910-18	Isabella Henderson[403]	1911-32	Miss Maclean
1918-45	Ann Thomson[404]	1932	Miss Walker
1945-62	Christina MacDonald[405]		
1962	Miss E Morrison		

Medical Superintendents

Dates	Med. Super.	Notes
1864-92	Dr Thomas Aitken	Died in service.
1892-94	Dr John C Mackenzie	Resigned along with chief nurse following 'a scandal'.[406]
1894-04	Dr Keay	
1904-08	Dr Robert B Campbell	Med Attendant 1896-7.[407]
1908-31	Dr TC Mackenzie	Wrote account of RNI.
1932-51	Dr William McWilliam	Assistant Medical Superintendent 1922 – 32.
1951-83	Dr Martin M Whittet	Appointed at age 32.
1984-00	Dr AW Scott-Brown	

Medical Attendants

From 1864, there was only one medical attendant in the Asylum but, in 1904, this increased to two. There was only one during the First World War but two from 1920 and three from 1921. 'Dr' is omitted due to space except where the first name is unknown.

1866-?	Dr Mitchell		**1907-8**	HC Weber
1871-3	Thomas MacDowall		**1909-9**	C Armit Masson
1875-6	Alexander MacKechnie		**1908-11**	AC McKillop
1877-8	James Mann		**1909-10**	James Davie
1878-9	David Hardie		**1910-12**	JC Simpson
1879-80	James F MacLaren		**1912-15**	WM Buchanan
1880-1	Hugh William ?Mann		**1912-14**	MR Mackay
1881-3	William Rob. Dalziell		**1914-17**	JG Elder
1883-5	A Hosie		**1916-19**	ES Pearce
1885-6	John Grant		**1919-22**	GWC Dunlop
1886-7	TH Mitchell		**1920-1**	Francis Sutherland
1887-90	David Macdonald		**1921-32**	WM McWilliam
1891	Samuel Elliot		**1921-3**	John P Chisholm
1891-2	William Peach Hay		**1922-4**	Geoffrey D English
1892-3	Geo Ernest Macleod		**1924-5**	WJ Mackintosh
1893-4	RH Watson		**1925-8**	James Gray
1894-5	WR Strapp		**1928-9**	M Rosenfield
1895-6	WC Hossack		**1929-34**	Marsh. AB Fenton
1896-7	RB Campbell		**1930-2**	Alex Wood
1897-8	Charles PB Wall		**1932-4**	WG Kennedy
1898-9	Charles Donaldson Law		**1934-5**	Fred H Taylor
1899-00	Alfred BS Powell		**1934-5**	J Leslie McLetchie
1900-1	Thomas FH Blake		**1935-8**	W Calder
1901-2	Kenneth DC MacRae		**1935-6**	John Battersly
1902-3	Sidney J Cullum		**1936-7**	WRM Couper
1903-4	Patrick Shaw		**1937-41**	FA Paul
1904-5	James Watson		**1938-9**	AF McCabe
1904-6	Lawrence Gavin		**1939-41-?**	MM MacRae
1905-7	Alfred Gray		**1941-2**	HS Dewar
1906-8	John A Macleod		**1942-?**	JT MacLaughlan

Craig Phadrig
1969

In 1912, Dr Mackenzie, superintendent of Craig Dunain noted the need for separate accommodation for 'feeble minded' patients.[i] In 1938, the Inverness Joint Hospital Board agreed that a new build was required for 'mental defectives' but the Second World War intervened.[408] A 1950 review of Highland psychiatric services raised the issue[409] and, by then, visiting commissioners were 'greatly perturbed' by the number of 'mentally deficient'[ii] patients housed at Craig Dunain. In 1951, there were 12 children below 12 years of age in this category and a further 12 below 18 years old. Children were growing up in a mental hospital.

Dr Whittet, medical superintendent, suggested using Kinmylies House as a temporary expedient[410] but it was not until 1965 that work started on a new Mental Deficiency Hospital with architects Alison and Hutchison and builder Alexander Hall.[411] Craig Phadrig (photo above) opened in

---

[i] Possibly due to the approaching Lunacy and Mental Deficiency Act of 1913.
[ii] Terminology and concepts have changed. They would now be described as having Additional Support Needs. Many would not be considered patients.

1969 on a 50-acre site with 229 beds[i] and was officially opened the following year by Princess Alexandra. The cost was £1.2m. There were around 100 staff under Physician Superintendent William Wright.[ii]

Patients stayed in 'villas' of 25 or 26 beds contained in single, 4 bed and 6 bed dormitories with shared kitchen. These were interconnected by ramped covered ways to overcome the problems caused by the steep site (see photograph on previous page). All buildings for patients were single storey for ease of access except the two storey administration block (top left in photograph) and staff accommodation (extreme top left) which consisted of a nurses' home and staff flats. The physician superintendent, his depute, senior nursing officer, resident engineer and porter all had houses on site.[412]

The hospital's facilities included an out-patients department, a physiotherapy department, an assembly hall, a school for up to 100 resident children[iii], recreation facilities and later a large swimming pool costing £85,000, which encouraged swimmers of a very high standard. Other sports were encouraged and residents successfully represented their country at international games. Occupational therapy was of prime importance and the hospital had a working croft with a range of animals and workshops which, among other items, produced decorative concrete slabs.[413]

By modern standards there seems to have been an initial lack of community involvement and it took time to establish networks[iv] and partnerships, e.g. with charities and voluntary groups, which we now take for granted.[414]

---

[i] It was planned with the capacity to extend to 400 beds but this never happened.
[ii] Retired 1982 and succeeded by Dr TE Baeker.
[iii] Education Authorities did not have responsibility for all children until the 1970s but the local authority had established a Junior Occupational Centre in the Leachkin for 'ineducable children' in 1958 (Whittet 1964).
[iv] Local authority social work departments were not formed until 1968.

However, the life of this long-awaited hospital was about to be curtailed. In the late 1970s and 1980s, there was a fairly profound and – from a historical perspective – rapid change in social policy which prioritised care in the community and social inclusion so that Craig Phadrig, like Craig Dunain, was no longer seen as necessarily the most suitable provision. Facilities were also developing elsewhere which reduced the need for resident patients. This included special schools and special units within mainstream schools from the late 1970s which accommodated the youngsters who had previously no local provision other than Craig Phadrig. In May 1988, beds were reduced from 200 to 180 and it closed in 2000 when New Craigs opened nearby.[415]

New Craigs Psychiatric Hospital can accommodate 234 patients in 11 separate single storey buildings which provides a 'barrier free range of buildings catering for a mix of acute, learning disability, rehabilitation and psycho-geriatric accommodation'.[416] However, as a recently established hospital – in historical terms - the hospital lies outwith the scope of this historical study and we have not attempted any analysis of this complex and multi-faceted facility.

Highland Hospice

Whilst not a hospital, Highland Hospice has links to the history of Inverness hospitals and some aspects of its operation are reminiscent of voluntary association hospitals before the NHS.

Highland Hospice purchased Ness House in 1986. This building has a long association with health care. In 1918, Miss J MacFadyen opened Ness House as a nursing home and, by the time it closed a decade later, she had also established there a large agency of nurses (page 145) who were hired out across the Highlands. In 1935, the RNI managers purchased Ness House for the hospital pathologist and then refurbished it in 1937 for the hospital's new Medical Superintendent (page 85). It was taken over by the NHS in 1948 along with all RNI assets.

Highland Hospice is a charity, as was the RNI, relying on fund raising, subscriptions and donations for the bulk of its costs. Like the pre-NHS voluntary hospitals, the cost of care would not be covered by charges – even if charges were made - and the raising of revenue is an incessant need. The effort for this required today is certainly no less than that applied by the RNI managers over the years as documented in this book.

Our present-day hospitals are state funded and the general public have often little notion of their financial needs and spend – other than the occasional newspaper headline. Highland Hospice reminds us of the time when all general hospitals required the public to directly support their local health care establishments.

Over the years, some aspects of medicine – such as infectious diseases - reduced as medicine advanced. Other aspects such as mental health and general medicine have expanded inexorably as public expectations have risen. The knock-on effect has been a continuing need to expand facilities and premises - a pattern which is being followed by Highland Hospice as it extends its building, facilities and services.

Conclusion

Despite its city status, Inverness is a relatively small settlement but it has always had ambitions to match the larger towns and cities of Scotland. This is particularly exemplified by the early establishment of the Infirmary and this ambition continued so that, in 1930, after a huge effort, it was one of the most modern in Scotland and few, if any, Scottish hospitals managed to achieve such a transformation at this time.

However, the Infirmary was always short of revenue - a reflection of its low population and poor hinterland and this also comes through in the development of public health facilities. While the establishment of the Citadel Hospital for cholera and smallpox in the 1870s was comparable with other towns, the Burgh continued to rely on the Infirmary for other fevers and, even when the 1889 Act required local authorities to be more proactive and successive Government inspections pointed out the inadequacies of the RNI fever wards, it took almost 30 years before Culduthel Hospital opened.

In terms of treating poverty related ailments, the Poorhouse and its successors were shockingly under-resourced until the 1960s and we cannot avoid the impression of a very stratified society with the poor only accommodated if they were 'deserving' and last in line for health care. This is not, of course, by any means unique to Inverness. In the 1960s, the refurbishment of Hilton hospital, seen as urgent in the early 1930s, did make considerable improvements but still seems less that what would have been achieved by the new build promised 30 years earlier. While the Asylum did not suffer from poverty of resources, it was deprived in terms of the isolation of the mentally ill both from everyday society and from other medical providers. However, even allowing for fairly generous resourcing, the Asylum was remarkable in its success and was over many years praised highly for its work as indeed was Hilton.

Facilities for mothers and children seem to have had a low priority. While the Infirmary formed a children's ward a decade after the Royal Sick Children's in Edinburgh there was apparently not a sustained effort in providing children's services and there was much reliance on local charitable work. Maternity services seem to have been resisted even after the 1937 Maternity Act and it took a World War and direct action by the Department of Health to have Rosedene Hospital established.

Although Inverness saw itself as the 'most centrical' place in the Highlands, this was not the view from all parts of the region, especially as Inverness had no local university to develop medical specialities, and it took local government changes and the expansion of the Highlands and Islands Medical Service to establish regional specialists there. Thus, the West and North Highlands were dragged into the Inverness sphere, not without some ongoing resistance to the process.

There has been much change over the past three generations. Not only has our main hospital moved from the RNI to Raigmore but there has been virtually a social revolution which has much influenced access to hospital care. The rights of the poor, and of other groups such as unmarried mothers, to equal medical attention have been much enhanced and town councillors, magistrates and church ministers no longer dominate decisions on an individual's social welfare and health care. Expectations have risen to a point that the system appears to be in constant financial crisis. However, even a cursory glance at the Infirmary records reminds us that health care has always been under financed and that no matter how much we have anticipated it over the years, we have still to find the 'magic potions' which will satisfy, if not reduce, our continually rising health care demands.

The omissions and problems over the years must not, however, allow us to understate the successes of the Inverness area which continues to offer an effective, advanced medical service to an area the size of Belgium but with a population of less than the average UK city. The success of this can be judged by noting that, a century ago, the Highlands was so comparatively poor in health services that special government intervention was required. Today, by contrast, many Highlanders would judge themselves better off than many parts of Britain in terms of medical provision.

Bibliography, sources and explanatory notes

Abbreviations used in this section (see also page iii)

BMJ	British Medical Journal	Abn.	Aberdeen
BJN	British Journal of Nursing	Com.	Committee
HAS	Highland Archive Service	Cour.	Courier
IRL	Inverness Reference Library	Edin.	Edinburgh
NLS	National Library of Scotland	Inv.	Inverness
NRS	National Records of Scotland	Jour.	Journal
Hosp.	Hospital(s)	Scot.	Scottish
NRHB	Northern Region Health Board		
IHBM	Inverness Hospitals Board of Management		

Newspaper reports and online resources
The main local newspaper sources are the Inverness Courier, Inverness Journal and Scottish Highlander. These and others are on microfilm in Inverness Reference Library and can be searched by keyword in Am Baile. At the time of writing some of the Courier is on www.britishnewspaperarchive.co.uk/ where much information can also be found in other newspapers.
Am Baile (www.ambaile.org.uk) and the Highland Historic Environmental Record (her.highland.gov.uk) have pictures and information on Highland hospitals.
Dictionary of Scottish Architects www.scottisharchitect.org.uk is a database of architects and their buildings from 1840 onwards.
Workhouses.org www.workhouses.org.uk has the most comprehensive and detailed overall information available on poorhouses in Scotland.
Historic Hospitals https://historic-hospitals.com contains a comprehensive survey of all Scotland's historic hospital buildings by Harriet Richardson who also wrote the book *Building up your Health* (Historic Scotland 2010). The book and much more is available at her website.
The legal framework. Advances in public health were often prompted by state legislation or major report. A list of key reports and acts of parliament as they affect Highland hospitals is at http://www.historyofhighlandhospitals.com
Highland Hospitals A list of all buildings identified as being used as a hospital in Highland can be found at http://www.historyofhighlandhospitals.com

General Bibliography

Burdett, Sir Henry	*Burdett's Hospitals and Charities (from 1931 Hospitals Year Book)* 1889 - 1930 Central Bureau of Hospital Information London
Day, JP	*Public Administration in Highlands & Islands* London 1918
Hamilton, AJC	*Surgery in the Highlands & Islands* Scottish Medical Journal June 1963
Hamilton, D	*Early History of the Highlands & Islands Medical Scheme* Scottish Medical Journal 1979 Vol. 24 (1) p64-8
Hamilton, D	*The Healers* History of Medicine Edinburgh 1981
Leslie, JC & Leslie SJ	*The History of Highland Hospitals* 2010 HAS
Mackay, S (Ed.)	*Inverness Our Story 1* Inverness 2004
Mackay, S (Ed.)	*Inverness Our Story 2* Inverness 2006
McRae, M	*Case for State Medical Services for the Poor. Highlands & Islands 1850* Royal College of Physicians Edinburgh 2008

Government and local authority materials

- *Report on Sanitary Conditions of the labouring classes in Inverness* – report to Poor Law Commission, George Anderson, 2nd April 1841 IRL
- *Report of the Highland and Islands Medical Services Committee* 1913 (Dewar Report) HAS
- *Hospital Services of Scotland* 1920 Nat. Insurance Health Commission NLS
- *Report on Hospital Services (Mackenzie Report)* Edinburgh Scottish Board of Health 1926 NLS
- *Committee on Scottish Health Service* (Cathcart Report) 1936 NLS
- *Scottish Hospitals Survey Report on Northern Region.* Edinburgh 1946 NLS
- *General Medical Service in Highlands of Scotland* (Birsay Report) 1967 NLS

Bibliography specific to individual hospitals

There are few accounts of individual Highland hospitals and much of the information in this publication has been gleaned from a large variety of sources. A bibliography of books and articles on the evolution of hospitals in Inverness can be found at http://www.historyofhighlandhospitals.com The main sources of information on Inverness hospitals are in local authority and NHS Highland archives both of which are managed by the Highland Archive Service. The following list omits those. Further sources are within the References section.

Craig Dunain (Inverness District Lunatic Asylum)
The asylum minutes, reports and other records held by Highland Archive Service are extensive.
- General Board of Control for Scotland – Annual Reports NRS
- Whittet, Martin and Macleod, I *Craig Dunain 1864 – 1964* Inverness HAS
- Philo, Chris *Scaling the Asylum - Inverness District Lunatic Asylum* University of Glasgow 2002
- Parr H, Philo C and Burns N *That Awful Place was Home* Scottish Geographical Journal 2003 Volume 119 Part 4 p341 – 360

Dunbar's Hospital Inverness
- Mitchell, A *Kirk Session Records of Inverness* R Carruthers and Sons Inverness 1902 HAS
- Wimberley, Captain *Hospital of Inverness* Northern Chronicle 1893 IRL
- Pollit, AG *Historic Inverness* Melven Press Perth 1980

Ida Merry Nursing Home
- Financial records c1926 National Records of Scotland.

Inverness (General)
- Fraser, G *History of Dermatology in the Highlands & Islands* Aberdeen Postgrad. Medical Bulletin, Volume 21 1987
- MacDonald, J *Medical History of Inverness 1919* in Transactions of the Inverness Scientific Society 1918 – 1925 Vol IX IRL
- *Inverness Burgh Directories* from 1873 until 1940s. http://archive.org
- Mackenzie, TC *Presidential Address to the Caledonian Medical Society AGM 20 June 1930* Caledonian Medical Journal Volume XIV July 1930

Raigmore Hospital

- Browne, WG. *'Old' Raigmore Hospital 1941 – 1985 A Fragment of History* Inverness 1988 Highland Archive Service
- Davidson, Andrew Chief MO Department of Health for Scotland *The Contribution of the Emergency Medical Services to Medicine and Surgery in Scotland* Edinburgh Medical Jour Vol XLIX p553 1942

Royal Northern Infirmary Inverness

The Highland Archive Service holds a large amount of Infirmary records and the two books below by Mackenzie give a detailed account based on these records. Neither are in print.

- Mackenzie, T.C. *History of a Scottish Voluntary Hospital* Inv. 1946 IRL
- Mackenzie, T.C. *Further History of a Scottish Voluntary Hospital* Inverness 1950 Inverness Reference Library
- Farrell, S. Architectural Building Survey Inverness Nov. 2002 IRL
- Knox, Dr *The Royal Northern Infirmary* Aberdeen Medical Journal 1975
- Opening of New Northern Infirmary Official Programme 1930 HAS
- Appeal for funds 1809 Earl of Seafield Cullen House documents NLS
- Various papers including Report by Dr Nicol 1820 NRS
- Report on fund raising committee 15 March 1831 NRS
- Minute of fund raising committee 1831 NRS
- Northern Infirmary Appeal for funding 4 January 1830 NRS

Nursing Homes

- Viewhill Nursing Home Ltd Company Papers NRS
- St. Margaret's Nursing Home Limited Company papers; Land and Premises: Acquisition Department of Health NRS

Index

Bold indicates main section. Italics indicated footnote.

248

References

Abbreviations (see page 241 are used to save space as required. Unless otherwise stated, all local authority and NHS Highland records are held by the Highland Archive Service. Note that in the text, the reference numbers are usually grouped at the end of a paragraph. The reference may therefore not refer to the sentence immediately preceding it.

[1]   Deed of 12 March 1589 in Inv. Burgh Documents (Am Baile): MacDonald Dr J MOH *Medical and Sanitary History of Inv.* in Transactions of the Inv. Scientific Society Volume IX 1919: Mitchell, A *Kirk Session Records of Inv.* Inv. 1902
[2]   Fraser, Rev J, *Chronicles of the Frasers The Wardlaw Manuscript* 916-1674 Edited by W. Mackay Edinburgh Scottish History Society Vol. XLVII 1905 The Internet Archive http://archive.org
[3]   Inverness Burgh Records   Highland Archive Service
[4]   Local Voluntary Hosp. Com. for Highlands & Islands Report c1922   NRS
[5]   Day, JP *Public Administration in Highlands and Islands of Scotland* London 1917 has a good analysis of the economics of Highland parishes and poorhouses.
[6]   Scottish Hospital Survey 1946 *Report on Northern Region.* Edinburgh   p25
[7]   *Report on Hospital Services of Scotland* 1920 National Insurance Health Commission NLS
[8]   Hamilton, AJC *Surgery in Highlands & Islands* Scot. Medical Jour. June 1963
[9]   *Report of Highland & Islands Medical Services* Com. Cd. 6559 1913 NLS
[10]   *Records of Inv.* Vol. II Mackay and Laing (Ed) New Spalding Club 1924 Aberdeen p288
[11]   Based on Ordnance Survey 1:25,000 map of 1961
[12]   Mitchell 1902 *op.cit.*: MacDonald 1919 *op.cit.*: Pollit AG Historic Inv. 1980
[13]   Macdonald 1919 *op.cit.*
[14]   Circular 9 Sept 1832 Inverness Board of Health: Inverness Jour. 10 Feb 1832
[15]   Inverness Jour. 8 July 1842, 15 July 1842, 08 Aug. 1845: Inverness Courier 26 Oct 1846, 13 Apr 1847, 20 Nov 1856: Parochial Board AR
[16]   Inv. Parochial Board Minutes: Scottish Archive Network www.scan.org.uk
[17]   Inverness Journal 8 Aug 1845: Inverness Courier 13 Apr 1847
[18]   Macdonald 1919 *op.cit.*
[19]   Inverness Parochial Board Minutes
[20]   Macdonald 1919 *op.cit.*
[21]   Mackenzie T.C. *Story of a Scottish Voluntary Hospital* Inverness 1946 p97: Decennial census: Inverness Journal 21 Apr 1848: Inverness Advert. 28 Apr 1848, 26 Oct 1860, 24 Nov 1860: Inverness Courier 8 Aug 1848, 9 Oct 1862
[22]   Inverness Advertiser 8 Dec 1858, 4 Oct 1859

23 Surveyed 1868-70, published 1874. National Library of Scotland
24 Inspector of Poor Report, Parish Council Minutes 1911: Inv. Cour. 5 June 1862
25 *Development of Poor Law Institutions*. Unsigned, undated document HAS
26 Inverness Poorhouse Accommodation and Alterations file HAS
27 *Development of Poor Law Institutions op.cit.*
28 Inverness Inspector of the Poor Report 1911: Inv. Poorhouse Governor AR
29 Inverness Courier 28 Feb 1917
30 Inverness Poorhouse Management Committee Minute
31 *Report on the Hospital Services of Scotland* 1920 *op.cit.* p37
32 *Development of Poor Law Institutions op.cit.*
33 Inverness Poorhouse Governor's AR 1942
34 Inverness Courier 15 Mar 1901
35 Inverness Poor House Minutes
36 Scottish Hospital Survey 1946 *op.cit.*
37 Governor and MO AR in Inverness Poorhouse Management Com. Minutes
38 Inverness Poorhouse Governor AR in Inverness Town Council Minutes
39 Inverness Public Health Committee 23 Dec 1939
40 Muirfield MO Annual Reports in Inverness Public Health Committee Minutes
41 Mackay, Sheila OBE (Ed) *Inverness Our Story* Bk 2 Inverness 2007
42 *ibid*
43 Northern Region Health Board General Purposes Committee 6 Sept 1956; Muirfield Hospital Dept. of Health Miscellaneous file NRS
44 Northern Region Health Board Minutes Vol. 15 p71, p108: Vol. 17 p29, p132
45 Highland Health Board Minutes 17 Oct 1984, 15Aug 1987
46 Muirfield Institution AR 1934, 1935 and 1938
47 Inverness Hospitals Board of Management 12 Nov 1951
48 Northern Region Health Board Medical Committee 3 Jan 1957
49 Alston, Dr David http://www.spanglefish.com/slavesandhighlanders/index.asp
50 Key sources are TC Mackenzie's - *Story of a Scottish Voluntary Hospital Inv. 1946* and *Further History of a Scottish Voluntary Hospital Inv. 1950* and Infirmary annual reports. These are only referenced in graphics or quotes.
51 Edinburgh Evening Courant 28 Dec 1797
52 Colvin, Howard *Biographical Dictionary of British Architects* 1600-1840 3rd Edition Yale UP 1997 courtesy of www.scottisharchitects.org
53 Clark, J The Town of Inv. in '*Views in Scotland*', Smith & Elder, London, 1823.
54 Inverness Courier 6 May 1799, 1 Jan 1926: Edinburgh Advert. 6 May 1799
55 Alston, Dr David *op.cit.*
56 Opening of the New Northern Infirmary 17 May 1929 Official Programme: Knox Dr *The Royal Northern Infirmary* in Abn. Medical Journal 1975 p4 HAS
57 Letter of 1805 from James Smith architect to Infirmary Managers NRS
58 Contained in trustees Appeal for Expansion Funds Jan 1830 (NRS). It appears that no changes to the building were made between 1804 and 1830.

59 Richardson H *Scot. Hosp. Survey* Unpublished RCAMHS Edin.: Richardson H
    Building up your Health Historic Scotland 2010: https://historic-hospitals.com/
60 Trustees Appeal for Expansion Funds Jan 1830. *op.cit.*
61 Address to Public Nov 1805 NRS: Caledonian Mercury 12 Nov 1804
62 Knox 1975 *op.cit.*
63 Northern Infirmary Report 15 June 1830 Fraser Papers HAS
64 Scottish Highlander 2 May 1889
65 Northern Infirmary Report 15 June 1830 *op.cit*
66 Appeal to the public for funds documentation 1809 National Library of Scotland
67 Northern Infirmary Appeal for funding 4 Jan 1830 NRS
68 Letter of 15 Jan 1805 from George Cumming NRS: Inverness Journal 11 Nov
    1808, 20 Jan 1809, 2 Nov 1821: Address to the Public Nov 1805 *op.cit.*:
    Caledonian Mercury 12 Nov 1804, 18 Jan 1806
69 Northern Infirmary Report 15 June 1830 *op.cit.*
70 Inverness Journal 4 Jan 1811, 25 June 1841
71 Inverness Journal 20 June 1817: Inverness Courier 6 Aug 1818
72 Minutes of fund raising committee NRS: Appeal letter 4 April 1839 HAS
73 Report on fund raising committee 15 Mar 1831 NRS: Fraser Mackintosh
    Collection NRS: Northern Infirmary Appeal for funding 4 Jan 1830 *op.cit.*
74 Inv. Courier16 Apr 1845: Gifford, J *Buildings of Scotland (Highlands and
    Islands)* Penguin 1992: Letter of July 1857 in Infirmary Correspondence HAS
75 Inverness Journal 17 Dec 1847
76 Inverness Courier 27 Mar 1833, 25 Sept 1856
77 Inverness Courier 1 June 1865: Abn Journal 28 Feb 1872
78 Inverness Jour. 14 Sept 1821, 09 Jan 1835: Inverness Advert. 24 Sept 1850, 28
    Nov 1884: Scottish Highlander 3 Jan 1889, 19 Jan 1893: Fraser Mackintosh
    collection HAS: Abn. Journal 12 Oct 1886: Abn. Weekly Journal 31 May 1887
79 Inverness Advertiser 22 May 1866, 31 May 1887
80 Inverness Advert. 26 Apr 1867: Inverness Courier 11 Nov 1846, 8 Nov 1870
81 Aberdeen Weekly Journal 24 Apr 1884
82 Aberdeen Weekly Journal 8 June 1877
83 Inverness Advertiser 25 May 1866
84 Scotsman 21 Sept 1891
85 Scotsman 21 May 1915
86 Lecture to the Highland Medical Society 1953. Courtesy of Dr David Bisset
87 Knox 1975 *op.cit.* p8
88 Inverness Journal 13 Feb 1835: Inverness Courier 20 Mar 1844: Nursing Record
    & Hospital World 6 Oct 1894: Burdett *Hospital & Charities Yearbook*.
89 Inverness Advert. 18 Sept 1868: Dictionary of Scottish Architects *op.cit.*: Report
    by Dr Dewar Inspector for the LGB 23 Dec 1910 in Inverness Town Council
    Minutes 1910-11 p274: Mackenzie 1946 op.cit. p110: p157

90 Arrangement with Infirmary Managers Regarding Fever Hospital 12 June 1902 and attached undated memorandum from the Infirmary Secretary HAS
91 Courtesy of Mrs Netta MacIntyre.
92 Burdett, HC *Hospitals and Asylums of the World* London 1893.
93 Northern Infirmary papers Highland Archive Service
94 Hamilton AJC 1963 *op.cit.*
95 Scottish Highlander 08 Oct 1896, 29 Jul 1897: Inverness Courier 10 June 1898, 14 June 1898: BJN 3 Oct 1896 p276: Aberdeen Weekly Journal 13 June 1898
96 Aberdeen Weekly Journal 7 May 1896
97 Aberdeen Weekly Journal 25 Jan 1899: Inverness Courier 17 Oct 1899 : Scottish Highlander 05 May 1898: Aberdeen Weekly Journal 25 Jan 1899
98 Aberdeen Daily Journal 14 Oct 1909, 12 Oct 1911
99 Scot. Board of Health - *Report on Hosp. Services of Scotland* Edinburgh 1926.
100 Hamilton AJC 1963 *op.cit.*: Aberdeen Journal 17 Jan 1925
101 BMJ 19 May 1928 p872: Inv. Cour. 27 May 1930, 13 May 1927, 30 Apr 1929
102 Inverness Advertiser 31 May 1867: 13 Oct 1868: 6 Nov 1868
103 British Journal of Nursing 28 Nov 1903 p438, 2 Sept 1922 p154
104 British Medical Journal 25 May 1929: Inverness Courier 12 Mar 1991
105 Hamilton AJC 1963 *op.cit.*
106 Inverness Courier 24 Mar 1931
107 Inverness Hospitals Board of Management14 Apr 1954
108 Infirmary Annual Report 1929
109 Hamilton AJC 1963 *op.cit.*: Knox 1975 *op.cit.* p10: Aberdeen Jour. 4 May 1916
110 Scottish Hospital Survey 1946 *op.cit.*
111 Hamilton AJC 1963 *op.cit.*: Knox 1975 *op.cit.* p13
112 Hansard 27th June 1922
113 Scottish Department of Health AR 1929-1931
114 Inverness Courier 15 Dec 1936
115 Hamilton AJC 1963 *op.cit.*: NRHB Specialist Medical Staffing 12 Jan 1949
116 Knox 1975 *op.cit.*
117 Scottish Hospital Survey Department of Health 1946
118 Cameron JM Personal memories of the RNI HAS: IHBM 30 Sept 1952
119 NHS Act 1947 Transfer of Hospital Northern Region NRS
120 NRHB Specialist Medical Staffing Report 12 Jan 1949
121 *Report of Committee on Post War Hospital* Problems in Scotland 1943
122 Nursing Mirror 20 Apr 1951: Mackay, Sheila 2007 *op.cit*
123 IHBM 16 Jan 1963: Northern Region Health Board GP 13 Jan 1972
124 Inverness Hospitals Board of Management(HAS) and DHS (NRS) files
125 P&J 11 May 1984: HHB Newsletter May 1986: Inv. Courier 12 Mar 1991
126 Inverness Journal Dec 1831, 29 May 1846: Inverness Courier 8 May 1844, 19 June 1851: Inverness Advert. 26 June 1868: Decennial census 1891: British Journal of Nursing 22 July 1905 p67, 26 Nov 1921 p340: IHBM 23 Apr 1953

[127] Inverness Courier 27 Dec 1849
[128] Inverness Hospitals Board of Management 6 Sept 1951
[129] Treasurers Cash Book Highland Archive Service
[130] Letter M Bethune to James Grant Chair Highland Archive Service: Inverness Journal 12 Mar 1813: Treasurers Cash Book Highland Archive Service
[131] Edinburgh Courant 13 Dec 1824: Inverness Courier 8 May 1928, 18 Apr 1850: Inverness Journal 1 May 1829: Treasurers Cash Book Highland Archive Service
[132] Inverness Journal 16 May 1828: Inverness Courier 29 Nov 1828: Fraser Mackintosh collection National Records of Scotland
[133] Inverness Courier17 Dec 1828
[134] Inverness Journal 7 May 1830
[135] Letter Highland Archive Service D863/6/1
[136] Inverness Journal 19 Aug 1836
[137] Inverness Courier 8 Feb 1843
[138] Inverness Courier 8 Mar 1843:   Inverness Journal 28 May 1845
[139] Inverness Journal 18 Apr 1845
[140] Inverness Journal 20 Nov 1846
[141] Inverness Courier 25 Jan 1848
[142] Nairnshire Mirror 22 Oct 1853
[143] Inverness Advertiser 05 July 1853
[144] Inverness Advertiser 04 Oct 1853
[145] Inverness Advertiser 13 Mar 1855
[146] Inverness Courier 25 Nov 1857
[147] Infirmary Correspondence D863/6/5 HAS Referred to as house clerk in letter of 22 Oct 1857: Weekly House Committee minutes 30 Jun1855.
[148] Chelmsford Chronicle 30 Dec 1921
[149] Inverness Advertiser 25 Dec 1860
[150] Inverness Advertiser 23 Dec 1862
[151] Aberdeen Journal 26 July 1865: Scotsman 7 May 1881
[152] Inverness Advertiser 26 June 1866: British Medical Journal 20 Aug 1904
[153] Inverness Courier 26 May 1870
[154] Decennial census
[155] Inverness Burgh Directory
[156] Inverness Advertiser 23 July 1878
[157] Inverness Advertiser 02 Nov 1880
[158] British Medical Journal 8 Feb 1941
[159] Scottish Highlander 05 Feb 1886: Scotsman 5 Feb 1886: BMJ 15 Nov 1930
[160] Scot. Highlander 03 Feb 1887: Inv. Advert. 26 June 1866: Scotsman 28 Jan 1887
[161] Scottish Highlander 30 Jan 1890
[162] Letter of 6 Jun 1892 in Infirmary Correspondence HAS D863/6/5
[163] Dundee Courier 21 Apr 1892: British Medical Journal 6 May 1922
[164] Aberdeen Journal 3 Aug 1911: British Medical Journal 23 Nov 1946

254

[165] Scotsman 19 Jul 1895
[166] Aberdeen Journal 3 Feb 1897
[167] Inverness Courier 24 June 1898
[168] Aberdeen Journal 15 Sept 1906
[169] Dundee Courier 17 Dec 1907: Inverness Burgh Directory
[170] Letter dated 20 July 1909 in D863/6/7 Highland Archive Service
[171] Dundee Courier 15 Oct 1909: Inverness Burgh Directory
[172] Aberdeen Journal 1 Apr 1913: Inverness Burgh Directory
[173] Dundee Courier 4 Sept 1914
[174] Knox 1975 *op.cit.*: Mackenzie 1946 *op.cit.* p214: Inverness Burgh Directory
[175] Inverness Burgh Directory
[176] British Medical Journal 2 Dec 1961
[177] British Medical Journal 17 May 1958
[178] Inverness Burgh Directory: Knox 1975 *op.cit.* p 11
[179] Aberdeen Journal 24 July 1924
[180] Inverness Burgh Directory
[181] Inverness Burgh Directory
[182] Inverness Burgh Directory
[183] Aberdeen Journal 19 Feb 1927
[184] Inverness Burgh Directory
[185] Inverness Burgh Directory
[186] Inverness Burgh Directory
[187] Inverness Courier Sept 1849
[188] Inverness Journal 2 Nov 1821
[189] Inverness Courier 13 Feb 1851
[190] British Medical Journal 28 Apr 1900
[191] Aberdeen Journal 5 Dec 1927: British Medical Journal 6 Mar 1943
[192] British Medical Journal 21 Jan 1905
[193] British Medical Journal 15 Nov 1930
[194] British Medical Journal 29 Apr 1911
[195] Scottish Highlander 02 Nov 1893
[196] Dundee Courier 17 Sept 1897: Caledonian Medical Journal June 1922.
[197] Knox 1975 *op.cit.* p9
[198] British Medical Journal 27 Dec 1924
[199] British Medical Journal 7 July 1928
[200] British Medical Journal 2 Apr 1927: Knox 1975 *op.cit.*
[201] Inverness Courier 12 Dec 1930
[202] Knox 1975 *op.cit.*
[203] Dr Theo Chalmers lecture to Highland Med. Soc. 1953. (Dr David Bisset)
[204] *ibid*: Knox 1975 *op.cit.* p1
[205] Inverness Courier 10 May 1929
[206] Aberdeen Journal 22 June 1929

[207] Inverness Courier 9 Aug 1929
[208] Knox 1975 *op.cit.* p11
[209] Knox 1975 *op.cit.*
[210] Knox 1975 *op.cit.* p13
[211] Aberdeen Journal 8 Jan 1947: 25 Dec 1947
[212] British Medical Journal 4 June 1960
[213] Leslie and Leslie *The Hospitals of Nairn* 2012: Cronin J *Origins and development of Scot. convalescent homes, 1860-1939*. PhD thesis 2003 Glasgow
[214] Scottish Highlander 29 Nov 1894: 6 Dec 1894
[215] We are most grateful to Miss E Luke and Mr JFM Macleod for kindly allowing access to their homes to observe the original features of the Home.
[216] Highland Times 9 May 1896
[217] Report on the Hospital Services of Scotland 1920 *op.cit.*:
Weekly reports from Matron of Convalescent Home 1909 HAS
[218] Leslie and Leslie 2012 *op.cit.*: Northern Counties Convalescent Home Minutes Nairn Museum
[219] British Journal of Nursing 3 Jan 1903 p7
[220] Architectural drawing of the hospital at Fort George 1862 NRS:
http://www.scarletfinders.co.uk/175.html
[221] Scotsman 4 Feb 1886: The Courier 10 Mar 1916;
http://www.scarletfinders.co.uk/175.html: Aberdeen Journal 9 Apr 1907
[222] Dundee Courier 6 Aug 1914: Aberdeen Journal 12 Jan 1916
[223] Inverness Courier 28 Sept 1915, 19 Jan 1917: Highland News 13 Sept 1916
[224] http://www.secretscotland.org.uk/index.php/Secrets/InvernessTrainingArea
[225] Highland News 12 Sept 1914
[226] Dundee Courier 24 Aug 1915, 5 Apr 1919: Inverness Cour. 15 Sept 1915:
Aberdeen Journal 5 Apr 1919, 27 Mar 1916, 17 Feb 1919, 10 Mar 1919
[227] Aberdeen Journal 2 Apr 1917, 25 Feb 1918, 5 Apr 1919, 24 Mar 1920, 8 May 1920: Inverness Courier 31 Aug 1917: Scotsman 30 Aug 1917
[228] http://www.thecaledoniancanal.org.uk/picture/number185.asp:
http://www.flickr.com/photos/rcahms/6213986733/: The Northern Barrage and Other Mining Activities US Naval Records Washington 1920: *The Northern Barrage* Annapolis US Naval Institute 1919
[229] RNI Management minutes 1940
[230] Crew, AF *The Army Medical Service* HMSO London 1952
[231] http://www.bbc.co.uk/history/ww2peopleswar/stories/63/a3930563.shtml
[232] Inverness Courier 29 Oct 1940: William Browne papers HAS
[233] Aberdeen Journal 2 Mar 1940
[234] Inv. Joint Hospital Board Minutes 13 Sept 1945: Raig. Hosp. Times Dec 1946
[235] Davidson Andrew Chief MO Dept. of Health for Scotland *The Contribution of Emergency Medical Services to Medicine and Surgery in Scotland* Lecture Reprinted in Edinburgh Medical Journal Vol XLIX p553 1942

[236] *ibid*

[237] *ibid*

[238] Browne WG *Old Raigmore Hospital 1941–85 A Fragment of History* 1988. In 1988 the last of the EMS brick wards (the maternity block) was vacated and Dr Browne (Oral Consultant 1961 – 1986) believed strongly that a history of the hospital to that point was necessary but in the absence of an official publication he set about the task himself. Unfortunately, the book is now out of print but it is available in the Highland Archives. Much of its information appears in this publication and the authors are most grateful to Dr Browne for his foresight. Because it is essential reading for anyone researching Raigmore's history we have not referenced it separately

[239] Raigmore Hospital Times Oct 1946 Highland Archive Service

[240] Raigmore Hospital Times Oct 1946

[241] Roundabout Raigmore Aug 1991

[242] P&J 17 Feb 1949, 14 Apr 1950: Scotsman 30 Sept 1948

[243] Maclean George Administrator Raigmore Hospital 1990 Unpublished notes HAS

[244] Raigmore Hospital Times 1st issue Oct 1946

[245] Letter of 13 Aug 1985 from Mrs Margaret MacDiarmid clerkess 1941–6 HAS

[246] Raigmore Times Dec 1946 HAS: Letter - Mrs Margaret MacDiarmid *op.cit.*

[247] Transfer of premises, Raigmore Hospital file NRS: IHBM 23 Apr 1953

[248] Northern Region Health Board Building Programme 1949 / 50

[249] Briefing paper for Sec of State's visit 11 Sept 1968 NRS

[250] Roundabout Raigmore Aug 1991

[251] Mackay, Sheila 2007 *op,cit.*

[252] Letter to Mr W Browne from RHJ Beale dated 5 Jan 1989.

[253] Information courtesy of the late Mr Donnie Fraser

[254] Department of Health files National Records of Scotland

[255] Paper by Richard Murray dated 23 Jul 1947 in Papers of W Browne HAS

[256] On schedule of hospital at hand over Apr 1948. National Records of Scotland

[257] Inverness Hospitals Board of Management 5 Mar 1951

[258] Fraser G A *History of Dermatology in the Highlands and* Islands Aberdeen Postgraduate Medical Bulletin, Vol. 21, 1st Jan 1987, pp. 4-8.

[259] Raigmore Hosp. Times Oct 1946: Roundabout Raigmore Aug 1991 HAS

[260] Nursing Mirror 20 Apr 1951

[261] Highland Health Board Minutes Apr 1979

[262] Memo from Patrick MacArthur in HOS/5/N/102 National Records of Scotland People's Journal 29 Oct 1955: opening ceremony papers HAS

[263] Diary of Brian Sturrock 1959 (unpublished) courtesy of his daughters.

[264] Correspondence file HOS/5/N/102 National Records of Scotland

[265] Inv. Cour. 20 Oct 1970: People's Jour. 15 Oct 1977: HHB Newsletter May 1886:

[266] Aberdeen Journal 23 Jan 1946

[267] Note of 3 Aug 1953 in Transfer of premises Raigmore Hospital file NRS

268 Joint Sub Com. of Northern Region Health Board and IHBM 26 Sept 1955

269 News Release, Rex Stewart & Associates 1 Apr 1970

270 Inverness Courier 27 Oct 1970: Central Board of Nursing File NRS

271 HHB Newsletter: Inv. Cour. 16 Aug 1985: Roundabout Raigmore Aug 1991

272 Roundabout Raigmore Dec 1991

273 Leslie and Leslie *The Hospitals of Lochaber* 2013

274 Nursing Times 7 Aug 1948 Volume XLIV p32

275 Dr EA Johnston in Raigmore Hospital Times 1946: Elemer Forrai unpublished autobiography courtesy of Mrs Pam MacIntyre: Aberdeen Journal 20 Sept 1949

276 Raigmore Hospital Times July 1947

277 Knox 1975 *op.cit.*

278 Inverness Parochial Board Minutes

279 Mackenzie 1946 *op.cit.* p186

280 Letter from Inverness town clerk in NI Management Minutes 8 July 1937

281 Inverness Public Health Committee Minutes 17 Jan 1941, 13 Dec 1937

282 Inverness Burgh Directories

283 Report on the Hospital Services of Scotland 1920 *op.cit.*: Scotsman 25 Sept 1918: Inv. Burgh Directory: Abn. Journal 20 Nov 1931, 30 Mar 1937, 26 Aug 1938

284 Inverness Courier Friday, 20 May 1927: Valuation Roll: Inverness Burgh Directory: MacDonald Dr J MOH 1919 *op.cit.*

285 Bill for nursing 23 July 1923 per Mrs Patterson: Inverness Cour. 12 Apr 1927

286 Company register: Receipt dated 29 Sept 1934 (Am Baile): Inverness MOH AR 1934: Inverness Courier 12 Apr 1927, 11 Mar 1930, 30 Aug 1935, 5 April 1938: Viewhill Nursing Home Ltd Company Papers NRS: Inverness Burgh Directory

287 Initial advertisement for the home Inv. Cour. 6 May 1927, 29 Apr 1930: Leslie and Leslie 2013 *op.cit.* pp 32,44: Valuation Roll: Scot. Hosp. Survey Department of Health 1946 *op.cit.*: Inv. MOH AR 1934: St. Margaret's Nursing Home Ltd Company papers: Land and Premises Acquisition Department of Health NRS

288 Dundee Cour. 12 Mar 1952: Inv. Public Health Com. 10 Jan 1939: Inv. Burgh Directory: Scotsman 6 May 1939, 21 June 1949: Inv. Cour. 18 Apr 1939: Scot. Hosp. Survey Department of Health 1946: NRHB Vol. 3 p170: Vol. 3 p259

289 Valuation Roll: Inv. Burgh Directory: Scotsman 13 Apr 1938: Highland Orphanage Trust 1985, Educational Endowments Commission 1931-36 NRS

290 Inverness Courier Friday, 16 Dec 1938

291 Inverness MOH AR: Public Health Committee minutes 13 Apr 1936

292 Much of the information in this section is from SSAFA Annual Reports held in the SSAFA Archive London

293 Fairrie, Col Angus *History of Fort George* Queens Own Highlanders Winter 1991: Cumming, Lt Col (Retd) OBE Highlanders Museum Fort George Personal communication 11 Mar 2009: BMJ Oct 18 1930 p662: Scotsman 9 Oct 1930: Caber Feidh Sept 1931 courtesy of Mr Bob Shanks

294 Inverness Courier 3 Aug 1928: Scotsman 4 Sept 1935

[295] Fort George Maternity Hospital Trust Settlement of Scheme 1965 NRS: The Courier 17 Feb 1912

[296] Caberfeidh Sept 1954: Inverness-shire MOH ARs: Cumming *op.cit.*: Personal communication (Kirkhill Mar 2014)

[297] Ordnance Survey 1:10,000 NH7656/7756 1964

[298] Mackenzie 1946 *op.cit.* p223: Valuation Roll: Inverness Courier 20 Aug 1940, 5 Dec 1941

[299] Inverness Courier 2 Oct 1925

[300] Ida Merry Maternity Home 6th AR 1925-26 NRS: Income tax Claim form 25 Jul 1924 NRS: Inv. Courier 15 May 1923, 2 Oct 1925, 3 Nov 1925, 8 Oct 1929

[301] British Medical Journal Apr 18 1925 p758: Inland Revenue Claim 1928 NRS: Ida Merry Mat. Home 6th AR 1925-26 *op.cit.*: Dundee Courier 10 Oct 1929

[302] Scotsman 20th July 1928

[303] Scotsman 5th Sept 1931: Inv. Courier 10 Oct 1930, 14 July 1931, 04 Sept 1931, 06 Oct 1931, 19 Aug 1932, 21 Oct 1932, 17 Mar 1933, 13 Oct 1933

[304] Ida Merry Maternity Home Cash Book NRS: Inverness Courier 23 Aug 1935: Scotsman 4th Nov 1937: Aberdeen Journal 14 Oct 1937

[305] Inverness Public Health Committee 8 Apr 1940: Inverness Courier 9 Aug 1940, 20 Aug 1940, 5 Dec 1941: Inverness Joint Hospital Board 11 Dec 1941: Scotsman 20 Nov 1941: Aberdeen Weekly Journal 29 Aug 1940

[306] Inverness Courier 11 Mar 1930, 19 Aug 1934

[307] Mackenzie TC 1946 *op.cit.* page 247

[308] Inverness Courier 19 Aug 1934, 28 Apr 1939: Aberdeen Journal 25 Oct 1938

[309] Aberdeen Journal 13 Dec 1923: Inverness Courier 28 April 1939

[310] Valuation Roll: Aberdeen Jour. 13 Dec 1923: Inverness Cour. 29 Apr 1997

[311] Inv. Cour. 23 Apr 1940, 29 Apr 1997the latter per Mrs D Paterson

[312] Inv. Cour. 24 Apr 1940. Quote by Provost Mackenzie at opening of Rosedene.

[313] Bryers, Dr Helen (unpublished thesis): Browne 1988 *op.cit.* p21: Scottish Hospitals Survey 1946 *op.cit*

[314] Inverness Joint Hospital Board Minute 14 Nov 1946: Dept. of Health file NRS

[315] Inverness Town Council minutes 8 June 1942: Inverness Joint Hospital Board administration papers: Scot. Hospital Survey (1946) Northern Region *op.cit.*

[316] Inverness Joint Hospital Board Minutes: The British Journal of Nursing Sept 1940: Northern Region Health Board Chairman's Committee 30 June 1949

[317] Scotsman 6 Mar 1947: Inverness MOH AR 1948 p7: Dept. of Health Scottish Hospitals Survey file Highland Archive Service

[318] Inv. MOH AR 1948 p7: Nursing Mirror 7 Sept 1956: Interview with sister Mary Macaulay on her retirement 28 Jan 1982 in George Maclean papers HAS

[319] Anderson G, *Report on the Sanitary Conditions of the Labouring Classes* (chapter on Inverness) 1842

[320] Inverness Parochial Board Minutes 1866

[321] Inv. Advert. 6 Nov 1866, 4 Dec 1866: Inv. Parochial Board Minutes 3/1/1867

[322] Inverness Advertiser 24 Mar 1865
[323] Inverness Advert. 1 Dec 1871: 26 Jan 1877: Inverness Burgh Papers HAS
[324] The photo was taken by George Gray and we are most grateful to Mr JFM Macleod for the copy which is used here and for information on its origins. The photo appeared in Inverness Field Club's *Old Inverness in Pictures* in 1978.
[325] Inverness Town Council minutes 7 Apr 1902
[326] Abn. Jour. 25 June 1881: Inverness Cour. 30 Sept 1892: Decennial census: Inverness Town Council minutes 13 Mar 1902: Macdonald 1919 *op.cit.*
[327] Scottish Highlander 14 Sept 1893: MacDonald 1919 *op. cit.*: MOH AR
[328] Inverness Town Council minutes
[329] Macdonald 1919 *op.cit.*: Skye District Committee Minutes
[330] Inverness Courier 5 Jan 1926, 12 Dec 1930
[331] Inv. Cour. 1 Jan 1929: BMJ Dec 7 1929 p1080: Inv. MOH AR 1934: Inv. Town Council July 1935 p544: Inv. Town Council Public Health Com. 13 Sept 1937, 14 Feb 1938, 14 Apr 1941: Abn. Jour. 10 May 1938, 24 Mar 1938: Air Raid Precautions Sub Com. 26 Jul 1939, 2 Oct 1940: Mackay, Sheila S OBE (Ed) *Inverness Our Story* Inverness Bk1 2004. Information on herring kippering from Mr Frank Syme who ran a nearby factory (courtesy of Mr Geoff Macleod).
[332] For information in the Invergarry sanatorium see Leslie and Leslie 2013 *op.cit.*
[333] Daily Record 26 Mar 1914
[334] Inverness Joint Hospital Board Minutes: Aberdeen Weekly Jour. 17 Sept 1915
[335] Inverness Courier 26 Jan 1923, 11 Nov 1927, 5 June 1928, 14 Dec 1928: Burdett's 1924-1930 *op.cit.*: MOH AR 1929
[336] Inverness Courier 22 Oct 1937: Department of Health AR 1937
[337] Inverness Joint Hospital Board Minutes
[338] Inv. Joint Health Board Minutes: Inv. Town Council Special Meeting 16/12/40
[339] Aberdeen Journal 9 June 1939
[340] Johnston Dr EA, *Report on the Tuberculosis in the Northern Region* June 1950
[341] Northern Region Health Board Minutes
[342] Highland Health Board Minutes 15 May 1987, 17Oct 1984: Roundabout Raigmore Aug 1991 Issue 16
[343] Aberdeen Jour. 2 Feb 1940: Inv. Hosp. Board Minute18 Mar 1953, 16 June 1965
[344] BMJ 13 Oct 1956: Inverness Cour. 12 Dec 1930: Abn Journal 8 Oct 1934:
[345] Abn Journal 15 Oct 1941: Dundee Cour. 23 Nov 1950: Scots. 22 March 1948
[346] MOH for Inverness-shire AR 1893-1900
[347] Inverness Courier 8 Jan 1834
[348] Inv. Jour. 2 Nov 1832, 3 May 1833: Hamilton, D *The Healers* Edinburgh 1981
[349] Inverness Advertiser 23 Oct 1868, 23 Oct 1868, 06 Mar 1868: Aberdeen Weekly Journal 18 May 1885
[350] Inverness Advert. 21 Dec 1880: Edinburgh Evening News 17 Dec 1880: Forbes Dispensary Trust papers 1952 National Records of Scotland
[351] AR extracts in press reports: Burdett's *op.cit.*: Hamilton 1981 *op.cit.*:

352 Aberdeen Journal 1 Dec 1904
353 www.scottisharchitects.org.uk: Scottish Highlander 8 Oct 1896: Inverness Burgh Directory:
354 Inverness Courier 27 Jan 1914
355 Inverness MOH AR
356 Northern Region Health Board Minutes Volume 3 p 12: NRHB administrative papers HAS
357 Inverness Journal 2 Nov 1832: Inverness Courier 1 Feb 1837: Inverness Advertiser 15 May 1874: Inverness Burgh Directory
358 Aberdeen Journal 30 Dec 1909
359 Inv. Advert. 9 May 1862, 16 Apr 1869: Inv. Cour. 5 Nov 1926: Scotsman 2 Aug 1938; Aberdeen Jour. 7 June 1945: Inv. Burgh Directories: Decennial censes
360 Barron, The Northern Highlands in the Nineteenth Century Inverness 1903
361 Hamilton the Healers op.cit.: Alison Darragh PhD Thesis *Prison or Palace Haven or Hell?* University of St Andrews 2011
362 Caledonian Mercury 12 Nov 1804: Northern Infirmary Address to the Public Nov 1805 National Records of Scotland
363 Appeal to public for funds 1809 Doc. of Earl of Seafield Cullen House NLS
364 Northern Infirmary Report 15 June 1830 Fraser Papers HAS
365 Darragh op.cit.: Inverness Journal 6 Mar 1818
366 Inverness Journal 2 June 1820: Northern Infirmary AR 1834, 1841
367 Royal Northern Lunatic Asylum List of subscribers HAS
368 Letter from WH Colquhoun 31 July 1845 in Northern Infirmary papers HAS
369 Plan of Ground at Charleston 16 July 1849 HAS: Abn. Journal 26 Dec 1849.
370 Inverness Journal 8 Aug 1845, 8 Oct 1847: Agreement dated June 1848 HAS: Mackenzie 1946 op.cit. p75, p115
371 Mackenzie TC Presidential Address to Caledonian Med. Society AGM 20 Jun 1930 Caledonian Medical Journal Vol. XIV July 1930
372 Ordnance Survey 1:2500 Inverness-shire Map XI.3 1872
373 Inverness Courier 9 June 1859, 23 June 1859
374 Inverness Courier 7 June 1860
375 Inverness Courier 26 Nov 1863
376 Inverness Courier July 1865, 6 Mar 1862: Banffshire Journal 12 June 1860
377 Inv. District Asylum General Register in Emily, Donoho PhD Thesis *Appeasing the Saint in the Loch and Physician in the Asylum* Glasgow University 2012
378 Inverness Courier 19 Oct 1865
379 Inv. Advert. 17 July 1866, 20 July 1866, 14 Aug 1866: Inv. Cour. 22 Apr 1869
380 Banffshire Journal 5 Jul 1859
381 Key sources are annual reports of the Asylum and bi-annual inspections of the Lunacy Commissioners. Also '*Craig Dunain 1864 – 1964*' (1964) by Martin Whittet and Ian Macleod. All are in HAS. We have not referenced these.
382 Quote courtesy of Alison Darragh op.cit.

[383] Banffshire Journal 11 June 1861
[384] Inverness Courier 10 Nov 1914
[385] There is actually no precise evidence of this (courtesy of Mr Rob Polson).
[386] Inverness Courier 16 July 1864, 28 Dec 1865
[387] Philo C *Scaling the Asylum*. Space Psyche and Psychiatry Conference Oxford Brooke University Dec 2002: www.scottisharchitects.org.uk
[388] Banffshire Journal 21 June 1864
[389] Whittet and Macleod 1964 *op.cit.*
[390] Lunacy Commission Report in British Medical Journal 17 Sept 1910
[391] Report on the Hospital Services of Scotland 1920 *op.cit.* p11
[392] Evening Telegraph 17 Aug 1895: Gifford *op. cit.*: Highland Times 9 May 1896: Inverness Courier 23 Aug 1898
[393] Report of visit by AA Hughes 27 Feb 1957 National Records of Scotland
[394] Northern Region Health Board Minutes Volume 5 p131, Volume 17 p132
[395] Whittet and Macleod 1964 *op.cit.*
[396] Rodger, T Ferguson *Requirements of a Psychiatric Service for the Northern Region* Northern Region Health Board 1950
[397] Northern Region Health Board Bk 23 1969 Appendices
[398] Northern Region Health Board Minutes 16 Jan 1964
[399] Highland Health Board Minutes 1985
[400] Highland Health Board Minutes
[401] Montrose Arbroath and Brechin Review 16 June 1865
[402] Dundee Courier 5 Oct 1888
[403] British Journal of Nursing 7 Jan 1911 p9
[404] Inverness Courier 17 June 1935
[405] Aberdeen Weekly Journal 7 May 1945: HAS catalogue
[406] Aberdeen Weekly Journal 5 July 1894
[407] British Medical Journal 2 May 1942
[408] Aberdeen Journal 8 Jul 1938
[409] Rodger, T Ferguson 1950 *op.cit.*
[410] Northern Region Health Board General Purposes Committee 18 Sept 1958
[411] Northern Region Health Board Minutes Volume 17 p132
[412] Hall, D Polson The Northern Regional Health Board unknown publication c1972 George Maclean papers Highland Archive Service
[413] *ibid*
[414] Craig Phadrig Department of Health file National Records of Scotland
[415] Highland Health Board Minutes 20 May 1988
[416] NHS website www.nhshighland.scot.nhs.uk